"A very engaging and readable book. Through their exploration of Christian and secular appropriations of the Eden narrative within the context of contemporary American advertising, dating websites, humor, and the sex industry, Schearing and Ziegler offer a thought-provoking contribution to ongoing studies of the Bible in popular culture."

—*Caroline Blyth, Lecturer in Biblical Studies,*
School of Theology, University of Auckland

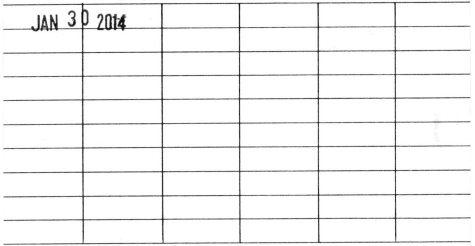

ENTICED BY EDEN
How Western Culture Uses, Confuses, (and Sometimes Abuses) Adam and Eve

Linda S. Schearing and Valarie H. Ziegler

BAYLOR UNIVERSITY PRESS

Scripture quotations are from the New Revised Standard Version Bible, copyright 1989, Division of Christian Education of the National Council of the Churches of Christ in the United States of America. Used by permission. All rights reserved.

Cover Design by *the*BookDesigners
Cover Image is courtesy of Shutterstock.
Book Design by Diane Smith

Library of Congress Cataloging-in-Publication Data

Schearing, Linda S.
Enticed by Eden : how western culture uses, confuses, (and sometimes abuses) Adam and Eve / Linda S. Schearing and Valarie H. Ziegler.
230 p. cm.
Includes bibliographical references and index.
ISBN 978-1-60258-543-0 (pbk. : alk. paper)
1. Sex role—Religious aspects—Christianity. 2. Sex role—Biblical teaching. 3. Adam (Biblical figure) 4. Eve (Biblical figure) 5. Eden. 6. Popular culture—United States. 7. Popular culture—Religious aspects—Christianity. I. Ziegler, Valarie H., 1954– II. Title.
BT708.S295 2013
261.8'357—dc23
                                    2012029216

Printed in the United States of America on acid-free paper with a minimum of 30% post-consumer waste recycled content.

To Brooks:
Teacher, Mentor, Friend

CONTENTS

ACKNOWLEDGMENTS

We have many people to thank, and it is a pleasure to do so. First on the list is Kristen Kvam of Saint Paul School of Theology in Kansas City. The three of us coedited our 1999 *Eve and Adam: Jewish, Christian, and Muslim Readings on Genesis and Gender*, which was a springboard for this project. Our interest in Genesis began at Emory University, where we were all students in the Graduate Division of Religion. A special thanks to its faculty for showing us how to be caring educators as well as responsible and ethical researchers. We also want to thank the Bible and Popular Culture section of the Society of Biblical Literature for providing us and other scholars the opportunity to think seriously about popular appropriations of biblical texts. The Pacific Northwest annual meeting of the American Academy of Religion, the American Schools of Oriental Research, and the Society of Biblical Literature allowed us to present and develop our research, for which we are grateful. We particularly want to express our gratitude to Ardy Bass of Gonzaga University, who chaired the PNW Women and Religion section and enthusiastically welcomed our contributions.

In Indiana, we received significant financial assistance from DePauw University. We offer our appreciation to the Faculty Development Committee and to VPAAs Neal Abraham and David Harvey for their support—it was invaluable. DePauw colleagues who provided much-appreciated aid and advice include Meryl Altman, Russell Arnold, Bernie Batto, Tamara Beauboeuf,

Dave Berque, Terry Bruner, Curtis Carpenter, Melanie Finney, Jason Fuller, Lyn Gram, Jane Griswold, Tiffany Hebb, Adam Hilkert, Tiffany Hodge, Leslie James, Tavian Lucas, Colleen Muir, Ibijoke Oke, Kerry Pannell, Carol Smith, Barbara Steinson, and Janelle Thixton. Thanks also to Bill and Lucy Wieland and the adult education class at Saint Andrew's Episcopal Church in Greencastle for working through the theological materials in this book. Outside Indiana, we owe a particular debt to Lunis Orcutt, whose KnowBrainer software and website made it possible for Val to dictate her sections of the manuscript. Val sends unending gratitude to the gang at Greencastle Physical Therapy, especially Brandon, Bridgette, Chet, and Lesley, for diligent care of the world's most persnickety forearms. In Michigan, Beth Hoger, Lisa Swem, and Pam Nelson have been incredibly and wonderfully supportive in imagining what's possible. In Great Britain, thanks to Carol Brady. To the extended family who enjoyed each other's company at a Dream Come True and who were generous enough to read chapter drafts, no words of gratitude are sufficient. We look forward to enjoying Iris' prose in years to come. Thanks also for the unerring support and love offered by Harold and Ruth Ziegler in Kentucky and by Bill Nunn Sr. and Joye Patterson of Columbia, Missouri. The family has suffered losses as well as gains recently. So welcome, Rachel, and farewell to Ruth and Joye, two utterly remarkable women whose passing is not something we would ever want to get over.

In Washington, special thanks are in order to Gonzaga's Religious Studies Department, whose faculty listened to and commented on the "Recycling Eden" materials in departmental colloquia. Their support and ongoing collegiality were important in their development. In addition, a variety of churches in the Spokane and Coeur d'Alene areas graciously invited presentations. One church in particular—St. Pius X Catholic Church in Coeur d'Alene—is especially appreciated.

Working with the staff at Baylor University Press has been an amazing experience. We especially want to thank Carey Newman, not simply for his superb editorial oversight, but also for his ambition and enthusiasm for this project. Carey's energetic engagement with our work spurred us to rethink and improve it in innumerable ways. We thank him for a fascinating intellectual exercise and for seeing us through to the end. Go Bears!

We want to acknowledge the deep debt of gratitude we owe our families. In Indiana, no words can express the depths of love or levels of support and sacrifice that Bill Nunn has unselfishly provided so that this book could be finished. Likewise, in Washington, without Angel Fitzpatrick's love and support this project would not have been possible. Special thanks are in order also to Sean and Brittany Fitzpatrick, whose patience and love enabled their Mom to work at the computer uninterrupted. You are the best!

Finally, we want to thank and praise E. Brooks Holifield of Emory University, to whom we dedicate this book. There was never a better mentor, friend, or advocate of clear expository prose. You are ever present in our minds as we craft thesis statements and analyze each other's writing. Those seminars paid off—thanks!

INTRODUCTION

Once upon a time, there was a Garden in Eden.
And the first man and woman were happy and helped each other.
It was Paradise.

But everything comes with a price, and the price of living in the Garden
was obedience.
One tree, one prohibition—a small price to pay for happiness and harmony.
But a smooth talking snake thought otherwise.
Why be happy with harmony when you can have power?
Why settle for helping others when you can rule?

The man and woman disobeyed.
As they left the Garden
A sentinel with a flaming sword barred the way to the tree of life.
There would be no going back. . . .

—L.S. & V.Z.

In Kansas, a citizen appalled by the state education board's decision to allow "supernatural" explanations in the teaching of science invents a new creator: the Flying Spaghetti Monster. The FSM's heaven contains a beer volcano and a stripper factory, and he prefers that his earthly followers dress in full pirate regalia. Soon Pastafarianism has adherents around the globe, giving school boards everywhere a new kind of "intelligent design" theory to ponder and promote.

In Florida, two middle-aged hikers slip and slide their way through the rugged nature preserve labeled the "Garden of Eden." Dripping with sweat and covered in mud, finally they reach the spot marked as the original Garden. They look around in disappointment. Who in the world designated this mosquito-riddled forest as the original earthly paradise?

In Washington, a teenager gives up dating, convinced that it is practice for divorce. Reading the creation stories in Genesis 1–3, he becomes convinced that the creator is a "God of romance" who will send his soul mate to him, just as God gave Eve to Adam. He embraces celibacy for the time being, eagerly looking forward to pure Christian honeymoon sex so heavenly that it can be described only as "worship in bed." Meanwhile, members of the Internet dating service Bigchurch.com respectfully contribute to the message board in hopes of encountering their Christian soul mates online, unaware that their site is owned by the racy magazine *Cosmopolitan* and that any member who explores the sponsored sites at the bottom of the Bigchurch.com home page is just two clicks away from lesbian.com and porn.com.

In California, a Jewish family celebrates Passover without the lamb, convinced that God created Adam and Eve as vegetarians. In Minnesota, a grocery shopper in the health food aisle ponders what ties Eden soy milk or Garden of Eatin' corn chips to the original Garden. Especially since she prefers Doritos.

In Connecticut, pilgrims climb a steep hill to visit a decrepit theme park called Holy Land USA. The site has fallen into such disarray that they can no longer locate the former Garden of Eden, where Satan wore a plastic Halloween mask and sported a green garden hose tail, while Eve and Adam were naked mannequins lolling around in an empty house trailer. Near Cincinnati, visitors to the Creation Museum study dioramas of Eve and Adam dwelling happily with dinosaurs.

In Kentucky, a woman advocates that husbands use corporal punishment on their wives and writes erotic Christian spanking fiction, believing that in Eden God designated Adam as Eve's disciplinarian. She gives up wearing slacks because they are too masculine, devises frilly pantaloons to wear under her dress in cold weather, and then creates a crotchless version of her pantaloons after her husband suggests she give up undergarments entirely so that she will always be available to him for intercourse. When she offers the crotchless pantaloons for sale on her website, one Internet respondent grumbles, "Don't look now but the Dark Ages are back!" while another confesses, "The Christian BDSM shop is so bizarre! I can't quit looking."[1]

What do these people have in common? They are all incorporating aspects of the biblical creation accounts in Genesis 1–3 into their own lives. Eden, Eve,

Adam, and the God who created them are such familiar figures to Americans that people routinely appeal to them to justify any number of practices: how to teach science in the public schools, how to choose a proper diet, how to find a partner, how to make love, how to dress, and even how to ask one's spouse for a spanking. Whether they realize it or not, Americans spend a great deal of time negotiating their world with Adam and Eve.

Recreating Eden

Adam and Eve pop up everywhere in American life, but for some people the original human beings are more than characters in a *New Yorker* cartoon. They represent all that is right and good about being human. And the desire to get back to the Garden means turning away from contemporary culture to recreate a simpler age when men were men and women submitted to them. For some of the loudest and most persistent voices advocating a return to Eden are conservative evangelical Christians convinced that the subordination of women to men was the central characteristic of life in the Garden. In creating man first, they insist, God ordained him to be woman's ruler. He is to take charge of woman, initiating and governing their relationship. Men are men when they act authoritatively. God designed woman, on the other hand, as man's helper. She must surrender to him and—literally—function as the passive receptacle of his desire. Women are women when they submit to male headship.

Nowhere is this model described more graphically than in T. D. Jakes' *Woman Thou Art Loosed!* commentary on Genesis 3. Jakes compares men and women to electrical outlets, explaining that "the receptacle is the female, and the plug is the male." As receptacles, Jakes explained, "women were made to be receivers," whereas God made men "to be givers—physically, sexually, and emotionally." Jakes cautions women, "Be careful what you allow to plug into you and draw strength from you. The wrong plugs can drain your power." Precisely because Eve allowed Satan to plug into her, Jakes concludes, today's women must avoid destruction by praying fervently for "the mighty power of God's Spirit" to plug into them.[2]

Most conservative evangelical discussions about gender are less obviously Freudian. But the insistence on man as initiator and head, with woman the passive recipient of his authority, is the absolute centerpiece of evangelical theology. Everything—*everything*—begins with the hierarchical creation God fashioned in Genesis. As evangelical theologian Duane Litfin has put it, "That the universe should be ordered around a series of over/under hierarchical relationships is His [God's] idea, a part of His original design. Far from being extraneous to the Word of God, a kind of excess baggage that can be jettisoned while retaining the essential truth of the Scriptures, these ideas are the essential truths of the Scriptures. To reject them is to reject the Bible."[3]

The single most important aspect of this hierarchy is that woman is a secondary creation designed to complement man as his helper. Advocates of this position have dubbed themselves "complementarians" to emphasize the centrality of this tenet. After the original human disobedience, they contend, God stressed gender hierarchy all the more, telling Eve in Genesis 3:16, "Your desire shall be for your husband, and he shall rule over you." They find additional support for the subordination of women to men in the New Testament. Ephesians 5:24 counsels Christian wives to be subject to their husbands "in everything," and 1 Corinthians 11:8 qualifies the Genesis 1:27 assertion that God created male and female in the divine image by arguing that man is the "image and reflection of God," but woman is merely the "reflection of man." A passage in 1 Timothy 2:11-15 ups the ante: "Let a woman learn in silence with full submission. I permit no woman to teach or have authority over a man; she is to keep silent. For Adam was formed first, then Eve; and Adam was not deceived, but the woman was deceived and became a transgressor. Yet she will be saved through childbearing." There are other texts in the Bible that reference the equality of men and women, but the forcefulness of the hierarchical texts above cannot be denied.

To Americans accustomed to democracy and egalitarianism, such passages can be discomfiting. People who find sexism offensive may well be tempted to leave conservative evangelicals to their own subculture, but they do so at their own risk. For that subculture wields enormous power, and its leaders are dedicated to recreating the hierarchical structures they believe God instituted in the beginning.[4] As Timothy Bayly, former director of the Council on Biblical Manhood and Womanhood, has commented, "Neither heterosexuality nor lifelong monogamy nor the headship of the husband are principles binding on God's covenant people alone; rather, having been instituted in the Garden of Eden, they are binding on all mankind. . . . Christian judges, legislators, and citizens must work not only to protect these truths from the encroachment of civil law, but also to proclaim them unashamedly in the public square."[5]

Recreating Eden necessitates reshaping American culture. At the very least, that involves teaching one's children to reject selected values of the larger society. In an article titled "Embracing God's Plan for Authority," evangelical theologian Tedd Tripp argues that "the dominant culture we live in has rejected God's plan for authority" and is thus unable to teach citizens that submission to divinely ordained authorities is "dignified and noble." If the larger culture cannot socialize children into willing submission to authority, then believers have two choices. They can either isolate themselves or seek to convert the dominant culture. In the first half of the twentieth century, hierarchical Christians largely chose the first option. More recently, they have dedicated themselves to the work of cultural transformation, both by entering the world of electoral politics and by creating alternative institutions that socialize believers into a cosmic pecking order in which, as Tripp has contended, "it is sweet and seemly to honor and obey those who are above us, and to govern those who are below us."[6]

But recreating Eden is not *all* about transforming American institutions, and in the twenty-first century it certainly does not require separating oneself from popular culture. Conservative evangelicals have enthusiastically embraced elements of contemporary life that have nothing to do with the biblical world, and have, in turn, been themselves recreated in the image not of God but of the larger culture they have gone to such pains to denounce. In the tug-of-war between transforming culture and being transformed by it, evangelical Christianity currently finds itself pervaded by secular values and practices. Capitalism, consumerism, mass marketing and media, patriotism, and militarism—to name but a few examples—are integral to conservative evangelicalism and represent the cultural captivity to which this crusading form of Christianity has surrendered.[7]

Hard as it may be to remember, there was a time when conservative evangelicals did not own broadcasting empires or theme parks, when Christian rock music was unknown, and when no one would have thought to consult an evangelical dating service, cosmetic brand, sex manual, fairy tale, cheerleading camp, creation museum, or Princess Bible.[8] But all of those options and more are available to believers seeking to recreate a hierarchical Eden today. Evangelical groups like PINC Ministries, Pure in Heart Ministries, and Becoming a Modern Princess teach girls to become passive princesses waiting for their lives to begin when the right Christian man initiates a relationship with them. "Stay-at-home daughters" learn to forgo college and careers, patiently serving their fathers until they are given husbands to oversee them.

In the world of Christian domestic discipline, husbands "rule over" their wives by regularly spanking them into submission. Celebrating the authority of fathers, the biblical patriarchy movement seeks to emulate Adam's headship over Eve by limiting voting rights in government, church, and family to men alone. The movement's goal is dominion—over the entire country. "Quiverfull" couples eschew birth control so that they can provide all the more soldiers in the campaign to recreate America in Eden's image. And Answers in Genesis, the parent company of the Creation Museum in Kentucky, works tirelessly not only to convince people that Eve and Adam dwelled with the dinosaurs in Eden a little over six thousand years ago, but also to require every public school in the nation to teach this version of origins.

In short, Adam, Eve, and the Eden are critical players in American life, not just in popular culture, but also in politics, education, religion, and family life. The conservative Christian groups dedicated to recreating the gender hierarchy they find constitutive of life in the Garden consider themselves representative of traditional Christian and American values. They are horrified at the ways American society has strayed from those traditional values, particularly with the presence of feminists (or, as they often put it, "feminazis"). And they are ready to go to war to restore the age when fathers ruled.

No organization better represents this impulse than the Council on Biblical Manhood and Womanhood (CBMW), an evangelical organization begun in 1987 for the sole purpose of opposing feminism and establishing the subordination of women to men as God's intention at the creation.[9] In the virtually innumerable articles, books, and conferences the CBMW has sponsored since then, it has repeatedly urged evangelicals to be warriors in the battle to reclaim American culture and has unashamedly exalted male privilege in ways extreme even among conservative evangelicals. In the CBMW's 2002 *Building Strong Families*, for example, evangelical radio personality Bob Lepine argued that the titles "prophet, priest, and king"—terms traditionally used to describe the redemptive roles of Jesus Christ—also applied to Christian husbands. As "king of heaven and earth," Lepine argued, Jesus was the model for how "husbands are to rule in our homes." Warning against passivity and a "soft view" of love, Lepine told husbands that, just as Jesus pronounced judgment on Israel, so they must confront "ongoing patterns of sinful behavior" in their wives and call them to repentance, no matter how "harsh and judgmental" that might sound. Husbands also, Lepine said, needed to summon up their "healthy, self-controlled aggressiveness" to become warriors in the culture war against egalitarianism.[10]

In 2012 Pastor John Piper of the CBMW announced that "God has given Christianity a masculine feel" in revealing God's self as "King, not Queen, and as Father, not Mother," as well as in creating man and woman and giving them the name of man: Adam. Celebrating the church's "masculine ministry," Piper called for the "*manly* affirmation of 'sharply cut doctrines,'" denounced "jelly-fish Christianity," and rejoiced in the "urgency, forcefulness, penetrating power" of masculine preaching and "firmness of principle." He assured women that this was all for their own good, as God had created them to flourish in a "masculine Christianity" that would offer them a "wide field of real, though unobtrusive, usefulness."[11] Given that rhetoric, it is easy to see how a disillusioned evangelical named Elizabeth Esther concluded, "When you start exploring these ideas of 'Biblical Womanhood,' what these books really promote is: *How to Subjugate Your Entire Being to the Dictate of Your Lord and Master (and we mean your husband, not God)."*[12]

No one should expect the CBMW to dial down its rhetoric anytime soon. As Mark Dever, pastor of Capitol Hill Baptist Church in Washington, D.C., wrote in 2008, a new and more militant generation of evangelicals committed to gender hierarchy has emerged. Complementarians in the 1980s, he said, had viewed women's ordination as an issue related to civil rights. But the new generation saw the ordination of women as a precursor to gay rights, and their central mission was to proclaim their opposition vigorously, no matter how often they were "shouted at publicly" or called "narrow, intolerant hate-mongers." The debate between gender egalitarians and complementarians, Dever concluded, had become the "watershed distinguishing those who will accommodate Scripture to culture, and those who will attempt to shape culture by Scripture." To preserve the gospel for future generations, egalitarian readings of Scripture must be driven from the marketplace of ideas.

Most Americans would not define that version of Eden as paradise, but for the conservative Christians who believe that gender hierarchy is at the heart of God's creation in Genesis 1–3, the subordination of women to men is normative. As they work to recreate the church and the larger culture in the Garden's image, their labor will impact every level of social discourse, from romance to science, from procreation to presidential politics. For this reason, whether they regard Genesis 1–3 as normative or not, every American has a stake in the conversation. To paraphrase Voltaire, we must all cultivate our gardens.

Recycling Eden

Conservative Christians are not the only ones who are attracted to Genesis 2–3. But not everyone believes Genesis 2–3 is authoritative because it is Scripture. They do recognize, however, that the Garden account is a *good story*. And, like good narratives everywhere, it has power based on its ability to address issues that shape how people understand themselves. Popular culture makes use of the symbolism of Genesis 2–3 in a number of different ways. Films, video games, music, comics, advertising, and humor are only a few of the media that use the biblical story and its characters. Rather than *recreating* Eden, however, these venues *recycle* the story quite blatantly for their own purposes. Sometimes that purpose is a rather crass consumerism, while at other times it might be a social comment on contemporary life and relationships. By repackaging the Garden story, the resulting artifacts say something *about* the culture in which they circulate while at the same time endeavoring to *shape* that same culture. This is especially true in terms of gender issues and how woman/Eve is imaged. Two examples of this recontextualizing of Genesis 2–3 that are particularly interesting are those found in advertisements and in jokes.

Adam, Eve, the snake, and the forbidden fruit are ubiquitous symbols in Western culture. Contemporary advertising commodifies these symbols to inspire consumerism and, at times, to establish market and brand identity. Products that use these symbols in their marketing campaigns range from the mundane (bathroom fixtures, chairs, automobiles) to the more titillating (gambling, alcohol, tobacco, sex industry). Understandably, this usage finds especially intriguing the ideas of "temptation/persuasion" and "sin/taboo" that are key to the Genesis 2–3 story. Many (though not all) of the ads that use Garden symbolism have one thing in common—they focus on a particular presentation of Eve and Adam. Since the biblical Eve gives the "forbidden" fruit to Adam, her actions become an analogue for the idea of sales. Seen in this light, the concept of temptation is evocative of a good sales technique. Ad after ad presents Eve as a temptress who employs sensuality as the vehicle through which the persuasion/sales is achieved. Sometimes in the ads, Adam is the focus of Eve's tempting actions. But at other times, it is just as likely that the reader/viewer will becomes an Adam surrogate.

In Western culture Eve/temptress stands for more than simply the "first female." Eve is frequently understood to be the prototype/template of *all* women. Thus, when ad after ad depicts Eve as a temptress/seductress, those ads are making a social comment about the nature of *all* women and reinforcing old cultural stereotypes. Frequently, in the end, this type of advertising reduces Eve to little more than a sex object. Even when ads change the biblical story line—and they sometimes do because they have no allegiance to the literal biblical account—they do so in a manner that perpetuates negative images of Eve/women.

In addition to the theme of persuasion/temptation, another Genesis 2–3 idea that gets used in marketing is that of "taboo/sin/forbidden fruit." Making something "forbidden" often serves to make it all the more alluring, and the story of Adam and Eve simply underscores this observation. Although they know they should not, Adam and Eve eat the fruit anyway. Since the biblical story is ambiguous about the type of *actual* fruit (ancient writers suggested all sorts of candidates), contemporary marketers find it easy to substitute their product for the forbidden one. Sometimes this substitution works better than at other times. Having apple juice or sour apple breath mints as "forbidden" connects with the idea of "apple" (a later suggested identity of the Garden's fruit) but does little to convey seriously the idea of "taboo." The same cannot be said of the gambling, alcohol, and tobacco industries' use of the forbidden fruit image. The products these industries peddle have the allure of the "dangerous" since all of them can lead to addiction. And, like the first man and woman, consumers of these products *know* they are dangerous and yet they do/consume them anyway. Products for these activities not only use Garden imagery, but also combine it with the Eve/temptress theme. Such usage goes beyond simple "persuasion" since the end goal is something that has the possibility of hurting the consumer. Unlike the Garden story, however, the end result is not expulsion but addiction.

Some interpreters in antiquity saw sex as either the sin of the Garden or a consequence of that sin. Contemporary opinion varies as to how one should view sex and sin. Marketers, however, realizing that "sex sells," find the juxtaposition of sex and sales a lucrative one. Not only do they use Eve's sexuality as a advertising strategy in their campaigns, but sexually related products also find the Garden a useful tool in their ads. This is especially true when it comes to the erotic/pornographic empire Adam & Eve. Whether this company succeeds in achieving its goal of being "sex-positive" or whether it simply repackages the old stereotype of Eve/woman/sex object/whore remains to be seen.

While jokes do not *sell* products they *are* products. As cultural artifacts they both describe and shape the culture in which they circulate. Although they sometimes entertain, they frequently represent a type of social commentary. In a subtle (and sometimes not-so-subtle) way, they can either support the status quo or challenge it. Since Genesis 2–3 is a story of origins, its characters become useful vehicles in supporting traditional gender roles or in attempts to subvert those traditions. Laughing at Eve is frequently another way of laughing at women. Such laughter supports the status quo and underscores the superiority of men. Laughing at Adam, however, challenges the idea that men are essentially superior to women. While making Eve the butt of a joke depends on stereotypes that men have of women, laughing at Adam does so by utilizing stereotypes that women often have of men. Finally, there are those jokes that make fun of both Adam and Eve while holding up all gender role expectations for examination. It is the nature of jokes to be able to explore dangerous/controversial topics with a sense of deniability—after all—"it's only a joke." In the end, however, jokes about Adam and Eve turn out to be jokes about us and no laughing matter.

Whose Adam? Whose Eve?

While Americans debate whether or not they live in a "Christian nation," there is no question that images from Genesis 1–3 saturate American culture. Whether they are working for or fulminating against the inclusion of intelligent design or creationism into science curricula, snacking on Eden food products or contemplating vegetarianism, admiring the one-chunk-out Apple logo on their MacBook, reading ads for alcoholic beverages, telling jokes about Adam and Eve, considering (or fantasizing about) sexual ecstasy, thinking about taking the kids to a Bible theme park, or watching Captain Kirk confront the Genesis Project in *Star Trek* reruns, Americans are surrounded by images of Eve, Adam, and Eden.

Eden, the first man, and the first woman represent not just sacred origins but also an idyllic type-time and type-place. As such they serve as a models for those who come after—whether it be people who find inspiration from them on how to live their lives, or marketers who blatantly use them for their consumerist goals, or comedians who poke fun at Adam and Eve in order to laugh at all men and women's relational problems. Of particular importance is the way interpreters define power dynamics in Eden. Describing the first woman as subordinate to the first man, for example, lends credence to gender hierarchy, just as in nineteenth-century America it provided support for another social hierarchy: African American slavery.[13] Similarly, reading Genesis 1 as literal history privileges creationism as a scientific theory, and arguing that Eden was geographically located in the United States contributes to the myth of American exceptionalism.

Popular images of Eve, Adam, and Eden wield power over any number of cultural artifacts and attitudes, especially the social construction of gender. Ultimately, commonplace images of Eden matter because those who have the voice to proclaim and the power to pursue their reconstructions of the Garden, or to recycle its symbolism, will irrevocably shape American society. It is not enough to note that references to Eden, Eve, and Adam are ubiquitous in our popular culture; what really matters is *whose* Eve, *whose* Adam, and *whose* Eden prevails.

~ RECREATING EDEN ~

The story didn't end when the first humans left the Garden.
It remained alive as long as people remembered it.
And people did remember it.

They went back to the Garden time and time again.
Oh, not to the *actual* Garden. . . . But to the *idea* of the Garden
And to the first human beings.

The story fascinated all sorts of people
for all sorts of reasons.

There were those who focused on Eve and Adam's relationship.

Some women imagined Adam as a real "prince" of a man
And tried endlessly to find him in the men around them.

Some men imagined Eve as a real "helper."
They domesticated women whenever they could,
And kept them in line when they couldn't. . . .

But the snake's promises of power and rule
Often poisoned these relationships.

Rather than recreating Eden's harmony and equality,
It was the post-Garden's hierarchy and oppression that they duplicated.

—L.S. & V.Z.

1

~

SOMEDAY MY PRINCE WILL COME
When Eden Becomes Camelot

Country music singers caution us about looking for love in all the wrong places. But what are the right places? Visit the religion section of your local bookstore, and you will find a host of writers pointing you to Genesis 1–3. Maybe you have never considered the creator God of the Hebrew Bible as the author of romance, or pondered the electrifying sexual chemistry God set alight in the Garden. Not to worry—popular culture is awash with evangelical Christian retellings of the original love-crazy couple: Adam and Eve.

As Joshua Harris, author of two hit guides to Christian romance, puts it, "Though we don't usually think of Adam and Eve's story as a love story, it is bursting with romance. . . . Can you imagine the moment their eyes first met? . . . Sparks flew. There was chemistry between those two like nothing you've ever seen. And here's the most incredible part: God was watching and rejoicing over it all. He was the one who arranged the original match. God, who spoke galaxies into existence, was finding joy in the beauty of romance between a man and a woman."[1]

If you have never pondered Eve and Adam as red-hot lovers, you may also never have considered the vitality of contemporary Christian lovemaking. But those who look to Eden as the birthplace of romance regard sexual desire as positively explosive and argue that evangelical Christians enjoy the most satisfying and frequent sex on the planet. For them, every Christian marriage is a recreation of the original mating in Eden, as each man learns to find, lead, and enrapture his wife. Here the success of marriage depends upon the recognition that, in the beginning, God created men to be initiators and women to be followers. Gender hierarchy is etched into the very structure of the universe, and people ignore it to their own detriment.

Though the celebration of romantic love is a familiar theme in American culture, the path to these evangelical marriages is anything but standard Hollywood fare. True to form, conservative evangelicals regard twenty-first-century American culture as hopelessly depraved, so enmeshed in sin that it is barely reminiscent of the golden age of Eden. Sexual immorality abounds, and much of the blame belongs to feminism, which these Christians regard as a gateway sin to a myriad of degradations. Women emasculate men when they refuse to submit graciously to them, and once the carefully crafted gender roles of Eden are abandoned, it is just as Cole Porter said: anything goes. Fornication, pornography, homosexuality, abortion, divorce, rape, bestiality, pedophilia, transgendering, bondage, and discipline—no practice is out of bounds for a godless culture.

Accordingly, though they celebrate the ideal of romantic love just as the larger culture does, conservative evangelicals have crafted traditions that are distinctive. Everything, of course, begins with the understanding that only men can initiate romantic relationships; women are to wait patiently for men to address them. Next comes the rejection of dating. These evangelicals argue that dating is nothing more than rehearsal for divorce, and they embrace courtship or betrothal in its place. People following this route to marriage are likely not to have kissed their spouse prior to their wedding. They distrust public education, often homeschool their children, and may also believe that, instead of going to college or pursuing careers, daughters should prepare themselves for marriage by serving their family in their father's house. And they frequently point to the figures of Princess and Prince Charming as role models for children, adolescents, and adults to emulate as they prepare for marriage.

This is a lifestyle with a heady mix of biblical and fairy-tale components. While these Christians regard Adam and Eve as prototypes of romantic love, they filter their understanding of life in Eden through extrabiblical images as well. Fairy tales, Walt Disney, Jane Austen, the gentility of a Victorian high tea, and life in a medieval castle all factor in. Even makeup and the color pink can be theologically significant. The reality is that Genesis 1–3 nowhere mentions love, much less proclaims God as the Creator of Romance. So while conservative Christians seek to be—and in some ways are—countercultural, their notions of romantic love and what it means to be a woman or a man are thoroughly permeated by American popular culture. In the quest to recreate life in the Garden, many Christians have confused Eden with Camelot and are more captives than transformers of American society.

A useful entry point into this world is to examine the way adults negotiate the path to marriage in the current evangelical "I Kissed Dating Goodbye" climate of romantic love and courtship. To understand how conservative Christians came to inhabit this world, it is helpful to investigate how they socialize their children to glorify women as passive Princesses and men as daring Prince Charmings. Also valuable is a consideration of how this fairy-tale context encourages stay-at-home daughters in the biblical patriarchy movement to renounce personal autonomy and embrace female submission with militant zeal. Finally, examining a version of evangelical romantic love that uses fairy-tale elements to problematize gender hierarchy provides an intriguing countervoice to typical conservative Christian renderings of Adam and Eve.

Passion and Purity

Sex and marital manuals have long been a preoccupation for evangelical Christian thinkers, who have for decades described conservative Christian sex as rapturous. The most recent crop of marriage guides springs from venerable roots, including Tim and Beverly LaHaye's 1976 *Act of Marriage: The Beauty of Sexual Love* and Ed and Gaye Wheat's *Intended for Pleasure: Sex Technique and Sex Fulfillment in Christian Marriage* (1977).[2] Both the LaHayes and the Wheats provide detailed physical instructions for Christian couples to ensure maximum enjoyment, and they counsel readers to expect frequent ecstasy. As Tim and Beverly LaHaye argue in their classic sex manual, "Spirit-filled Christians do not have an obsession with sex . . . [but] they enjoy it more on a permanent lifetime basis than any other group of people."[3]

The LaHayes trace the roots of blissful Christian sex to the Hebrew Bible, particularly to the creation. "Mutual pleasure and enjoyment are God's purpose in designing us as He did," they explain. "He has made that clear in His Word."[4] Thus, they advise, "It may be hard for us to think of Old Testament saints as being good lovers, but they were."[5] Indeed, how could they help it? After all, the LaHayes conclude, "God is the creator of sex. . . . God Himself brought Eve to Adam . . . [and] commanded them to make love."[6] Careful examination of Proverbs 5, which urges the husband to rejoice in the wife of his youth by letting her breasts ever satisfy him, leaves the LaHayes in no doubt that God, as they put it, "intended the act of marriage to be the most sublime experience two people could share on earth."[7]

In *I Kissed Dating Goodbye* (1997) and *Boy Meets Girl* (2000), Joshua Harris continues the LaHayes' enthusiastic description of God as the creator of good sex, but he adds his own twist, urging Christians to abandon dating in favor of courtship. Harris was only twenty-one when he wrote *I Kissed Dating Goodbye*, and as a single, homeschooled young man preparing for the conservative evangelical ministry, he became the cover boy for a new movement. Harris was not the first Christian writer to argue against dating, but the enormous popularity of *I Kissed Dating Goodbye* catapulted the Christian courtship movement into public consciousness.[8]

Harris confesses in *I Kissed Dating Goodbye* that he owes a great debt to Elisabeth Elliot, the author of another iconic text of Christian marital romance: *Passion and Purity* (1984). Though she does not provide a "how-to" section in her works, no author is more celebrated in the field of marriage advice than Elliot, who gained fame in the 1950s with her accounts of her first husband Jim Elliot, who was killed by the Aucas, a remote Ecuadoran tribe whom he was missionizing.[9] Harris' mother gave him *Passion and Purity* when he was sixteen, hoping to encourage him to break up a dating relationship she found inappropriate.[10] As a teenager, Harris was less than thrilled to receive Elliot's story of her very long and very chaste courtship. Contemporary readers can sympathize, given that Elliot's premise—"it is possible to love passionately and to stay out of bed"—promised little titillation.[11]

The book delivered on its pledge, outlining an exceedingly virtuous romance. The early stages were decidedly unpromising. Upon confessing his love for Elisabeth in the spring of 1948, Jim promptly determined that he was called to a life of celibacy and announced that they should no longer see or write to one other. Eventually Jim decided that they could resume writing, but it was not until January 1953 that he proposed, and then only under the condition that Elisabeth learn Quichua, a native Ecuadorian language. Elisabeth said yes to both proposals, and the couple enjoyed their first kiss. A period of diligent language study followed, and in October 1953 they were married in Ecuador. The wedding night, she tells us, was "unspeakably worth the wait."[12] After Jim's death in 1956, Elisabeth went on to write several books about Jim as well as numerous theological works. In 1976, at what she called the "height of the strong feminist movement that swept through our country," Elisabeth published *Let Me Be a Woman*, a book of advice to their daughter Valerie as she faced marriage.[13]

Let Me Be a Woman returns to many of the themes outlined earlier in *Passion and Purity*. To explain how she and Jim managed to remain pure (though passionate) prior to marriage, Elliot credits their knowledge of Genesis 1–3. "The notion of hierarchy," she says, "comes from the Bible." In fashioning the world, God gave every entity its place in the cosmic hierarchy. And when it was time to create people, God first created man and then made woman "from and for" him. From the beginning, therefore, God fashioned the male "to call forth, to lead, initiate, and rule," and the female "to respond, follow, adapt, submit." Indeed, Elliot concludes, even "if we held to a different theory of origin, the physical structure of the female would tell us that woman was made to receive, to bear, to be acted upon, to complement to nourish."[14] Apart from biblical revelation, therefore, the natural shape of our bodies nonetheless proves the Genesis message that men are initiators and women are passive receivers.

Moreover, an unbiased study of both biology and Scripture, Elliot is convinced, reveals that man and woman are also polar opposites. Genesis 2 merely poetically states what every honest person acknowledges: woman's "desire" for a husband is an "inextinguishable hope for recognition, response, protection." Conversely, in the man there is "always the restlessness to wander, experiment, conquer."[15] Inevitably man's love differs from woman's. Woman seeks rest in man, but as Jim Elliot once wrote Elisabeth, "Love is not all a resting in me. It is a tenseness and a daring, a call to crush and conquer."[16] Thus, Elisabeth contends, God created the woman as "totally other, totally different, totally God's gift to man . . . [so that] each stands in relation to the other."[17]

Given this premise, Elisabeth concludes that wives must submit themselves to their husbands. "It is," she insists, "the will of God that woman be subordinate to man in marriage. Marriage is used in the Old Testament to express the relation between God and His covenant people and in the New Testament between Christ and the Church. . . . Tremendous heavenly truths are set forth in a wife's subjection to her husband, and this use of this metaphor in the Bible cannot be accidental."[18] Rather, God has given each gender special instructions. "It all makes up the pattern—God's pattern."[19]

Elliot concedes that submission is not easy, but since God's pattern for man and woman is embedded in the created order, it is essential to human happiness. Gender hierarchy and complementarity are simply a cosmic reality, and if people hope to flourish they must embrace them. Elliot explains, "The roles are not assigned on the basis of capability. They were determined at the beginning of Creation to be a man's role and a woman's role and . . . we are not free to experiment, tamper with, or exchange them. . . . We can count on the God who issued the order to provide the strength to carry it out."[20]

Elliot can take a perverse pleasure in the necessity of yielding to God's will. At one point she suggests that people ought to welcome the suffering that unconsummated love provides—after all, if suffering was good enough for Jesus, it ought to help us mature spiritually.[21] And she is horrified at the gender role confusion she finds rampant in American culture: "There are signs of confusion far worse than women chasing men," she says. "Homosexuality, teenage pregnancy, divorce, abortion, the new 'house-husband' role, new translations of the Bible to eliminate 'sexist' language, women suing the New York fire department because they flunked the test for 'firepersons'—signs that the congruous has become incongruous. The order disordered. The complementarity competitive. The glory of our sexuality, in short, is tarnished."[22] In other words, once God's clearly demarcated gender roles are muddled, all hell breaks loose.

Worship in Bed

No one is likely to accuse Elliot of lacking zeal for the subordination of women to men. In approaching this material, Joshua Harris strikes a more winsome tone. He is just as convinced that gender hierarchy is God's will, but he is far less likely than Elliot to heap scorn on women for coveting autonomy. Elliot describes this desire as a "damnable kind of pride" and notes in self-loathing detail that "women are always tempted to be initiators. . . . If we can't dragoon our men . . . we plead, we get attention by tears, silence or withholding warmth and intimacy. We have a large bag of tricks."[23] Harris works hard, on the other hand, to explain that both genders face challenges. "Girls," he says, "don't struggle with the same temptations we struggle with. We wrestle more with our sex drives while girls struggle more with their emotions."[24] He also contends, "a man's biggest temptation is to be passive, a woman's biggest temptation is to take control."[25]

Like Elliot, Harris turns to Genesis to discover what it means to be a man or a woman, and in Eden he sees gender roles encompassing male leadership and female submission. God, Harris observes, "made Adam first, signifying his unique role as leader and initiator. He created Eve from Adam and brought her to Adam to be his helper. . . . She was made to complement, nourish, and help her husband. God's greatest gift to man was 'a helper suitable for him' (Genesis 2:18). This doesn't minimize a woman's role, but it does define it."[26]

Conceding that such roles are sometimes difficult to accept, Harris promises more than suffering for the faithful; the reward for honoring God's design, both by accepting one's gender role and by refraining from dating, is marital ecstasy. "Why," Harris queries, "does God ask single Christians to face the daily struggle of controlling their sexual appetites until marriage? One answer is that He's committed to great sex!" Harris provides enough personal information to assure readers he knows what he's talking about. "I've read," he says, "that honeymoon resorts are having to provide more and more activities for newlyweds who, since they didn't wait, are bored by sex by the time they get married. While many sexually promiscuous couples greet the marriage bed with a yawn, the chaste fall into it with cries of delight. On our honeymoon, Shannon and I didn't need a schedule packed with activities. We rarely left our hotel room!"[27]

In a chapter subsection titled "Worship in Bed," Harris expounds the point. "God," he says, "celebrates pure sex within marriage. He invites us to do the same." In marriage, at long last, Christian couples find pleasure rather than frustration. After all, Harris explains, God made sex drives "for our enjoyment and His glory. Because He's very, very good. He could have made the means by which we procreate as brief and boring as sneezing. Instead, He gave it more sizzle than the Fourth of July. And when the husband and wife revel in and thank God for the gift of sex, they glorify Him. Their love-making becomes a jubilant, two-person worship service!"

The key to this jubilation, naturally, is adherence to biblical principles. "To plan ahead for a great sex life," Harris counsels, "we have to realize that the message of Scripture is not for us to disdain sex, but to love God's original design so much that we see the world's perversions of it as revolting."[28] In the season of courtship, God calls Christians to store up their passions. "Each time you feel as though you're *denying* yourselves, you're actually *blessing* yourselves," Harris contends. Purity now means increased passion in marriage later. So as couples think biblically about sex and accept God's plan, they are setting the stage for "thrilling, God-glorifying sex."[29] Harris does not doubt that God rejoices in such ecstasy. "'Enjoy pure sex!' God practically shouts in Proverbs 5:18-19. . . . Be captivated, be ravished by the body of your spouse. . . . Be entranced by the true and lasting pleasure of the marriage bed."[30]

In the end, for Harris, marriage reveals God's sovereignty. Just as God gave Eve to Adam in the Garden, so today God gives to a Christian man the woman God calls him to marry. Harris begins *Boy Meets Girl* with an imaginary conversation between Adam and his great-great-granddaughter Elanna, who wonders how she will find a mate pleasing to God. Adam responds that, when people live in obedience to God, they will recognize the mate God has chosen for them just as clearly as he identified Eve. "When the Maker brings you your husband, you'll be aware that it was He who made you for each other and He who planned your meeting. And in that moment, just as we did, you'll want to sing a song of praise to Him."[31]

The purpose of *Boy Meets Girl* is to describe how Josh and Shannon experienced that moment. "Our love story, like all real love stories," Josh explains, "was arranged by God. All the coincidences that made it possible were interventions of His grace. Our story was His story."[32] It is a simple tale, Josh concedes, but it was not always easy: "Two people learning to trust God. Two winding paths that God made straight. Two straight paths that He chose to cross at just the right time. We watched Him do that. For all the moments of difficulty it involved, we wouldn't trade the experience for anything." And, of course, Harris observes, "God wants to do the same for you. Yes, you. The Creator of romance, the Maker who arranged the first 'boy meets girl' in the Garden so very long ago, is still at work."[33]

Having established Christian marriage as bliss, in his next book Harris broke the bad news: marriage is not the end of sexual temptation.[34] In *Not Even a Hint* (2003), written after he was already the father of two children, Harris relates his ongoing agonies: he is fascinated by lingerie catalogues that arrive in his mail, by good-looking women at his gym and at the beach, and even by innocent hugs from women at church. He sadly concludes that "a Christian man seeking to resist lust never reaches a state where he's unaware of a female's body."[35]

The only answer is to separate oneself from the sources of temptation. Harris advises men to ask their wives or mothers to sort through the mail to be sure sensual catalogues hit the trash before they catch the eye; he tells Christian women to dress modestly and not to hug men, even at church; he decides to vacation at less desirable beaches where the women are not as pretty; and he resolves never to "counsel or correspond" with a woman (except his wife) about lust. That meant he had to hire a female researcher to interview women for *Not Even a Hint*.[36]

For Harris, women are such potent temptations that safety comes in sticking with one's own kind. For men, that means assuming roles of leadership in the church and in the family; for women, it means embracing lives of submission. Married women should focus on the home. Though Harris' wife Shannon is active as a singer in the church he pastors, they do not share a ministry or even a website.[37] Josh is currently the senior pastor at Covenant Life Church in Maryland, overseeing a large staff of male pastors; Shannon is a wife and mother who also sings. Given the incredible volatility of the male sexual drive that Harris describes, a separation of male and female spheres would be a practical necessity even if he did not also regard it as a theological mandate. Women will always be temptresses for Harris; they represent threats to male power and purity.[38]

Central to Harris' reading of Genesis 1–3 is the articulation of hierarchical gender roles that can lead to romantic unions so ecstatic that participants call them forms of worship. In this world, purity outside of marriage, passion within it, rigorous channeling of the volatile male sex drive, diligent harnessing of the female yearning for autonomy, and a willingness to see the story of Adam and Eve as a tale of both promise and peril constitute the theological foundations undergirding God as the Creator of Romance.

Someday My Prince Will Come

Enticing as fairy-tale endings may be, one might imagine that the prospect of being a subordinate helpmeet would be less than alluring for evangelical women. But evangelical girls are groomed from an early age to regard themselves as princesses awaiting their special Prince Charming. They have been dressing in pink, wearing crowns, and attending an array of royal ceremonies for as long as they can remember. Few if any New Testament exegetes would recognize the color pink or the image of a princess as critical to Christian identity. But that failure would put them sadly out of touch with popular American Christianity, where girls and women are constantly encouraged to consider themselves divine princesses and to embrace frilly pink smocks as God's clothing of preference. No image could better serve the evangelical insistence on women as passive recipients of male initiative then these fairy-tale renderings of the Princess in her lonely castle, waiting and praying for Prince Charming to set her free. Gender hierarchy is thus the foundation for recreating Eden as Camelot.

Despite the rhetoric identifying Christian romance as countercultural, in their pursuit of all things pink and princess, evangelical females are in lockstep with secular society. As Peggy Orenstein notes in her despairing book, *Cinderella Ate My Daughter*, the color pink attracts today's girls "like heat-seeking missiles," drawing them into a world where becoming a princess represents their highest aspiration. Orenstein paints a bleak picture of that ambition. "Princesses," she says, "avoid female bonding. Their goals are to be saved by a prince, get married . . . and be taken care of for the rest of their lives. Their value derives largely from their appearance. They are rabid materialists."[39] At a loss to explain why popular American culture so strongly urges girls to embrace this identity, Orenstein suggests that these royal images speak to parents' "unspoken, nonrational" desires and fears. "The desire to encourage our girls' imperial fantasies is, at least in part," she suggests, "a reaction to a newly unstable world. We *need* their innocence not only for consumerist but for *spiritual* redemption."[40]

Whatever redemption might mean for American society as a whole, in Christian circles, princesses replay the original encounter of man and woman in Eden. But this time, the story has a happy ending. The new Eves are passive, obedient, and resplendent in long-flowing gowns. The new Adams are enterprising and commanding, prepared to govern their wives firmly. A return to paradise—now envisioned as a medieval castle rather than an idyllic garden—is at hand. It is hard to imagine a greater trivializing of the Christian faith.

To ensure that Christian girls are effectively socialized into this scenario, they are bombarded by products that reinforce it. The color pink, for example, is ubiquitous in Christian girl culture—pastel T-shirts, hats, kitchen magnets, and coffee mugs proclaim their users to be a princess of the divine King. Even Bible covers come in pink, and there are Bibles marketed exclusively to the Christian princess.[41] Some Christian enterprises raise the color pink to ontological status, as in the case of PINC Ministries. Aimed at girls aged twelve to eighteen, the PINC website is a festival of pink bubbles, including a pink cat inscribed with the words, "Pink isn't just a color . . . it's an ATTITUDE!"[42]

PINC hopes to persuade girls to become PINC princesses by convincing them that "being a godly girl is the 'cool thing' to do." PINC offers conferences, "Yes and No Fashion Shows," cheerleading camps, mother-daughter activities, tips for eating less during the holidays, and a "PINC Boutique" with "awesome products" including "real tiara's [*sic*]," all designed to exhort girls to set themselves apart from the larger culture by embracing sexual purity and modest clothing. The PINC strategy is clear. It incorporates activities and fashions popular in girl culture—such as the color pink, which it dubs the "universal color for female"—to draw girls into becoming princesses for Jesus.

Innumerable ministries follow the same tactic. Christian purity culture may be inspired by the biblical characters of Adam and Eve, and it may champion the subordination of women to men, but it is the appeal of fairy-tale princes and princesses that gives it social capital among Christian girls. Nancy Leigh DeMoss' Pure in Heart conferences provide another example. A popular evangelical author and speaker, DeMoss has two syndicated radio shows, has sold millions of books, runs the Revive Our Hearts ministry for women, and is a prominent leader in the True Woman movement, an offshoot of Revive Our Hearts.[43] Central to the True Woman ministry is the True Woman Manifesto, which cites texts from Genesis 1–3 in arguing that "men and women were designed to reflect the image of God in complementary and distinct ways" that involve female submission and "God-ordained male leadership in the home and in the church."[44]

Pure in Heart conferences are yet another dimension of DeMoss' work. The conferences are one-day events targeting girls aged seven to twelve and their mothers, grandmothers, and mentors. The conferences promise to teach girls "practical, biblical wisdom to help them make choices for purity" and to provide "practical take-home tools that will help prepare children to combat the conflicting cultural messages they face each day."[45] Naturally there is merchandise for sale, and conference materials assure attendees that opportunities will be provided throughout the day for mothers and daughters to shop.[46]

Conference videos at the Pure in Heart website focus on princess and purity themes. They show girls dressed in pink, wearing tiaras, learning about the "royal love story," singing with their mothers, and offering testimonies to the importance of being pure, dressing modestly, and knowing God. Mothers express gratitude for the conferences' stress on purity but fret about their inability to transmit that message to their daughters. In response, videos promise that the conferences will help mothers win their "special princess's heart" and that with their daughters they will "explore together their identity as beloved daughters of the King."[47]

Other materials associated with Pure in Heart ministries include the popular *Princess and the Kiss* books, part of a curriculum designed to teach sexual purity to Christian girls.[48] *Life Lessons from the Princess and the Kiss* guides girls through twenty-one sessions that lead the young princess from preparing her heart to know God's love to—finally—marrying the prince God has chosen for her and starting a family. This blessed literary conclusion is to be followed by a real-world *Princess and the Kiss* Ceremony. Mothers are urged to decorate the ceremony site with "royal decor," including a throne and a princess tiara or headdress. Mothers and even fathers are encouraged to dress as queens and kings. During the ceremony, daughters kneel or sit before their mothers, who bless them, present them with a Revive Our Hearts Princess Prayer Box neck-lace, and then pray over them.[49]

Life Lessons from the Princess and the Kiss quotes Scripture frequently, stressing absolute sexual abstinence prior to marriage and exhorting the prin-cess to avoid the disobedience of Adam and Eve by submitting herself to God, to her parents, and to her future husband.[50] It is a sobering book—hardly the stuff of popular youth literature—but *Princess and the Kiss* materials have sold well because of their success in presenting gender hierarchy in the guise of a story of a cloistered Princess awaiting Prince Charming.

Pure in Heart resources are just the tip of the iceberg when it comes to Christian princess culture. A teenaged girl who wanted to spend more time in Camelot/Eden could, among many other options, visit a homeschooled girl's blog to sign the "Committed to Being Christ's Valentine" petition, indi-cating her willingness to "remain faithful to your future Prince Charming."[51] She could go to Facebook to interact with fans of the *Christian Princess Molly* books.[52] She could read *Before You Meet Prince Charming: A Guide to Radiant Purity* and learn how to reject the "world's way" for "God's way" by honoring God's plan for the creation and waiting for Sir Valiant, her future husband, to initiate their relationship.[53]

Or the teenaged girl could consult Focus on the Family, the venerable con-servative Christian institute founded by James Dobson, and its Becoming a Modern-Day Princess program—"a biblically based rite-of-passage program for teenage girls." The back cover of *Raising a Modern-Day Princess* situates parents and mentors in the land of make-believe, asking, "Sleeping Beauty, Cinderella, Snow White—how many girls, at some point, dream of being a princess like these fairy tale characters?" *Raising a Modern-Day Princess* out-lines a dizzying array of rituals and curricula to help girls "realize their place as daughters of the King—true Modern-Day Princesses."[54] Central to this program are purity balls and purity rings designed to help unmarried girls embrace chastity enthusiastically, using romantic rituals to promote an ethic of abstinence at odds with the sexual permissiveness of the larger culture.

Nevertheless, abstinence can be a hard sell, so other Modern-Day Princess activities unabashedly embrace popular youth activities. Makeup nights in particular are important events both for the budding princesses and for their leaders, and the authors acknowledge that learning table etiquette and natural beauty tips are "always a highlight of the journey" in Becoming a Modern-Day Princess. These activities are popular, they say, because "etiquette training enables a girl to act like a princess; makeup enables her to look and feel like one!" The authors especially urge readers to purchase Mary Kay products.[55] Apparently the emphasis on beauty and makeup works. One mother remembers how reluctant her daughter was to become a part of the Modern-Day Princess program; fortunately, makeup provided a pivotal incentive. "We dragged Sarah to the first meeting but it turned out to be a fun-filled night of makeovers and manners with friendly girls close to her own age. After the evening concluded and we drove home, she decided not to drop out."[56]

And it is not just the girls who enjoy Mary Kay products. One Modern-Day Princess mentor explains her love for makeup and her joy in teaching girls how to look and act like ladies:

> Being a part of the makeup and manners night was right up my alley. I have had my hands in makeup since I was three years old, and my hands, I guess, just never came out. The manners part would later follow when I started auditioning for pageants, interviewing for jobs, and meeting influential people. So needless to say, this night was one of my favorites and I loved teaching the girls how to apply makeup and behave like a lady.[57]

This emphasis on beauty and manners is hardly limited to Becoming a Modern-Day Princess. Danna Gresh's Secret Keeper Girl's *8 Great Dates for Moms & Daughters*—a book James Dobson spiritedly endorsed—promises to help mothers "replace our culture's lies with truth and make a lasting connection with your tween girl." Gresh urges readers to "think facials, tea parties, shopping challenges!" as they pursue mother-daughter activities designed to ground girls in spiritual wholeness and to answer critical "real-life questions" such as "what is real beauty?" and "how do I take care of my hair?"[58] Gresh manages to connect hair care to female submission by reminding readers that the Apostle Paul advised women to wear a sign of authority on their heads because in Eden woman was created from and for man.[59]

Being submissive does not, however, entail depriving oneself. For the first date, Gresh advises mothers to "thoroughly pamper" their daughters at "an exclusive little teahouse or a swank hotel" where they will enjoy "an extravagant tea." Date two, devoted to learning "the discipline of skin care," includes a "special, pampering facial" and, if possible, a meeting with a Mary Kay consultant. Gresh urges mothers to give their daughters ten to fifteen dollars to spend on Mary Kay lip gloss and skin care products and reminds them to "treat yourself to something too!"[60] In addition to the usual references to royalty ("*Key thought:* God calls me a princess"), Gresh also addresses the saving power of pink. "We need to make sure that we don't clothe ourselves in dark and dreary attire," Gresh counsels. "Since a Secret Keeper Girl loves Jesus, she represents life. So we vote 'no' to darkness and skulls and bottom crossbones." Of course, sometimes a girl just wants to get down with a little punk rock. In that case, Gresh recommends, "instead of all the death and dark colors, try bright pink with the touch of black."[61] Tea parties, pampering, extravagance, Mary Kay, and pink: these are the "countercultural" values of Gresh's Christian princess and her Jesus.

Yet Gresham is not alone in focusing on manners or tea times. The Purely Woman School of Grace also provides insight into the connection between Genesis and etiquette. Founded by Jordyn Wilson, who describes daughters as "regal princesses," the Purely Woman School of Grace celebrates the splendor and refinement inherent in God's design of femininity. The weeklong school elevates etiquette and beauty to theological virtues. "The ladies will learn how to create lovely environments of welcome and beauty and learn the basics of etiquette, grace, and hosting," Wilson explains. "We will practice the charm of posture and mingling, the art of valuing others, asking wise questions, how to formally set a table, host with grace and many other venues of beauty." Participants note that the class taught them "what God calls us to be as woman," and a mother enthuses that she and her nine-year-old daughter "regularly discuss the content [of the School of Grace] in our mother/daughter tea times." Wilson herself observes that she "loves a good cup of tea."[62]

But the self-proclaimed purveyor of a "High Tea without equal"[63] is an organization called Vision Forum.[64] Led by Doug Phillips and based in San Antonio, Vision Forum offers a dizzying array of products and blogs dedicated to what it calls "the timeless truths of biblical patriarchy." Central to biblical patriarchy are the maleness of God; man's headship over woman as established in the creation of Adam and Eve; man's sovereignty over woman in the family, church, and state; a rejection of birth control, given God's command in Genesis 1 to "be fruitful and multiply";[65] a rejection of public schools in favor of Christian education in which "fathers are sovereign over the training of their children"; and the limitation of woman to the domestic realm as the God-ordained "helper to her husband, the bearer of children, and a 'keeper at home.' "[66] In this world, tea parties represent the "great domestic sciences of Christian civilization" that every daughter should master.[67] And daughters learn to serve and please their fathers, who in turn represent both God and Prince Charming to them. If that seems a bit confusing, welcome to the world of father-daughter high teas and "stay-at-home daughters," as explicated by Vision Forum and its most prominent advocates: Doug Phillips, Geoffrey Botkin, and Botkin's daughters Anna Sofia and Elizabeth.

If You Want to Be Princesses, Start by Loving Your Daddies
Stay-At-Home Daughters

Each spring, Vision Forum holds a father-daughter retreat, replete with "unity games" like croquet matches in which "the daughter played and the father corrected when needed"[68] or trust walks to foster daughters' reliance on their fathers.[69] High tea served in porcelain cups, accompanied by a variety of delicate snacks, with fathers and daughters dressed to the nines, is a highly anticipated event.[70] There are also catered meals and speeches, and sometime during the weekend Anna Sofia and Elizabeth Botkin will play the harp, greet admirers, and, after being introduced by their father Geoffrey, give an inspirational talk about biblical femininity. Authors of a popular book (*So Much More*), DVD (*The Return of the Daughters*), and blog (visionarydaughters.com), the Botkin sisters are stars of the biblical patriarchy movement. The sisters are in their twenties and as yet unmarried, and their insistence that daughters must reject higher education and careers in favor of serving their fathers until they are given to their husbands is so enthusiastic that detractors have accused them of infecting adherents with Botkin Syndrome, a form of covert incest.[71]

Certainly the Botkin daughters are blunt. The creation account in Genesis 2, they claim, reveals that God designed women to help and complete men.[72] Therefore, they tell young women, "[Y]our destiny will always be tied to the vision of a man." They praise their mother for choosing to be overshadowed by their father and exhort girls to say goodbye to "useless, selfish, autonomous 'adulthood.'"[73] Individuality, they explain, is for kids. "Any two-year-old girl has a mind of her own," they observe, just as every "woman knows her own mind—it's part of being Eve's daughters." Feminism is thus the fruit of Eve's rebellion in the Garden, and the Botkins call upon Christian girls to reject it and embrace true femininity instead. Exercising autonomy, they insist, is "toddler stuff"; true femininity is "about helping men fulfill their calling." And real maturity involves giving your heart to your father, claiming his vision for your own, and joining with your family to act as a "powerful weapon for Christ's glory and Kingdom."[74]

The time between completing homeschooling and getting married provides a special opportunity for stay-at-home daughters to give their hearts to their fathers. Anna Sofia and Elizabeth know a number of stay-at-home daughters whom they cite as exemplars of this process. One is named Ruth, who asserts that "Daddy is my God-given authority." It is important for her to know and appreciate her daddy's views, Ruth explains, in order to "understand and articulate what I believe." This knowledge extends even to matters of dress. "If he, for instance, has a preference in colors that I wear, I seek to honor him by finding that out and dressing in a way that would please him." Hannah, another stay-at-home daughter, explains that submitting to her father as the "king of my home" allows her to "know my place and glory in my duties." Hannah claims that this knowledge has increased her love for her father. Formerly, she says, "He was just my dad." But now, he is "my friend, my guardian, my priest, and my knight in shining armor. I give glory to God for my dad."[75]

The Botkins also cite Jasmine Baucham, daughter of evangelist Voddie Baucham. Jasmine admits that, as she grew up, she dreamed of going to NYU and becoming a screenwriter. Staying at home instead and submitting to her father was, as she puts it, "something that I fought against. It felt weak, it felt wrong." In the end, however, Jasmine came to believe that submitting to her father was a good thing. As Voddie himself explains, the Bible commands women to be submissive because Eve, the first woman, sought to usurp her husband's position. Therefore, he had to rein Jasmine in as she sought independence: "What I need to foster in my daughter is not the sin to which she's prone; I need to foster the biblical pattern that she must learn. . . . Jasmine has gifts, she has abilities, and those are being developed as she works with and serves her father."[76]

As the founder of Vision Forum, Doug Phillips further explicates these patterns. Essential to the Scriptures, he claims, are two eternal relationships: the parent/child model exemplified in the connection between God the Father and God the Son, and the bridegroom/bride model first articulated in the creation of Adam and Eve and then consummated eschatologically in the book of Revelation, when Christ the Lamb marries the Church, his bride. These biblical patterns, Phillips insists, are absolutely critical to the Christian life; they are also exemplified in the relationship between a godly father and his submissive daughter.[77]

For Phillips, the central element in the relationship of God the Father to God the Son is the Father's authority to command the Son and the Son's willingness to obey. In Christian families, Phillips argues, earthly fathers must imitate God the Father by daily exercising their authority over their daughters.

And daughters must imitate Jesus, who submitted to God the Father even unto death. Just as Jesus "gave his heart to the Father," says Phillips, "daughters must give their hearts to their dads." Phillips describes this winning and giving of hearts with the language of romantic love. Think of a girl's father, he invites, as a knight in armor, riding an enormous white horse. It is his job to "woo" and "win" his daughter, the princess. Phillips urges Christian men to pull out all the stops. "Are you appropriately physical with your daughters?" he asks. "Do you come up, do you love them? Do you hug them? Do you put your arms around them? Do you kiss them? . . . I'm probably overzealous. I just grab my girls, throw them up in the air, smother them with kisses, and they do the same with me. . . . They tackle me, they deck me, they knock me to the ground, and they pummel me."[78]

For biblical patriarchy, all of this is essential if daughters are to embrace submission with joy. As Geoffrey Botkin elaborates, when daughters give their hearts to their fathers, they are learning how to submit to God and are preparing themselves to submit to their future husbands. "The father-daughter relationship," he contends, "is crucial to God's design. It is primarily where girls learn God's ways and how to stay on track."[79] It is here, too, where girls learn to be princesses. As Anna Sofia puts it,

> If you girls want to be feminine, if you want to be real ladies, if you want to be princesses, start by loving your daddies. That's the most feminine thing that you can do. Love your Daddy. Love his vision. Serve him. Do right, so that his heart can safely trust in you. If we don't get that right, then it doesn't matter how girly our clothes are, or how good our manners are. If it's not about putting our husbands, fathers, or families first, it's not femininity as God designed it.[80]

Doug Phillips concurs, noting that a properly trained daughter will be ready, when it is time for her to marry, to submit to her husband just as the Church will submit to Christ, the heavenly bridegroom, in the eschaton. At marriage, Phillips says, a father gives his princess to a new Prince Charming— her husband. Here the biblical pattern of bridegroom/bride merges with the secular fairy tale of prince/princess. Phillips recounts with relish officiating at a wedding in which the bride's father unveiled a huge sword modeled after the one Mel Gibson carried in *Braveheart*. Commanding the groom to kneel, the bride's father said,

> In the name of the Lord Jesus Christ I commission you to take my daughter. . . . You are to be the loving Lord in your home and over her. Cherish and love her and never forget what a rare gift God has given to you. Keep the sword in your house forever.

When your children rise up and ask you "father, whence comes this sword," you must answer them that "This sword was given as a charge by my father to me as a reminder that our family would forever be followers of the Lord Jesus Christ, and that the covenant of marriage is sacred and never to be broken."[81]

While it is tempting to unpack all the metaphors at work here, suffice it to say that the gender hierarchy basic to this theology portrays the male head of the home as God's royal commander. When daughters and mothers are obedient, they empower their commanders to use the principal weapon God has given them—the patriarchal family—to advance the sacred vocation to which God has called them—recovering Christian civilization.[82] There is no greater or more desperate cause in the universe. For while the principles of biblical patriarchy may be timeless, American society has fallen away from the sanctity of its Puritan founding. Thus God's kingdom hangs in the balance; the times call for men of exceptional courage and daring. Daughters who give their hearts to their fathers, Elizabeth Botkin argues, give them confidence to be "more dominion-minded, more visionary, more entrepreneurial, more full of faith, and bolder" in their leadership.[83] In return, Doug Phillips remarks, these fathers share with their daughters their own warrior spirit, and invite them to serve God by helping their fathers to rule.[84]

In this way, stay-at-home daughters may be delegated considerable power and responsibility. "Dominion," the Botkin sisters explain, "means taking responsibility for your generation and subduing it. . . . It means subduing the media, the fashion industry, the economy, the government, bring everything in submission to Christ." Their father concurs, lamenting that American society has abandoned the gender complementarity integral to God's creation and calling upon Christian fathers and their daughters to proclaim and practice the gender hierarchy basic to biblical patriarchy. "Dads," he exhorts, "you and your daughters have the responsibility of disciplining our generation and the next generation to correct and reform what's missing, what's wrong."[85] In modeling biblical femininity to an unbelieving world, Elizabeth Botkin explains, the Christian daughter "wants everything she does to inspire and edify others, and glorify God, and so she radiates regal serenity, grace and poise, a gentle and quiet voice, discretion, self command, sincerity, peace, cheerfulness, and humility." At the same time, she does not shrink from dirty work. "Understanding that there's a time for everything, she is balanced, flexible, ready to serve tea or to take up a tent peg against an enemy."[86]

The Botkin sisters are extraordinary ambassadors on behalf of biblical patriarchy. Their public prominence demonstrates how stay-at-home daughters can function as weapons in their fathers' arsenal in the battle for this particular version of Christian civilization. Poised and talented, Anna Sofia and Elizabeth Botkin are very much at the forefront of the crusade to renounce female autonomy and subject Eve's daughters to male authority. As long as they are single, the Botkin sisters are free to learn and speak their father's mind. Ultimately, however, stay-at-home daughters will be called to wed, and they will be expected to bear and train as many children as possible in the service of what they call "mission-driven marriage and multigenerational family fruitfulness." Like their mother, the Botkin sisters will practice "dominion femininity" and "militant fecundity," allowing themselves to be overshadowed by their husbands and even their children.[87] And public focus will pass to the next generation of princesses for Christ.

All of this happens through the incestuous rhetoric of fathers wooing and winning daughters' hearts, serving as Prince Charming both to their wives and to their daughters while celebrating their daughters' grace and etiquette as foundational virtues to conquering the world. There is, to quote the Botkins one last time, "a time for flowers, chocolates, ruffles, tea, but these are not the sum total of femininity. . . . It's not for us to escape into fantasy worlds. This crooked and messed up generation, this world, is the battleground that God chose to put us into, and we should be grateful for it."[88]

In the world of biblical patriarchy, when Eve's daughters go to tea, they also go to war. Ostensibly dedicated to recreating Eden, these Christians unapologetically conflate the fantasy world of Camelot with the biblical Garden. For all the talk about fidelity to Scripture, the ruling metaphors here derive from secular fairy tales and romanticized versions of Victorian womanhood, not the Bible. Men in the biblical patriarchy movement are in cultural captivity to these images, as are their women. But the women face another kind of subjugation, for they must learn at an early age to renounce selfhood and to objectify themselves as weapons in their fathers' battle to transform American society into a realm of exclusive male privilege and power. Here daughters must sacrifice their identities to their daddies, forswearing education, careers, and even their favorite colors to make themselves over in their fathers' images. This is a new version of the biblical creation story indeed, with fathers and husbands standing in for God. Whatever the biblical patriarchy movement lacks in Bible, it more than makes up for in patriarchy.

When God Writes Your Love Story

Before leaving the enchanted world of Jesus, Prince Charming, and worship in bed, it is important to examine a conservative evangelical view of romantic love that wholeheartedly adopts fairy-tale elements at the same time that it reimagines much of the gender hierarchy typical of evangelical theology. Popular Christian authors Eric and Leslie Ludy have, as Eric's online biography modestly puts it, "been jointly representative of purity, beauty, and excellence in marriage since their inspiring pre-marriage relationship culminated in covenant vows in December of 1994."[89] Their books include *When God Writes Your Love Story, Romance God's Way, Teaching True Love, The First 90 Days of Marriage, When Dreams Come True,* and *A Perfect Wedding.* The Ludys helped popularize courtship and the notion of waiting till the altar to share the first kiss. They are well known in the evangelical world as speakers, recording artists, authors, and, in more recent years, explorers and purveyors of radical spirituality.

Much of what Leslie and Eric Ludy say about Christian romance and marriage will sound familiar. They believe that God created men and women as complements to one another and that "the entire Bible is a picture of a beautiful romance between the Bridegroom and His bride." But the Ludys do not contend that daughters should subjugate themselves to their fathers' visions of Christian dominion, nor do they believe that wives should give up their individual ministries in order to devote themselves solely to their families. And while they do profess a fondness for Mel Gibson (Eric's last solo book was *The Bravehearted Gospel: The Truth Is Worth Fighting For*), they argue that Christian women need to become warriors while Christian men need to connect with their feminine sides.[90] "As much as a great man must learn to listen, cry, be sympathetic, and allow compassion to ebb in his being," Eric claims, "so a great woman must have a brave heart. She must have the grit, the growl, and the gusto of God drilled into the bedrock of her soul."[91]

The foundation of all Christians' endeavor, the Ludys contend, should be a profound spiritual relationship with Jesus, their heavenly Prince. The deep yearning that people experience for romantic love is merely a temporal manifestation of an everlasting desire; it is "precisely the longing we should have to be with our Lord, our true Bridegroom, for all eternity."[92] Jesus is, in short, the divine Prince and Lover with whom all Christians should have their primary intimate relationship.[93] For women, the relationship with Jesus is relatively uncomplicated. Being female, Leslie Ludy explains, means having "a deep, unshakable, intrinsic longing to be tenderly cherished forever by a noble prince to whom we may entrust our heart."[94] Thus, Leslie insists, *"An ongoing, passionate romance with our true Prince, is the foundation for success in every other area of life."* Her language can become quite ardent: "I never really understood what true worship was until I experienced deep daily intimacy with my Prince in my inner sanctuary. . . . [S]uddenly I couldn't help . . . falling on my knees in awe before him." Ultimately, Leslie contends, surrender to and passionate intimacy with Jesus gives a woman vision to see the man Prince Jesus has chosen for her. Marriage will be the wedding of her passive longing with her husband's heroic striving.[95]

For the Ludys, men must also have a primary love relationship with Jesus before they enter into Christian marriage. But the metaphor of Jesus as Prince Charming is problematic, since men's goal is to *imitate* Jesus as Prince, not to play princess to his prince. The Ludys suggest that for men Jesus is a heroic "warrior-poet."[96] "Just as young girls dream of becoming princesses, young boys dream of becoming warriors," Eric explains. The first rule of military life is submission to one's commander, and men in Jesus' army must learn to yield completely to his authority. They must therefore learn to value tenderness and intimacy, for in addition to being a great warrior, Christ is also a "compassionate, gentle, and eternally loving Poet." As Eric observes, unmarried men— even Christian men—are often interested in only one thing (sex); they must also learn to be poets "trained to understand the intimate and sacred sanctuary of a woman's heart" while pursuing "the same intimacy with Christ" in their own hearts.[97]

Particularly in the wife that God gives them, Eric believes, men will see what "God-designed femininity" truly is; and then they will know what they "must become as men in order to honor, protect, and love that kind of womanhood." Women, in short, hold the key to masculinity. "The map to the city of 'Great Manhood' lies right in front of us—*in the form of a woman,*" Eric explains. He argues, in addition, that sex should not be the primary focus of marriage, since sex is but an "occasional reminder" of marriage's greatest benefit: "the beauty of shared love." Eric also contends that, in the bedroom, husbands should not be leaders. "If sexual intimacy were defined by a man's body clock," he claims, "the entire act would be over and done with in less than five minutes. That is why a man must allow his wife to define the pace of awakening and enjoying romantic love. God designed the woman to be the pacesetter in of the bedroom."[98] It is hard to imagine Harris, Elliot, or the biblical patriarchalists of Vision Forum agreeing.

The Ludys do believe that the Bible depicts man as the head of woman, but they do not think that Scripture calls wives to subjugate themselves to their husbands. "Far too many men today limit the potential of their wives," Eric argues. "They mentally fence in a woman's potential impact and subconsciously assume that a godly woman can be nothing more than a wife and a mother."[99] Rather than focusing on separate spheres of dominion, it makes more sense to think of a married couple as a team. "To thrive as a team," Leslie advises, "you might have to surrender your preconceived ideas of what areas your spouse is to be in charge of." Eric agrees, noting, "as the husband, I may be the head of our home, but that doesn't mean I run our home according to my personal agenda and force my wife into subservience." Instead, he insists, "I am responsible for drawing my wife out in fully appreciating all that she is capable of bringing to her marriage. As the head of the home, I am her prince, her greatest advocate, and her most reliable confidant."[100]

Eric is passionate about advocating for Leslie's work with young Christian women. He regards Leslie as a wonderful wife and mother, but insists that she is far more than that:

> She is designed by the Almighty to impact this world for Him. She aches for a lost world. She is a talented communicator, an accomplished artist with the brush of truth. It is my great delight as her husband to fully appreciate these qualities and fan them into flame within her life. I make room in our schedule for her to grow her ministry to young, set-apart women. I protect her time at the piano so she can create music that makes God smile. I encourage and assist her when she writes a life-changing book. I am awed when I see her impact on this culture. I don't feel threatened by her life and her influence. . . . *I treasure it.* I am her biggest fan. Leslie doesn't aspire to center stage. She doesn't try to claim the head position in our home. She is merely a woman functioning the way God built her to function, secure in her God's and her husband's adoring love and approval.[101]

Eric ends with a challenge to Christian men who would limit their wives to the domestic realm: "A man is the prince of the home, and, therefore, he holds the noble role of laying down his life for his bride. Guys, don't fear that in doing this you will lose your masculinity."[102]

The Ludys advise each partner to spend time alone with Jesus each day, for a Christian romance between husband and wife is always a triangulated relationship, founded upon a primary love for Jesus. That foundation, the Ludys believe, enables Christian marriages to endure. "I do not put unhealthy pressure on Eric to fill a place in my life that can be filled only by my true Prince," Leslie concludes. "Eric does the same thing in reverse—he finds his purpose, fulfillment, and security in his relationship with Jesus Christ alone. This created the freedom for us to have unhindered intimacy in our marriage. We are not focused on selfishly meeting our own needs through our relationship." Accordingly, the Ludys find that "no matter what difficulties we go through, our love flourishes, our commitment lasts, and our intimacy only grows stronger."[103]

The result, the Ludys contend, is an extraordinary partnership in which they share a public ministry together as Christian speakers and recording artists. Though the Ludys highlight differences between men and women, they do not stress female subordination to men. The triangulated nature of romantic Christian love means that primary submission is to one's intimate love relationship with Christ. If the Ludys fear anything, it is that they do not spend enough time alone with Jesus or with one another. "We say no to many outside invitations and commitments," Leslie explains, so that they can truly "rest and enjoy each other."[104] Where Harris worries that lust pursues him throughout life, in spite of a richly satisfying marriage, the Ludys argue that "married boys are shaped into married men when they finally realize that the buried treasure isn't the act of sex—the buried treasure is knowing, loving, and sharing the most intimate aspects of life with that woman sleeping next to him every night."[105] And where biblical patriarchalists confine wives to thinking their husbands' thoughts and working to further their husbands' vocations, the Ludys are comfortable developing the gifts of both the prince and the princess of the home.

Evangelical Christians looking for love turn to Adam and Eve, the archetypal sweethearts, as models for their own lives. Yet Genesis 1–3 never mentions romantic love or depicts the original human beings as sexual athletes, much less as medieval royalty. Nevertheless, in their desire to recreate contemporary American society in the image of Eden and what they imagine to have been its rigid gender hierarchy, conservative evangelicals have read the biblical narrative of creation as though it were the story of a gallant Prince Charming wooing his pliant Princess. The single most important characteristic of life in this American Eden is woman's wholehearted submission to man. When believers imagine God as the Creator of Romance and Eden as a medieval bastion of male privilege, it is no wonder that they see Eve and Adam—as well as themselves—as characters in Camelot.

2
~

THIS ONE SHALL BE CALLED SOUL MATE (OR WILL SHE?!)
Adam, Eve, and Online Dating

Then the Lord God said, "It is not good that the man should be alone; I will make him a helper as his partner. . . ." So the Lord God caused a deep sleep to fall upon the man, and he slept; then he took one of his ribs and closed up its place with flesh. And the rib that the Lord God had taken from the man he made into a woman and brought her to the man. Then the man said, "This at last is bone of my bones and flesh of my flesh; this one shall be called Woman, for out of Man this one was taken." Therefore a man leaves his father and his mother and clings to his wife, and they become one flesh. And the man and his wife were both naked, and were not ashamed.

—Genesis 2:18, 21-25

The bad thing about using Adam and Eve as role models for romance is that they are an impossible act to follow. Since they were the only two people on earth, the first man and first woman had no trouble finding one another, and they certainly did not have to question whether they were meant to be together. Locating one's soul mate in a world populated by billions, however, is more complicated. And conservative evangelicals face particular difficulties. Those committed to courtship or betrothal refuse to date altogether, which raises the level of difficulty in finding a desirable life partner. And those who are willing to date are hampered by the hierarchical gender roles that forbid women from initiating relationships with men. Indeed, whether conservative evangelical women date or not, they find themselves in an unenviable position: desirous of marriage, yet prohibited from actively seeking it.

And that is not the only problem. Notwithstanding the widespread regard for Joshua Harris' work, many conservative evangelicals who agree with his rejection of recreational dating do not see the story of Adam and Eve as "bursting with romance," nor do they resonate with Harris' claim that the electric chemistry between the first man and woman was "like nothing you've ever seen."[1] These Christians have no inclination to regard Christian singles as Princesses and Prince Charmings. Rather, they disdain romantic love, downplay the importance of sexual attraction, and present marriage not as an experience of personal fulfillment but rather as a divine obligation instituted with Adam and Eve. One of their deepest fears is that writers like Harris and Eric and Leslie Ludy have written so lyrically about the ecstasy of uniting with one's soul mate that single Christian men are refusing to settle for anything less—and, as a result, are remaining unmarried and childless.

That is no way to practice dominion. When married evangelical men look at American culture, they see feminists running rampant and the gender hierarchy ordained at creation under siege as never before in history. It galls them that the single Christian men who ought to man up, marry up, and father up are all too often too timid, too absorbed in enjoying an extended adolescence, or too hung up on finding the perfect mate to heed the biblical mandate to be fruitful and multiply. Meanwhile, single evangelical women waiting patiently for love fear that no one will ever ask them out, much less propose to them. Unsure that the time-honored paths to marriage are sufficient for the present age, large numbers of unmarried evangelicals are doing what everybody else does when looking for a mate: heading for places where they can find people who share their interests. In the twenty-first century, that includes the Internet, a hazardous venue for crusaders pledged to counteract, not surrender to, the siren call of popular culture. As they engage online dating services, Christians seeking their own personal Adam or Eve sound a familiar refrain, reprising the debates about gender roles and romance regnant in the offline evangelical world.

Walking the Cyber Aisle

Online dating services aimed at evangelicals take many forms. Some, like a site called Adam Meet Eve, focus on conservative Christians and assure members that they will find the perfect soul mate that God has created for them. Media giant eHarmony, on the other hand, eschews the language of soul mates and claims to offer patrons something even better: scientific precision in matchmaking. Then there are sites like ChristianCafe, which is aimed exclusively at Christians and willing to accommodate a wide variety of views on romance and gender roles, but wary of making promises it cannot keep. Members may be seeking soul mates, but ChristianCafe management does not promise to provide them. Finally, small sites like Marry Well denounce the search for romance and soul mates as unbiblical and have an Internet presence only because they believe conservative evangelicals need an alternative to the courtship movement.

People who join online dating services learn about and interact with prospective partners in a number of ways. Member profiles reveal personal information about individuals, and discussion boards provide extended conversations among members. Many sites have chat rooms, and many provide email services as well. Some sites also furnish editorial advice, such as essays or letters posted by the sites' owners, or by linking the sites to materials related to romance or to particular theological positions.

The sites exist to make money. Some sites are free to members; these sites earn money through advertising. Others charge a monthly fee. Typically, these sites offer free seven- to ten-day introductory subscriptions, but they reserve key elements (such as the ability to respond to emails from prospective dates, or to access search engines) to paying members. Many of the sites offer more than one level of membership, so that those who opt for the most expensive membership level receive special favors. Sites produce revenue in other ways as well. Some, for example, post ads asking other websites to run their banners.[2] Some sites, which seem autonomous, like Adam Meet Eve,[3] funnel people to another website when they click the "Join" button. Still other sites, which seem independent, belong to owners who operate numerous online dating ventures. Spark Networks, the owner of ChristianMingle, for example, owns thirty other sites.[4]

Confusing as all this may be, online dating services are important to many Americans. According to an extensive Pew Center study, 11 percent of American adults who used the Internet had gone to an online dating website. Of online Americans interested in dating, 74 percent had used the Internet in some capacity to seek romance, and 31 percent of all American adults knew someone who had used a dating website. Of all Americans, 15 percent knew someone who married or established a long-term relationship with a partner they met online. Most people who dated online said they had positive experiences and that online dating websites provided distinctive experiences because members had access to many more potential partners than they could have otherwise met.[5]

Finding Your Personal Adam or Eve

A single Christian searching for online dating services that reference Adam, Eve, or soul mates will find several from which to choose. Such sites include SoulmatesforChristians, AdamAndEveSingles, ChristianSoulmate, ChristianSoulmates, AdamMeetEve, and Christianity Oasis Soul Mate Searchers,[6] a hybrid search site dedicated to linking Christians searching for soul mates to online dating services that can help. The Soulmate Searchers' commitment to the myth of soul mates could not be clearer. Adam and Eve, the site claims, were originally one soul. Separated at creation, their task was to reunite and become one flesh in marriage, as designated in Genesis 3:23-24.[7] Recognizing that, after the fall, it is difficult for people to find their other halves, and conceding that the bar scene is good for drinking and dancing but not for soulmate hunting, Soulmate Searchers argues that online dating services are a good means to its ultimate end: "To help you find YOUR Christian Soul Mate, not just another meaningless date." Soulmate Searchers provides links to secular sites like Mature Singles Only, Mature Professional Singles, Compatible Interests, SeniorPeopleMeet, Top 10 Best Dating Sites, Double Your Dating, and Catch Him and Keep Him, as well as ads for ChristianMingle, Christian-Cafe, eHarmony, and CatholicMingle.[8] Clearly Soulmate Searchers ascribes to the "any means necessary" approach.

Another enthusiastic operation is Christian Soulmates. "We want," the site explains, "to use every tool available to us so the awkwardness in getting to know other christian [*sic*] singles is completely removed."[9] Whether browsers are hoping to marry or just to enjoy a casual relationship, Christian Soulmates urges them to "experience Christian romance today." Somewhat disturbingly, the site assures people that "when you're ready to find your soulmate," Christian Soulmates can offer thousands of "Christian girls [?!], women and men."[10] Once they join, members will find an astonishing array of services, including chat rooms, instant messaging, emails, video chats, photo transfers, friend lists, ignore lists, member categorizing, private rooms, and, best of all, a "Soulmate Searcher" engine that promises to perform custom searches for members even when they are offline.[11]

But the most enthusiastic view of Christian romance belongs to Adam Meet Eve. The home page masthead reads, "God, the best Matchmaker of all, created your perfect soul-mate, your personal Adam or Eve." Promising over seventy thousand "active" single members with whom prospectives may communicate, the site notes that if "you believe in your heart that God . . . has created someone in this world who is not only compatible with you, but someone who is your perfect compliment [*sic*], your 'soul-mate,'" then "the person you are seeking could be just a few clicks away."[12] Here there is no question that God created Eve for romance, not for mere compatibility. "We all want God's best for our lives, and for dating," the site explains. "In Genesis 2:18 we see that when God created Eve it was not so that she could cook meals for Adam or mend his clothes. . . . Eve was created for companionship, deep friendship and intimacy."[13]

Therefore, the site exhorts, "Christian dating does not have to be so difficult. We are here to help you find your personal, special Adam or Eve to be your life-long soul-mate God wants for you in godly marriage!"[14] Testimonials with headlines like "Praise the Lord, I Found My Soulmate Online" tell of marriage proposals on second dates,[15] and resident pastor Jim Rives recommends books like *Dear God, Send Me a Soul Mate.*[16] The site's statement of faith, with its emphasis on biblical inerrancy and Jesus' sacrificial death, is aimed at conservative Christians. But members will look in vain for exhortations to women to refrain from contacting men they find interesting.[17] When one's potential soul mate is only a click or two away, it is no time to worry about creation order; success goes to the intrepid. Therefore no Christians, the site insists, should feel guilty about pursuing their soul mate. "If God has planted in your heart the desire for a mate there is nothing 'wrong' with seeking a mate, or dating single Christians. Jesus is the only Matchmaker or Dating Service you need, and if He chooses to use AdamMeetEve Christian Singles Dating, it is only one of many tools in His capable, loving hands."[18]

Of course, Adam Meet Eve is not free. But the site argues that a ninety-day membership costs less than fourteen cents a day, which is little enough to pay for a dating service in which people are paired in "much the same way that God brought Adam and Eve together in Genesis chapter 2." And the ten-day trial membership costs nothing. A three-month subscription costs about fifty cents a day,[19] which browsers should consider to be cheap. "After all," the service argues, "God did not charge Adam much for the privilege of meeting Eve."[20] And for those Christians who believe in soul mates, the Creator of Romance is still ready, willing, and able to present them with partners from paradise.

eHarmony
When Soul Mate Means "True Compatibility"

While plenty of evangelicals are looking for their personal Eve or Adam at eHarmony, officially the site redefines the myth of soul mates. Neil Clark

Warren, the founder of eHarmony, is an evangelical Christian who originally worked with James Dobson's Focus on the Family to get eHarmony off the ground in 2000. Warren has since severed his ties with Dobson, and conservative Christians often complain that Warren has also watered down his adherence to the gospel.[21] eHarmony's 2008 decision—after being sued for discrimination—to add a section called Compatible Partners for same-gender couples has provided only more proof of its heterodoxy.[22]

Nevertheless, eHarmony has made a name for itself as a dating service highly successful at finding its members marriage partners.[23] The membership list is huge—over twenty million people—and eHarmony claims credit for inspiring 542 Americans per day to marry, or almost 5 percent of American marriages. eHarmony is proud of its ethnic, racial, and religious diversity.[24] Explicitly Christian discussion threads (such as "biblical view on masturbation?") exist and thrive at eHarmony, but many members reference other religious traditions—or none at all.[25] eHarmony is happy to market itself to all comers. Googling "Christian dating services," for example, will produce a link to eHarmony Christian Dating. But that is just one way to access an eHarmony home page. eHarmony offers distinctive portals for Jewish, Asian, African American, senior, and Hispanic browsers. There are also generic home pages. Googling "eHarmony" leads to a page with a smiling woman who says, "It all starts with you" or "Date smarter, not harder" or "Find someone right for you." Like the Apostle Paul, eHarmony is happy to be all things to all people.

People who click to enter eHarmony discover that the site is huge. There are discussion boards, advice boards, and virtually innumerable articles by eHarmony experts on what would seem to be every conceivable question anyone might raise about love, frustration, lap dancing, dating while wearing an air cast, middle-aged virginity, the dangers of being too nice, and the allure of Tim Tebow—to name just a few. There are discussion boards on any subject anyone cares to pursue, including cougars, creative writing, romance and the freethinker, stupid conversations, sex, weight loss, foodies, and flip-flops. If it is possible to identify a niche audience, eHarmony is eager to serve it.[26]

Ironically, for all of eHarmony's zeal to connect people, it uses the language of romance and soul mates only to lure people into the site. Googling "find your soul mate" will yield hits like "eHarmony Online Dating—Your Soul Mate Is Out There" and "Find Your Soul Mate—Trust eHarmony for Dating Online."[27] In 2008 clicking on those links led to home pages that also spoke of soul mates. The welcome page for Christians began, "When you're ready to find your Christian soul mate," and the generic welcome page promised, "It *Is* Possible to Find your Soul Mate."[28] eHarmony has since toned down that language. The current entry portal for Christians only hints that your soul mate is waiting for you. "As a single Christian," it asks, "do you feel like God has someone special in mind for you but you just haven't found them yet? Well that someone is out there looking for you too. And at eHarmony we can help you find each other." The site then explains that eHarmony is not about dating, but about finding "long-term, committed relationships." And the key to success is that "unlike traditional Christian dating sites, eHarmony matches singles based on compatibility." Left to their own devices, eHarmony argues, people can spend years trying to determine if they are compatible with their partners. But eHarmony claims that it can, with scientific precision, swiftly sort through thousands of Christian singles to identify the special few who are exceptionally suited to you.[29] The only thing eHarmony members have to do to meet these special someones is fill out a long Compatibility Matching System survey, which claims to measure twenty-nine "key dimensions" of personality.

As Neil Clark Warren explains in his book, *Falling in Love for All the Right Reasons: How to Find Your Soul Mate*, the Compatibility Matching System eliminates 99.7 percent of eHarmony members. The ones who remain are keepers. "With eHarmony doing all the hard work," he explains, "you get to relax and focus on the chemistry of falling in love." Only at that point are conversations about soul mates appropriate—and then only if soul mate is redefined to exclude romance. Instead of searching for Prince or Princess Charming, Warren urges members to search for broad-based compatibility.[30] "When you find the person with whom you can have the most genuine harmony on the twenty-nine dimensions of a good relationship," Warren concludes, "you have found your soul mate."[31] Well, that's one way to look at it.

In an online "Expert Advice" article titled "Is There One Perfect Person for Me?," Warren challenges members not to fall for the romantic myth of soul mates. "I think this idea is more fantasy than reality, more storybook whimsy than real-world wisdom," he insists. "I don't believe that you could only be completely and blissfully happy with one person to the exclusion of all others." Pointing to the eHarmony Compatibility Matching System, Warren observes, "Out of all the women in the world, there must be at least 500 with whom I would match on all 29 items. And there are probably thousands more I'd match with on, say, 26 or 27 items and still be quite satisfied." In the end, Warren concludes, "You start with the ingredients for a highly-compatible, successful relationship, and then you work to develop closeness and intimacy. Does this mean you lower your standards when it comes to finding a partner? Absolutely not! It simply means you 'expand your field of vision.'"[32]

Where does this leave Adam, Eve, and the Creator of Romance? Most eHarmony conversations about Eden are conducted by members, not by Warren or other eHarmony experts. The diversity of membership is reflected in discussion boards that are willing to analyze Genesis 1–3 in a variety of ways. A discussion thread called "Adam and Eve: A Story, Parable, or Historical Fact?" would be unthinkable in more theologically conservative settings. Likewise, in a thread titled "Interpreting the Story of Adam and Eve," a member named deistdreamer argued, "I don't think that it is a bad thing or something for Christians, or Jews or Muslims to worry about that there is not one way, or two, or four or even 100 ways to understand the story of the Garden of Eden. This is the beauty of stories." In "I Read It Once," deistdreamer rehabilitated Eve in ways no evangelical would attempt. "I always rooted for Eve," deistdreamer explained to a member named notyet. "She was curious and wanted to learn more[.] She was not content to remain a child. She went ahead of her man and dragged him reluctantly along with her . . . it led to both of them setting out into the real world as grown ups. So if you are comparing me to Eve: I say thank you. The world needs more Eves, more women capable of thinking for themselves."

None of that is reminiscent of evangelical discussions of Genesis 3. Neither is the eHarmony experts' blog "'We're So in Love, We'll Work It Out' and Other Dating Myths," which references Genesis 1–3 as a cautionary tale. "In the Beginning, there was the illusion of perfection," the writer argues. In the first three months of a relationship, infatuation and "fairytale romanticism" run rampant. Unfortunately, "fairytale beliefs about love lead to quick burnout in reality." The myth of soul mates—believing that there is only one ideal partner—is, the author concludes, "a great way to turn yourself into a neurotic mess by 35. There are many compatible relationship partners for someone out in the world." Ultimately, at eHarmony God can write your love story in many different ways with any number of potential partners. Romantic attraction is not a good indicator of love. Chemistry follows compatibility. First, find someone who is like you; then, learn to love him or her. And forget all about love at first sight. When Adam first glimpsed Eve, he did not think she was hot; he thought she was like him. "This at last is bone of my bones and flesh of my flesh," he said, paving the way for compatibility as the ultimate turn on.

If eHarmony's notions of romance are relatively modest, its levels of success are not. Each day 542 eHarmony members get married, and for most people that is probably enough of a fairy-tale ending.[33]

"If Christian Men Can Write This Pile of Tut, I'm Seriously Reconsidering My Membership Here"
Gender Hierarchy at ChristianCafe

ChristianCafe is the largest Christian online dating service—depending on how one defines "Christian." For number of hits or online visits, Christian-Mingle is the biggest site. But ChristianCafe argues that it is the largest Christian site owned and operated by Christians, as well as the largest exclusively Christian site. Founded in 1999 by Canadian Sam Moorcroft and his brother Philip, ChristianCafe has been entrepreneurial, acquiring a number of other Christian dating services, including, in 2009, Christian Single Network, the original destination site for Adam Meet Eve. An evangelical himself, Moorcroft knows that conservative Christians are suspicious of online dating, but he argues that, like it or not, millions of Christians are using the Internet to search for love. "Our take," he explains, "is that since Christian singles are online anyway, shouldn't Christians be matching Christians, rather than the world doing it? That's why we're so proud of being Christian-owned-and-operated."[34]

Moorcroft estimates that 80 percent or more of ChristianCafe's market is conservative evangelical Christians,[35] and he maintains—conveniently—that "if you're even half-serious about your faith and you want to meet someone who shares what you believe," exclusively Christian sites are the only way to go. He counsels Christians to be careful their dating services are not promoting groups he deems heretical, like Mormons and Jehovah's Witnesses. The presence of those groups on a dating site, he contends, "guarantees the owners aren't Christian. Do you want to be on a website where you can potentially meet someone who considers him- or herself a believer, but they're from a background that we regard as an apostate faith?"[36] This barb is aimed at Christian-Mingle, whose parent company owns two dating sites directed at Mormons (LDSMingle and LDSSingles) and two for Jews (JDate and JewishMingle). Moorcroft's insistence on orthodox confessionalism did not, however, deter him from launching JewishCafe in 2002 as a rival to JDate.

Though ChristianCafe aims at a Christian clientele, it does not, as sites like Adam Meet Eve do, provide a testimonial on biblical inerrancy or delineate a statement of faith. Moorcroft considers such doctrinal material distracting. "Are we going to make this dogmatic or practical?" he asks. "Do we want people agreeing with the Nicene Creed, or do we want people who consider themselves Christians?" With his eye ever focused on the bottom line, Moorcroft argues that the most important element in success for an online dating site is a "critical mass" of customers. ChristianCafe, he says, can boast one hundred thousand members in any three-month period and annually grosses in the seven figures.[37] ChristianCafe charges members $34.97 per month or $107.97 for a year's subscription.[38] Moorcroft concedes that some Christians prefer to use free dating sites, but he dismisses those souls as foolhardy. "Funny how people spend $1.50 to $5.00 on a coffee/latte/whatever drink a day, but can't find $.30 to a buck to meet their soul mate!" he grumbles. "Talk about misplaced priorities."[39]

ChristianCafe did not offer members discussion forums until March of 2011, so for most of its history the tone of ChristianCafe has been provided largely by Moorcroft himself. He has a breezy style. As members compose their personal profiles, he urges them—literally—to smile and be happy. "Be positive in [writing] your profile, even about your faults," the site advises new members. "We all have our faults and those who dwell on their faults are not fun to be around at the best of times." Fun is an important virtue at ChristianCafe. Moorcroft encourages members to "smile when you are writing" to demonstrate that you "are happy and well adjusted, and that you would be an excellent person to share one's life with." The site also instructs people to be effusive. Instead of quietly claiming, for example, that you are a Christian with a good sense of humor, ChristianCafe suggests that you say things like "Are you the type of person who loves Roller Coasters? I love the excitement and thrill of it all!" or "I LOVE talking about advances in science and how they continually point to God's power. What really gets your blood pumping about God or Nature?"

The last heading in ChristianCafe's tips on how to write an appealing dating profile is "Take the Initiative." Here members—both women and men— are advised, "[T]he best way to get mail from others is to send mail yourself. . . . Everyone on the site is waiting to receive mail, so overcome your shyness and send off some letters!" ChristianCafe also urges clients to use instant messaging, to join in chat room and forum discussions, and to log into their accounts as often as possible. Apps are available for Android and iPhone users, so that even when people are away from their computers they can still access their potential life partners. The main thing is to get busy. "Those who are online more often, involved in letter writing, make use of Instant Messaging, and join in on the chat room discussions consistently report making more friends in the

Cafe—including meeting that special someone ☺."[40] To ensure that people have abundant conversation partners, when members click on "quickmatch," the search engine provides profiles of the thousand members it deems most compatible to them. While it is possible for users to run more discriminating searches, success at ChristianCafe depends upon volume and frenetic activity, not upon the surgical precision hyped by eHarmony.

Now about that special someone: ChristianCafe members regarded Adam and Eve as the first married couple, but they were not at all certain that the first man and woman were soul mates or if soul mates even existed. Some people passionately believed that God had set aside one person and one person only for them. Other members argued that they could happily wed any number of like-minded partners. Some people worried that they might not recognize "the one" when they met; others were convinced they would have a burning-bush revelation upon meeting. Occasionally members argued that the best way to find "the one" was to search for him or her diligently, while others insisted that success depended upon trusting God to present one's mate. Many members questioned whether women should take the initiative to ask men out, at the same time that others were certain that women should. Still others wondered why men were so hesitant these days to approach women. And a few people denounced the whole notion of soul mate as unbiblical Hollywood hokum.[41]

Perhaps the most significant thing about these discussions is how much less certain ChristianCafe members were that God would write their love story or present them with their personal Adam or Eve than were the court-ship advocates Leslie and Eric Ludy or Joshua Harris. While many users were looking for romance, a segment of ChristianCafe users rejected the notion of soul mates altogether. And some who clung to it feared they were shooting too high. As apkerr536 confessed, "I am willing to accept that my chances of finding 'the one' on the internet are slim to none. I'm also willing to admit that my definition of 'the one' (and my stubborn refusal to broaden that definition to include 'anyone') is quite probably the main reason I've had no success."[42]

Members were also divided on the question of gender hierarchy. As ever, the problem was how to understand Eve's relationship to Adam. Genesis 2:18 says that God created woman to be man's helper, and after the man and the woman ate the forbidden fruit, God told the woman in Genesis 3:16 that her husband would rule over her. Clearly those texts are critical to defining norma-tive gender relations, but members could not agree on what message to draw from them. Calling upon the New Testament texts that referenced the Garden story did not help. Paul argues in 1 Corinthians 11:2-16 that the husband is head of the wife and that woman was created for the sake of man. But he adds that "woman is not independent of man or man independent of woman. For just as woman came from man, so man comes through woman; but all things come from God." And Paul recognizes that women were empowered to pray and prophesy when Christians worshiped together. Members could plausibly argue from 1 Corinthians either that God created men to have authority over women or that their relationship was one of mutuality.

Another New Testament book that references Genesis 1–3 is Ephesians. In 5:21-33, the author of Ephesians cites Genesis 2:24 to compare the union of Christ and the church to that of husband and wife. The author admonishes wives to be subject to their husbands as the church was subject to Christ; but he also cautions husbands to love their wives sacrificially as Christ loved the church and as they love their own bodies. It is hard to establish this text as a clear-cut example of hierarchy or mutuality. Appealing to the history of interpretation is no help, as these passages from 1 Corinthians and Ephesians are ambiguous enough that readers throughout Christian history have interpreted them as examples of both gender hierarchy and gender equality.

This passage at 1 Timothy 2:11-15, however, seems unequivocally subordinationist:

> Let a woman learn in silence with full submission. I permit no woman to teach or to have authority over a man; she is to keep silent. For Adam was formed first, then Eve; and Adam was not deceived, but the woman was deceived and became a transgressor. Yet she will be saved through childbearing, provided they continue in faith and love and holiness, with modesty.

But if 1 Timothy argues for gender hierarchy, Galatians 3:27-28 seems clearly egalitarian. In referencing the "male and female" from Genesis 1:27, Paul avows that following baptism, gender distinctions and gender hierarchy have passed away. "As many of you as were baptized into Christ have clothed yourselves with Christ. There is no longer Jew or Greek," he says, "there is no longer slave or free, there is no longer male and female; for all of you are one in Christ Jesus."

No one knows exactly how—or if—these texts should be balanced. Whether wives must subordinate themselves to their husbands or women may function as church leaders equal to men provides twenty-first-century Christians endless grist for sermons, conferences, and late-night radio rants. There are occasional dissenting voices, like Eric and Leslie Ludy, who are willing to soften gender hierarchy within marriage. But most evangelical conservatives enthusiastically champion gender hierarchy and trace it back to Adam and Eve. Given the overwhelming predominance of conservative evangelicals at ChristianCafe, users were expected to contend that, from the beginning, God intended women to be subordinate to men. And certainly that argument appears on the site. But what is most remarkable about ChristianCafe is the fierce insistence on gender equality displayed by many members.

This can readily be seen in a long discussion on feminism. Showing more zeal than sense, a man with the moniker uslover878 launched a thread titled "Well, I know this is a very dangerous subject and i have to weight [sic] my words, very carefully here! God! Lead me here! My postulate is that many christian marriages have been destroyed by feminism." He then invited the women of ChristianCafe to respond. If uslover878 was hoping for affirmation from fans of 1 Timothy, he had woefully misread his audience. Kelles619, the first member to speak for the women, tried to give him an out. "We shouldn't try to blame dissolution of marriages on a movement that was simply trying to give women equal opportunities to education and careers," she observed. "Afterall [sic] women are also children of God. I'm sure God would not condone unfair practices on women in some societies or discrimination."[43]

Uslover878 was not buying it. "Feminism IS still a great problem," he insisted. In his view, after feminists in the late 1970s won better social and political opportunities, they craved still more power and more rights. So they turned their husbands into "soft" men and presumed to be the "boss" of their households. "And believe me," uslover878 warned, "there are [a] lot of them today, also in the church i can tell you."

Kelless619 responded that she was unaware of any women who had more rights than white men, and a member named lavendergreen suggested that "if men in the past had behaved in a Godly manner, there would not have been any need for a feminist movement." Lavendergreen pointed to the suffrage movements of the late nineteenth and early twentieth centuries as critical to establishing basic human rights for women. "The christian women who formed the suffragist movement were imprisoned, beaten, force fed with metal tubes, and locked in mental institutions," she declared, and as far as lavendergreen was concerned, those women were heroes. "That's the feminist movement," she concluded. "Thank God for raising up such brave women."

Uslover878 disagreed. "Feminism," he insisted, "is a thing, created in the deepest of Hell, disrespecting the word of God." To which lavendergreen replied, "glad you finally came out of the closet and exposed yourself as a misogynist. . . . Feminism was driven by christian women who were trying to help downtrodden women living with a plethora of children in poverty. If you think that God is opposed to that, you might want to count up all the passages relating to widows and orphans." Not surprisingly, lavendergreen had no sympathy for uslover878's "soft" men. "Feminism did not create weak men," she said. "Casinos and alcohol did that. Feminism just empowered women to deal with it."

"Amen to that[,] Lavender!" Maranot685 enthused. "Feminism is to women . . . what the Civil Rights movement was to the black man—equalizing opportunity, period." Wittyk352 joined in, arguing that the notion that Christian wives were not equal to their husbands was not only unbiblical but was also "destroying the church from within." Maronot685 then turned to the stay-at-home daughter movement. "I lead a homeschool group," she explained, "and we had a meeting last night where we discussed what to do with girls who feel they don't need to be educated because they will be married. Well, what happens if they don't get married? What happens if their husband leaves them? What happens if they are widowed? And why would God want them to become less than he created them to be?"

By now uslover878 was running scared. He was willing to agree that women deserved political rights and insisted he was targeting only those feminists who wanted to usurp men's leadership "or at least degrade the man to a partner, not the spiritual leader in the home! So please[,] ladies," he pleaded, "don't misunderstand me, okay? ☺ . . . I am not trying to commit suicide in here.☺" Of course, by then, for most of the women, he already had, prompting one of the men to laugh, "Uslover, You certainly have a way with the ladies!!!" Uslover878 gave it another try the next day: "I want a partner, a soul mate, a woman, equal to me," he averred. "Only in important issues, where we can't agree, will I take charge." But uslover878 could not get past that pesky second-wave feminism, with its hateful and bitter women determined to destroy the institution of marriage. "I still claim [it] was plan[n]ed and fabricated in the deepest of hell," he reiterated.

Lively conversation on this thread continued for another six months. In the background were Genesis 1–3 and the New Testament passages that commented upon it. Posters could imagine that God had created Eve equal to Adam; they could also imagine the opposite. They could postulate that faith in Christ restored the gender equality present at creation; conversely, they could conclude that Christianity mandated fidelity to a gender hierarchy embedded in human nature from the beginning. And uslover878 did have supporters who agreed with the typical conservative evangelical view that feminism was demonic. Indeed, a member named dannyspl652 managed to inflame the rhetoric by arguing that feminism was not only a lesbian movement designed to usurp masculine power but also "the main reason for our social, personal and existential problems." He then posed this question to the membership: "Has feminism caused women to emasculate men?"

That question, predictably, almost induced apoplexy. Welshprincess143 responded, "Some have said feministic ideologies are from hell, but I say this so-called 'male role,' or 'being in charge' is actually the idea that originated in the very bowels of hell." In her view, the New Testament commanded husbands to love their wives sacrificially, as Christ loved the church. "A woman," welshprincess143 contended, "is to submit to THAT LOVE," which has "nothing to do with men being in charge." Pronouncing herself sickened by dannyspl652, welshprincess143 announced, "If Christian men can write this pile of tut, I'm seriously reconsidering my membership here."

Or, as lavendergreen put it, "Feminism is about women being equal image-bearers of the Living God." Given that ChristianCafe largely consisted of conservative evangelicals, members' continued willingness to advocate feminist interpretations of Christianity was striking. For those brave souls, Eve and Adam walked side by side, and finding a soul mate meant finding one's equal.

Boundless Angst
Return of Focus on the Family

While ChristianCafe users were pondering gender hierarchy and equality, in November 2011 they noticed a new link called Dating 101 on the menu bar. Clicking on it delivered members to a site offering a view of marriage that was astonishingly grim. Whereas eHarmony had steered people away from overreliance on soul mates, Dating 101 denounced "soul-mate-ism" as sinful, insisted that marriage was an obligation for Christians, and dismissed romantic attraction as a transient emotion certain to die within months. Authors at Dating 101 fretted that the courtship movement had failed miserably. They were frantic that Christian men were shirking their responsibility to identify life partners and marry them expeditiously, and they feared that Christian women were increasingly tempted to abandon marriage in favor of careers. Though these authors looked to Adam and Eve as exemplars of God's institution of marriage, they worried that, in a fallen world, Christian men and women could never recover God's original intentions for them.

This new link was Boundless, a ministry of Focus on the Family charged with providing young adults a "vibrant vision for the single years." Started in 1998 by Candice and Steve Watters, Boundless was a webzine offering articles, blogs, and a weekly podcast. It was connected to Marry Well, a small online dating service begun in March 2010 by the Watters and two other couples associated with Focus on the Family. In its own words, Boundless was "uncompromising" about the "very distinct" roles for men and women it believed God established at the creation.[44] Whereas Sam Moorcroft described ChristianCafe as a place where "people" were free to initiate dating relationships, Boundless insisted that only men should do so.[45] Articles like "Pursue Her" and "Why Women Should Never Ask" belabored the point. Boundless authors also uniformly denounced feminism as a product of humanity's fall into sin. In contradistinction to ChristianCafe, Boundless users were not instructed to have fun or smile while they wrote, and no one was suggesting that dwelling on one's shortcomings was problematic.

Despite these differences in institutional cultures and theology, Boundless and ChristianCafe had struck up a partnership.[46] Boundless materials would be linked to ChristianCafe through Dating 101, and ChristianCafe would serve as Boundless' "exclusive online dating site."[47] The alliance held promise for both organizations. The relentlessly entrepreneurial Moorcroft had made no secret of his desire to acquire or merge with his competitors,[48] and Focus on the Family had long chafed at losing eHarmony. Now Moorcroft had access to the enormous Focus on the Family empire, and Focus on the Family could reach users at the largest explicitly Christian online dating site.[49] If the two organizations could smooth over their differences, ChristianCafe could become a blockbuster.

Though the ChristianCafe site blog enthusiastically urged members to check out Boundless' "fantastic dating advice" at Dating 101,[50] many members were distressed to learn of the partnership with Focus on the Family. Both men and women complained, and lavendergreen laid out the worst-case scenario: "I guess it will attract more members from the Religious Right, which means that those of us who lean left will be even more persecuted on the forums. I'm getting tired of being called a feminist every time that I suggest that women aren't doormats." Conversely, other members were already familiar with Boundless and welcomed its presence at ChristianCafe. Many users also were comfortable with Focus on the Family. And one member managed to bewilder everyone by complaining that Focus on the Family was more left leaning than he would prefer, prompting incredulous posters to ask if the John Birch Society and Bob Jones University fell into the left-wing category as well.[51]

In any case, the Boundless materials introduced a new theological paradigm of marriage. Albert Mohler, president of Southern Baptist Theological Seminary in Louisville, had laid down the gauntlet in a 2004 speech on "The Mystery of Marriage." Worried that conservative Christians were not marrying until their late twenties, Mohler argued that "from Genesis to Revelation, the Bible assumes that marriage is normative for human beings."[52] For Mohler, this meant not only that marriage was not "primarily about our self-esteem and personal fulfillment," but also that it was not "just one lifestyle option among others." Rather, in the beginning, God created man and woman and gave to them the institution of marriage as "both opportunity and obligation."

After the customary deprecation of "radical feminists" who devalued marriage, Mohler turned to his central target: young Christians, particularly men, who deliberately postponed marriage to enjoy an "extended adolescence" into their late twenties and early thirties. This, Mohler insisted, was "the sin I think besets this generation." He decried the young men who avoided becoming the household heads God created them to be and instead focused on "career, friends, sports, and any number of other satisfactions when they ought to be preparing themselves for marriage and taking responsibility to grow up, be the man, and show God's glory as husband and father." For Mohler, until a male followed in Adam's footsteps, taking responsibility to lead and provide for a wife and children, he would never be more than a boy, and an irresponsible one at that.

Mohler had produced quite a jeremiad on marriage, and, as one of the most visible spokesmen in the conservative evangelical world, his words carried considerable weight. Southern Seminary has long been considered the flagship seminary within the Southern Baptist Convention, and as Mohler's website modestly noted, Time.com had dubbed him the "reigning intellectual of the evangelical movement in the U.S."[53] As president of Southern, Mohler had overseen its transition from a moderate theological institution to one that refused to hire—or to continue to employ—anyone willing to entertain the possibility of the ordination of women. In denouncing the state of evangelical marriage, Mohler could expect full cooperation from Boundless, since founders Steve and Candice Watters lived in Louisville, where Steve worked for Mohler as Director of Publications and Strategic Initiatives at Southern Seminary.

Mohler could also expect support from the Council on Biblical Manhood and Womanhood. The council was housed at Southern Seminary, and Mohler and several other Southern administrators served as officers. CBMW's mission was to refute feminism and champion gender hierarchy as God's will for the creation. No phrase in evangelical conversations was more recognizable than "biblical manhood and womanhood." If Mohler had determined that the next phase in recreating the male headship and female submission that marked life in Eden involved challenging young Christian men to get serious, get married, and get their wives pregnant, then that would be the new rallying cry in the battle for biblical manhood and womanhood.

Not surprisingly, Boundless authors were quick to develop Mohler's argument. Alex and Brett Harris (younger brothers of Joshua Harris) disparaged the male "kidults" still living with their parents after graduating from college as "Peter Pans who shave." Self-absorbed and focused on pleasure, these men needed, the Harrises said, a dose of biblical reality. Fortunately, they would not have to read very far in Scripture before they hit Genesis 2:24, which directed men to leave their parents and cling to their wives. "The biblical pattern," the Harrises insisted, "is for young people to leave their parent's [sic] household in order to begin their own."[54] Boundless' propensity for castigating men who delayed marriage was so rote that, when its online dating service Marry Well published an article on quarterback Tim Tebow, a member named Psalm67 claimed to be "pleasantly surprised" that it failed to accuse Tebow of living an extended adolescence. "After all," Psalm67 noted, "he's delaying marriage for the sake of establishing his career, spending all his time playing recreational sports instead of seeking a spouse, and shirking his God-ordained responsibility to pursue marriage."[55]

Boundless' authors produced a steady stream of "grow up and get married" articles. In "Pursue Her," columnist Drew Dyck addressed men's reluctance to ask women out. He wrote of talking to an attractive Christian woman who asked, "What's wrong with Christian guys? They never go after you!" Dyck challenged Christian men to "man-up," promising that God designed women to enjoy male advances. "God created you to be a pursuer," Dyck contended, and now was the time to get moving.[56] Michael Lawrence of Capitol Hill Baptist Church sounded similar notes in "Real Men Risk Rejection." Imagine, he asked readers, the moment when God presented Eve to Adam. Adam was man enough to take charge. "He doesn't flirt with her," Laurence asserted. "He doesn't ask her if she likes him. Instead he shoulders the risk, steps up to the plate, and declares his intentions . . . for marriage." In a fairly terrifying delineation of masculinity, Lawrence challenged male readers to accept the risk and agony of being a real man:

> Some of you men are thinking at this point, "Wait a minute. Are you saying that all the risk is mine?" Yes I am. "Doesn't that mean that she can just tell me no and leave me twisting in the wind?" Yes it does. Welcome to leadership. Welcome to trusting God. Welcome to being a man.[57]

If that were not intimidating enough, Boundless discussions of love and romance could at best be called sobering. The first cultural construct to be jettisoned was "soul-mate-ism."[58] Gary Thomas of Houston's Second Baptist Church labeled searching for "the one" as idolatrous, dismissed falling madly in love as an "infatuation binge," and insisted that in the Bible people were presented good and bad choices for marriage, not "one right choice."[59] Scott Croft upped the ante, advising that caution, not chemistry, should mark the early stages of a relationship. He conceded that his advice sounded "cold" and "uninviting."[60] And everyone agreed that dating as practiced in the secular world was selfish. Instead of seeking a partner to serve, people invariably searched for someone who would make them happy.

Next on the chopping block was physical attraction. Since the point of marriage was to fulfill God's command to be fruitful and multiply, what mattered most in a spouse was Christian character, not physical appearance. "In Scripture," Capitol Hill Baptist Church's Scott Croft asserted, "love is described not as a mere emotion based on personal desire (i.e., 'attraction'), but as an act of the will that leads to selfless actions toward others." The best example of such love was Jesus' willingness to die on behalf of sinful humanity. "His perfect love of us was a choice," Croft contended, "an act undertaken despite our *lack* of attractiveness."[61] (Trust Focus on the Family to make ugliness a virtue.) Boundless writers acknowledged that physical attraction spurred sexual desire, which in turn could encourage people to marry. But they advised that being head over heels in love was a "temporary emotional disposition," a release of pheromones that at most could last eighteen to forty-eight months.[62] In the end, Christians needed to understand that love was not an emotion but "a policy and a commitment that we choose to keep."[63]

Boundless writers worked hard to show readers that spiritual compatibility was the basis of a good marriage. "If you feel that you're not initially attracted to a man who initiates with you, OK," Scott Croft told women, "but at least ask yourself why that is. Are you considering biblical characteristics in that decision? Do you have enough information to know that you could not marry this man?"[64] Freelance author Suzanne Hadley Gosselin prodded women to "do your very best to be receptive to every guy who shows interest."[65] And Boundless founder Candice Watters urged women not to focus on men's looks but instead to ask, "[W]ho would be a godly husband, strong partner and good father?" Physical appearance was secondary. After all, she contended, a "face is just wrapping paper. . . . Sometimes the tackiest wrapping covers the best gift."[66]

Michael Lawrence laid it on the line. "Men, you may feel like the passive victim of your own internal sense of attraction but you're not. Your sense of attraction is skewed. And it's your fault!" In the beginning, Lawrence explained, Adam had found Eve's godliness and purity a "turn-on." After the fall, however, men came to fixate on women's physical appearance. That obsession needed to end, Lawrence warned, for "God holds each of us morally accountable for . . . [our] misshapen sense of attraction."[67] Or as Scott Croft put it, "Forget the fantasy. . . . Let the *Inventor* of attraction and beauty reform your thinking, and your marriage will be rich."[68]

Even once all of this was achieved, people still needed to remember that there was no returning to Eden. Boundless' *Girl's Guide to Marrying Well* depicted a young woman studying an apple she held in her hands and warned readers, "Expect to marry a sinner." Indeed, said the *Guide*, "it may be helpful to think of 'The One' as someone who's sinful, just as you are."[69] Dwelling on sin was a task at which Boundless excelled. In a Marry Well article, "You Never Marry the Right Person," Candice Gage reminded readers that "any two people who enter into marriage are spiritually broken by sin" and warned that "the biblical doctrine of sin explains why marriage—more than anything else that is good and important in this fallen world—is so painful and hard."[70] Beyond the conviction that God required men and women to marry, no idea resonated more with Boundless contributors than the certainty that married life was fraught with difficulties. Even so, there was no getting around it. As Gary Thomas concluded, "Marriage is God's creation, not man's, and we should surrender to it as part of our worship."[71]

If the Men Won't Step Up, Pull a Ruth

For some evangelicals, this was just too much. Columnists at *Christianity Today* found Boundless' theology of marriage so off-putting they wrote "Is Singleness a Sin?" to refute Mohler and "God Loves a Good Romance" to decry a "vision of marriage as a duty—and little else."[72] Gina R. Dalfonzo, editor of the Break-Point Blog on Christian understandings of current events, contributed a brilliant fable about a "good Christian girl" who had diligently followed the last fifteen years of Christian dating advice. First, she was told that God considered her a princess, and she pledged herself to sexual purity. When she reached dating age, she was told that good Christian girls did not date but waited for the perfect Christian boy God had chosen to court her. After that, nothing happened as "all the guys in her church were apparently still waiting for the divine signal to initiate courtship." So she consulted dating websites, being careful to avoid men who were immature in their faith.

At that point, the good Christian girl was told that she was too picky. So she spent a great deal of time with Christian men, trying to "give every reasonably decent guy every chance she could." And she was told that she spent too much time being friends with guys. When she let men know that she was romantically interested in them, she was told that Christian men "don't like it when you do the pursuing." So the girl tried to be passive, and no one paid much attention to her. When she hit thirty and was still single, she was dismissed as a career woman and derided as a princess who would only be happy with Prince Charming or possibly Mr. Darcy. She was also told that girls like her who delayed marriage "were the trouble with her generation, with Christianity, and with the country in general." So at last, Dalfonzo concluded, "she ran off with the first non-Christian man who showed her some interest, asked her out, and treated her with respect. And the knowing ones shook their heads and said, 'What happened to her? She used to be a good Christian girl.'"[73]

Dalfonzo's critique hit the mark. The reality was that online dating was not working well for the conservative evangelicals Boundless targeted. At Marry Well, women initially outnumbered men ten to one until management offered men free trial memberships and gave away Starbucks gift cards to anyone who successfully recruited two men.[74] When management asked women about their experience of online dating, women said things like "don[']t have. haven[']t been asked!" and "My online dating experience has been that I have met a lot of great ladies on Marry Well who are very intentional about making friendships with other ladies."[75] Motte Brown, one of the owners of Marry Well, said in January 2011 that women currently outnumbered men two to one at the site and suggested that the "low activity level among the men here makes it [the female to male ratio] seem worse." In reply, one man argued, "I think the name of the site could be intimidating some guys. . . . Guys generally are not quite to that level like females immediately and want to ease into the whole idea. It is my prediction that at some point Marry Well will change its name once they get marketing information."[76]

It was that kind of attitude that made people despair. Marry Well constantly emphasized the need for men to initiate relationships,[77] and there was a limit to how often men's timidity or laziness could be attributed to feminism. Articles like "Soul Mate Standard Leaving Many Americans Unmarried"[78] conjured up the dreaded specter of soul-mate-ism, and both columnists and members blamed the courtship movement for introducing that particular obsession into evangelical Christianity. Author David Murrow went further, accusing female youth leaders, the antidating movement, and the "super virginity movement" of driving red-blooded Christian boys out of the church. Murrow castigated the popular story of God giving Eve to Adam as the basis of the "crazy teaching" that God would personally provide a mate to every Christian who patiently waited. Since Christian men might (and undoubtedly would) wait forever without hearing from God directly, Murrow said it was no wonder that Christian men, given the choice between a Christian girlfriend "with all her fantasies and prohibitions" and a "regular girlfriend who will pucker up," were increasingly dating outside the church. "Ladies," he said, "I feel your pain. The dating scene in the church is grim. Christian colleges are becoming convents."[79]

Marry Well co-owner Steve Watters asked members what they thought of an article in which Susan Olasky, senior writer for the Christian news magazine *World*, argued that the popularity of Joshua Harris' *I Kissed Dating Goodbye* had made the courtship model virtually mandatory for serious Christian students. The result, she said, was that Christian men felt paralyzed and pressured. They were either scared or disinclined to ask women out, fearing both rejection and the possibility of missing out on an even better woman if they waited a while.[80] Many Marry Well members agreed with Olasky. A man named ehaven wrote, "People get skittish when they are under the gaze of the thousand eyes, and when they feel pressured to get too serious to quickly. . . . This has caused me to think that what is needed in some Christian circles is more casual dating."[81] A female member commented, "I find myself saddened and a little angry that at the beginning of this movement, some seemed to lack the foresight to notice the young kids drinking up all the admonishments toward caution and multiplying them to the nth power."[82] MissLea asserted, "I think I would have been much better off skipping 'When God Writes Your Love Story' and reading something along the lines of Boundless' Biblical Dating series."[83] And lydiann confessed that she had left Joshua Harris behind and would be willing to date more than one person simply to get to know men better. "I understand," she said, "why that sounds so worldly to some . . . to go on a date without the purpose being leading to marriage . . . it used to sound that way to me, so I get it. But I see it differently now."[84]

Though the owners of Marry Well did not admit it, courtship was not the only classic practice under attack at their site. For all the rhetoric about male headship and the initiative, women members at Marry Well were learning how to contact men and push them toward marriage. In some instances, women were reluctantly choosing to do so. As MissLea observed, "I find it disturbing how much of the 'contacting' us ladies have to do on Marry Well. Each new half-way attractive guy who joins is promptly descended upon by a host of welcomers. . . . It just seems sad to me that us ladies have to put . . . so much effort into something that shouldn't even be our job."[85] On other occasions, Marry Well itself was advising women to take the initiative. "We encourage the women of Marry Well to be proactive in searching profiles, wall conversations, and Lodge chats where men in our community are interacting," management explained. "Leaving a comment on his wall draws his attention to your profile and gives God the opportunity to point him in your direction . . . there's no sin in being the first to say hello."[86] To those who would disagree—and many did—Marry Well cited the example of a woman member who changed her mind about initiating contact being a man's job after she joined Marry Well, waited two weeks, and received no communication from anyone. "It was clear my approach was pointless," she acknowledged. Marry Well agreed. "Meeting people online has enough challenges," management observed. "Let's not add to them by complicating a simple 'hello.'"[87]

People could reasonably disagree about the theological implications of saying hello. But another Marry Well policy overtly gave women power to push men toward marriage. It was called "pulling a Ruth," and it was first described by Boundless cofounder Candice Watters. Frustrated as a college student that her close friend Steve had not made his intentions toward her clear, and encouraged by a mentor who argued that the Bible nowhere prohibited a woman from expressing her desire to a man, Candice gave Steve an ultimatum. Either he officially declared that they were dating and moving toward marriage or she would no longer spend time with him. Within a day, Steve replied that he did want to date; and six months later he asked Candice to marry him.[88] (For readers unfamiliar with Ruth, she was a destitute widow in the Hebrew Bible who convinced an affluent man named Boaz to marry her by sleeping at his feet.)

Candice later claimed that she had not meant to suggest that she had pursued Steve or taken the lead in their relationship; rather, she had merely been "responding to all the strong cues he was giving me." And she conceded that her story was not ideal. But neither are the times in which we live, with their gender confusion, lack of biblical literacy, and widespread delaying of marriage. "Because Ruth's is a story of getting to marriage amidst harsh realities," Candice contended, "I still believe it offers help in making sense of the current singles culture."[89]

It was, however, not only in her advice about pulling a Ruth that Candice pioneered avenues for evangelical women to engineer their own marriages. As Marry Well members knew very well, Candice's 2008 book, *Get Married: What Women Can Do to Help It Happen*, devoted 196 pages to teaching Christian women how to "nurture" a man into proposing to them.[90] An objective observer would be hard put to see how "nurturing" was different from the verboten "taking the initiative." Moreover, Marry Well defined its mission as providing "coaching advice" and "support for people who connected through our site, but then had questions about how best to move forward."[91] It was no secret that, as radio host Dennis Rainey of Family Life Today explained to listeners before interviewing the Watters in 2010, Steve and Candice Watters' job at Marry Well was to "coach men and women to think biblically about marriage."[92] How Marry Well or its parent company Focus on the Family could reconcile Candice performing that task with 1 Timothy 2:12-13 ("I permit no woman to teach or to have authority over a man; she is to keep silent. For Adam was formed first, then Eve . . .") was anybody's guess. No matter how loosely one might define "teaching" or "authority," the reality was that men and women were paying Candice to interpret Scripture for them and to help guide them toward marriage. Hermeneutical acrobatics would be required to square that with 1 Timothy's prohibition of women teaching or having authority over men.

Whether in her book or online, Candice's message was clear: when Christian men failed to move toward marriage, Christian women had to step into the breach—just as Boundless and Marry Well were teaching them. For all the rhetoric about biblical manhood and womanhood, evangelical men were failing miserably as marital initiators, and Christian couples were marrying later and later in life. Evangelical women were understandably—though, by their own lights, sinfully—losing their patience. All too often, whether they were courting or trying to date, these women found that neither God nor man was writing their love stories.

And so, more and more, it seemed as if there was no way back to the Garden at all. God may have presented Eve to Adam, and the chemistry between them may have been just as amazing as Joshua Harris described, but the joys of that first meeting of man and woman were forever gone. What remained was the bad news of the fall, with man charged with unrelenting labor and headship over woman, while woman's lot was pain and subservience to man. At Marry Well, neither gender was proving particularly faithful to those roles. Rather than reprising life in the Garden, members were capitulating to secular notions of manhood and womanhood.

In the end, despite all their claims to biblical fidelity, Boundless and Marry Well had failed to devise a distinctively Christian approach to dating. Anyone who thought to compare the advice offered at Marry Well to that at eHarmony—Focus on the Family's original online dating service—would have been struck by the similarities. Evangelicals could revile eHarmony as apostate all they wanted, but the advice they gave at their own dating services replicated the eHarmony formula: find someone who shares your values, try to learn to love him or her, and avoid the trap of expecting too much. Both eHarmony and Marry Well found ways for women to initiate relationships with men. And both steered clear of the romantic thrill involved in searching for soul mates, offering instead the relatively dull and risk-free proposition that compatibility could lead to intimacy. Whether Christians were courting or dating, the giddy expectations that they would "worship in bed" with the perfect soul mate that the Creator of Romance had expressly designed for and delivered to them was threatened on all sides. Where once Christian marriage had promised ecstasy, it now settled for compatibility. As we said in the beginning, Adam and Eve are a tough act to follow.

3

~

ADAM AS ALPHA MALE

Christian Domestic Discipline and the Erotics of Wife Spanking

> Your desire shall be for your husband, and he shall rule over you.
>
> —Genesis 3:16

It takes a lot to get attention from the *Colbert Report*, but Pastor Ed Young and his wife Lisa made the program in January 2012.[1] Ever alert for ways to publicize their "sexperiment" ministry—in which they exhort married Christians to have sex for seven days in a row—the Youngs celebrated the January 10 publication of their new *Sexperiment* book with a twenty-four-hour bed-in on the roof of their megachurch in Grapevine, Texas.[2] Announcements about the bed-in were provocative enough that *Sexperiment* spent a day on the Amazon best-seller list.[3] The bed-in itself on January 13 was not without incident. Unfortunately, before the twenty-four hours had expired, Pastor Young suffered a slight eye injury and the couple had to abandon their live-stream broadcast prematurely.

Christians interested in sex ministries barely had time to overcome their disappointment before they were drawn into the next brouhaha. On January 22, Pastor Mark Driscoll and his wife Grace of Mars Hill Church in Seattle saw their new primer on marriage and sex reach number one on the *New York Times* best-seller list for hardcover advice books.[4] Much of *Real Marriage* covered familiar ground, with Grace marveling at Mark's prodigious sex drive and exhorting wives to "glorify God by submitting to our husbands." Things got a tad strange when Grace confessed to a personal history of promiscuity and sexual abuse that had, by the time she married Mark, led her to regard sexual activity as "gross." Fortunately, Grace confided, the Holy Spirit had known how to heal her, directing Grace to overcome her trauma by having frequent sex with Mark.[5] That disclosure was perhaps more than readers needed or even wanted to know, but intimate revelations are to be expected in tell-all accounts of one's faith journey.

What readers did not see coming was chapter 10, "Can We _____?" This chapter began with a warning: "If you are older, from a highly conservative religious background, live far away from a major city, do not spend much time on the Internet, or do not have cable television, the odds are that you will want to read this chapter while sitting down, with the medics ready on speed dial." After detailed discussions of the joys and dangers of masturbation and oral sex, the Driscolls went on to address anal sex, menstrual sex, role playing, sex toys, birth control, cosmetic surgery, cybersex, sexual medication, and sexual assault. The only item on the list they condemned out of hand was sexual assault. All the others, they advised, had the potential to be pleasurable and uplifting for Christian couples.[6]

The Driscolls' positive assessment of anal penetration for both husbands and wives appalled and titillated many of their fellow evangelicals, who were not predisposed to regard such pleasuring as godly.[7] Moreover, readers invariably imagined Mark and Grace performing the various sex acts they described in the book, prompting one reviewer to conclude that its "cringeinducing . . . extreme oversharing" had "something to offend everyone,"[8] while another critic suggested that *Real Marriage* was not so much an analysis of married life as it was "a cry for help."[9] Still, *Real Marriage* did make the *Times* best-seller list. Love them or loathe them, the Driscolls had managed to move the spotlight from the Youngs' rooftop sexperiment onto themselves.

Weird and confessional as all that was, there was yet another side to Christian sexuality that the Driscolls failed to address: spanking. Though there are significant Christian online communities practicing wife spanking and writing spanking fiction, for the most part practitioners of Christian domestic discipline (CDD) have avoided public scrutiny. Nevertheless, CDD is rooted in a theology of gender complementarity that will be quite familiar to readers. Practitioners of CDD, like other conservative evangelical Christians, look to Genesis 1–3 for their understanding of gender roles. They believe God created men to be initiators and women to be their submissive helpers. They also contend that God created romance. When a CDD husband rules his household and his wife obeys his dictates—including his command to fetch the paddle and assume the position—they understand themselves to be laying the groundwork for intense sexual love. For a CDD wife is aroused by her alpha-male husband exercising his God-given mandate to rule over her, just as her husband is thrilled when his wife surrenders to his authority. The result, they believe, will be ardent marriages marked by comforting intimacy and ecstatic lovemaking.

While evangelical Christians seek to transform popular culture by invoking Adam and Eve as models for love, they are frequently beguiled by secular, not biblical, renderings of the first couple. Many embrace the myth of Prince Charming to explain the rapturous love that united the first man and woman. CDD enthusiasts also point to Adam and Eve as models for romance, but here it is Tarzan and Petruchio who are reigning in Eden, not some royal dandy. Nevertheless, whether evangelical Christians emulate Tarzan and Jane or Prince Charming and Sleeping Beauty, they are working from the same theological presuppositions: that God created men to rule over women and that women's acquiescence to men's authority makes pulchritudinous marriages possible. Most people would be shocked at the way CDD practitioners revel in the physical chastisement of women. But evangelicals should not be. CDD is a logical extension of the valorization of romance and wifely submission typical of evangelical discussions of biblical manhood and womanhood.[10]

Leah's Corner
Dedicated to Biblical Womanhood

Many civilians got their first glimpse of CDD as a result of a question posed by Kentucky homemaker Leah Kelley at Yahoo Answers in July 2006:

> What misbehavior could a wife commit that would deserve a spanking from her husband? I am an author of spanking fiction and want to know what the general public feels is worthy of corporal punishment. PLEASE no bashing. If you don't like spanking or feel like it is abuse in a marriage, don't waste your time or mine by answering this question. For a free spanking story chapter go to my site at Christian Domestic Discipline Fiction.[11]

With that post, online users got a glimpse of a world that many assumed or at least hoped was a hoax. Visitors at Kelley's website could observe firsthand the erotic dimensions of Christian romantic spanking fiction and peruse the learned debates regarding the preferability of "sting" versus "thud" in spanking implements. They had multiple opportunities to contemplate Christian marriages in which husbands plied their wives' backsides with paddles, belts, straps, loopy johnnies, miniblind rods, spatulas, wooden spoons, and paint stirrers. And they were asked to believe that CDD wives adored their husbands for giving them this special attention.

If that was not astonishing enough, Kelley's enthusiastic embrace of female submission and her claim (or was it a boast?) that CDD was inherently erotic made her seem like a visiting alien to those outside CDD.[12] Skeptics simply could not take Kelley seriously when she wrote passages like this: "Does your husband like pirates? Be the sexiest wench he's ever laid eyes on. Does he like to spank your bottom? Put on some drop-seat pantaloons and lay out the paddle. . . . And don't forget that sex starts *outside* of the bedroom. When was the last time you played footsies with your husband under the table or subtly rubbed up against him in public?"[13]

Once people began visiting Leah Kelley's website, they could not stop. Many joined a Yahoo CDD group (hereinafter known as "the Yahoo group")[14] where Kelley was active so that they could monitor discussions there as well. People also followed Kelly's blog at Amazon.com and ordered her books at Lulu.com. By the spring of 2007, Kelley's website was going full bore, replete with an array of articles on CDD, biblical womanhood, and biblical manhood; guest writers; a guest book; a fiction and nonfiction CDD book store; a clothing shop called Heirloom Intimates offering lingerie and "flirty" baby doll dresses that Kelley sewed herself; miscellaneous CDD products like soothing gel for spanking aftercare; a forum for discussions; "Leah's Life Blog," which kept people up to date on events in the Kelley family; and "Leah's Corner," a pastel wonderland dedicated, Kelley said, "to Biblical Womanhood where I can be as girly as I want."[15]

It is no wonder people flocked to Kelley's website once they heard about it. Some visitors contended the site had to be a parody; as one proclaimed, "Fun stuff! She's a great porn writer."[16] Others professed horror. Blogger Anne Johnson labeled Kelley a "vile creature" and denounced Kelley's website as "possibly the most nauseating content I've ever seen on the World Wide Web."[17] Jesus' General proclaimed Kelley "Christopathically detached from reality,"[18] while another respondent said, "It's slashfic for the Christian set."[19] Greta Christina called Kelley's site "creepy" and began her blog with this paragraph: "Christian spanking porn. Not three words I ever expected to string together."[20] Meanwhile mathman was largely speechless, mumbling, "wow. just wow."[21]

Naturally visitors sought a frame of reference through which to understand CDD. Some people associated it with BDSM. But CDD was distinct from BDSM, which emphasized role-playing. In BDSM, women could play either dominant or submissive roles, and, if they chose, practitioners could switch roles. BDSM also stressed the importance of creating safe words for submissives to use if they felt discipline had become too painful. Moreover, BDSM was not necessarily a lifestyle. If they wished, people could practice it in the bedroom (or the dungeon) without letting it spill over into the rest of their lives. And while BDSM focused on hierarchical relationships, it did not limit women to submissive roles or argue that male headship was divinely ordained.[22] In all these ways it differed from CDD.

Not surprisingly, CDD did share many characteristics of domestic discipline (DD). Reading Jules Markham's insider's account, *Domestic Discipline*, for example, was akin to reading Leah Kelley. Like Kelley, Markham disparaged feminism,[23] waxed nostalgic for the golden days of traditional gender roles when men and women complemented one another, and credited DD with an astonishing list of accomplishments. These included rejuvenating relationships, creating loving intimacy, eliminating arguments, dispelling angst, improving communication, providing forgiveness and euphoria, and improving couples' sex lives.[24] But there were also significant differences between the two forms of DD. Markham maintained that either the woman or the man could function as head of household (HOH), and she was not buying theological claims about CDD. Markham had this to say to people who averred that religious duty obligated them to serve as an HOH: "This is probably more about them wanting to assert themselves as the HOH rather than anything tied to fact."[25]

Compared to BDSM and secular DD, the thing that made CDD distinctive was the same feature practitioners regarded as its very heart: biblical manhood and womanhood. Male dominance and female submissiveness were not mere roles in CDD; they were attributes of cosmic reality put in place by God at the creation, and they revealed the essential nature of what it meant to be male and female. When CDD couples attempted to recreate themselves in the image of Adam and Eve, they were not only endorsing but also enacting a divinely ordained hierarchy fundamental to reality itself. CDD spanking, therefore, was not simply punishment or just an erotic activity. It was a symbolic rendering of and vital participation in the really real: the cosmos as God experienced it. And CDD demonstrated—indeed, incarnated—the coercive and abusive drive essential to biblical manhood as well as the submission and victimization that defined biblical womanhood.[26]

In the Beginning, God Created Adam HOH

However one situated CDD in the fetish world, there was no denying the addictive quality of Kelley's website. Her personal posts were, if possible, even more outlandishly fascinating than her discourses on CDD. Kelley kept readers updated on family vacations, menus, budget constraints, and discipline sessions with her husband, providing thought-provoking commentary such as, "Silicone Spatulas are Evil!!!"[27] At one point in her CDD journey, Kelley decided to jettison all her slacks and wear only skirts and dresses. Finding warm and feminine undergarments for the cold months proved problematic until Kelley decided to create frilly pantaloons for winter wear. Then her husband suggested that it would be exciting if she quit wearing underwear altogether, so that she would always be available to him for intercourse. That prompted Kelley to create the crotchless pantaloons she sold at her website.[28]

The open-mouthed visitors at Kelley's website found her adventures in submissive undergarments endlessly amusing. Kelley quickly lost patience with them. In her June 2007 newsletter, she observed that so many people had joined her forum "for no other reason than to aggravate and challenge our lifestyle" that opponents of CDD and arguments against it were no longer welcome. She took particular aim at Jesus' General. His blog, she said, had sent record amounts of traffic to her website, and sales had spiked. To autism266, an emailer who called her a "nutjob" with a "severe mental illness," Kelley announced that her "poor mentally ill children" were "some of the best adjusted teenagers I know." Her oldest son, she said, was "engaged to a submissive woman . . . who loves her crotchless pantaloons," and her younger son "would most certainly pick up on your feminazi-ness and mess with you." Promising to block future emails from autism266, Kelley concluded, "I have work to do. Besides working on a pair of crotchless pantaloons that have to go in the mail Monday, I have to make a dress, read two new story submissions, and publish five more. So if you're still curious, I guess you'll just have to read the website or buy the books (wouldn't that be funny)."[29]

Kelley did not need to waste time wondering if people like Jesus' General or autism266 thought she was a nut case. That was guaranteed. But even her cultured despisers had to concede that she was an ambitious and prolific defender of the hierarchical gender roles integral to conservative Christian evangelicalism. And in the end, it was not sexual kinkiness that really bothered Kelley's critics. It was her theology. Some Christian critics were open to erotic spanking and others were not. But what uniformly galled them was Kelley's biblical defense of CDD. One deemed it "Biblical hogwash,"[30] and another denounced the depiction of CDD as a biblical practice "that has gone on since Adam and Eve" as "utterly and blatantly unBiblical and clownish."[31] Secular critics echoed those complaints. Few objected to consensual erotic spanking, and some, like blogger Greta Christina, were fine with fantasies about nonconsensual sex and violence. It was CDD's theological claims that she could not abide. As she said,

> My big problem with the CDD stuff really isn't the fiction. It's the non-fiction, where they proselytize about how God wants everyone to have this kind of relationship, and strongly imply that consent isn't really necessary or important. That's what makes it cross the line from "this is weird, and I think it's kind of unhealthy, but whatever" to "this is potentially abusive and profoundly f**d up."[32]

Or, as another secular critic said, "Your idea of God is purely evil."[33]

Readers were correct to focus on Kelley's emphasis on female subordination since Kelley's site offered as classic a defense of gender complementarity as existed in the evangelical world. For Kelley, CDD was a natural consequence of biblical manhood and womanhood. "A true CDD marriage," she said, "begins with God's Word. Before a couple should even consider something as radical as CDD, they must be committed to living in the roles God ordained for them."[34] Kelley feared that feminism had infiltrated American Christianity, and like many conservative Christians, she rejected the notion that husbands and wives were equals. Instead, she contended, God created man to be the head of his wife, while the wife's job was to submit to him. Christians' failure to appreciate the complementary nature of gender roles had led, Kelley asserted, to a high divorce rate. "So please don't be swayed by this lie from hell," she urged—egalitarianism had no place in a Christian marriage.[35]

Kelley grounded this claim in Genesis 2–3. God created woman to be man's "help meet" in Genesis 2:20. Designed to follow and serve her husband, woman was actually "hard-wired" for this role. Thus, Kelley explained, women could be happy only when they were in submission. Unfortunately, in Genesis 3 Eve disobeyed God and developed what Kelley called a "sin nature." Now all wives wanted to control rather than follow their husbands. As a result, in Genesis 3:16 God declared that Eve's husband would "enforce his leadership" by ruling over her. Because women continued to share in Eve's sin nature and still sought to usurp power in their marriages, their husbands must check their rebellion by subjecting them to DD.[36]

Like other advocates of CDD, Kelley marshaled a number of New Testament texts to support this reading. The household codes in Colossians 3 and Ephesians 5 command that wives to submit to their husbands, and Titus 2:3-5 adjured wives to be obedient to their spouses. Passages at 1 Corinthians 14:34 and 1 Timothy 2:11-12 instructed women to be silent in worship and obedient to their husbands, 1 Peter 3:1 ordered wives to accept the authority of their husbands, and Romans 13:1 admonished every person to be subject to the higher powers that God had ordained. Hebrews 13:17 also directed Christians to submit to their leaders, noting that the leaders charged to watch over believers' souls would have to give an account of their conduct.[37]

Kelley found the Hebrews text particularly significant. "If a husband has authority over his wife by God, and must watch for her soul and give account for her, is it fair," Kelley asked, "that he have no *real* control over her, only what she willingly submits to him (as is thought by many in the mainstream churches today)? If he has no means of enforcing his authority, how can God, in all fairness, hold him accountable for her actions? Authority without the means of enforcement is a sham, and the person in the position no more than a figurehead. True authority always comes with the means of enforcement." Kelley noted that Proverbs 10:13, 26:3, and 29:15 all allowed for the use of a rod on wrongdoers, and observed that Jesus himself drove the money changers out of the temple with a whip. Moreover, in Revelation 3:19, the Son of Man stated that "I reprove and discipline those whom I love."[38] Scripture was replete, in short, with proof texts that gave those in authority license to discipline their charges.

Being subject to the authority and the discipline of their husbands should not be bad news to women, Kelley claimed. "Since God is a loving God and He created us to be followers, it is inbred in us to be happiest in that role. . . . CDD puts us back into the place where we can submit and willingly follow; thus we are happy again. That is why we are so peaceful after discipline . . . why we can curl up in his lap and feel forgiven and clean, all our rebellion with all its ugliness gone." Indeed, Kelley concluded, there was nothing like a spanking to excite one sexually. "Since spanking connotes authority in our society," she explained, "I believe that is why there is such a great sense of eroticism surrounding it for some women . . . it puts us in the roles God created for us in the most basic way. That is why I think you'll hear a lot of women say they don't like the spanking itself, but afterwards they're extremely sexually attracted to their husbands."[39]

Kelley focused on four kinds of spankings: play, maintenance, preemptive/reminder, and punishment (highlighted by the "avoid at all costs" variety).[40] While no couple was obliged to use all of these types of spankings, she said, they worked together to provide a predictable rhythm of discipline. Maintenance spankings were regularly scheduled spankings that gave wives frequent opportunities to practice submission. Punishment spankings were severe and were intended to correct specific offenses. Preemptive spankings were given before situations in which wives had previously acted out and reminded them to be on their best behavior. Play spankings could occur at any time. They were gentle, but they served to remind wives of the gender roles appropriate to Christian marriage, in which husbands were initiators and wives were submissive receivers. When incorporated into sexual activities, play spankings also had an erotic element.

Kelley argued that the severity of a spanking as well as the implements and positions to be employed were up to the husband. Safe words were not an option, nor could a wife decide to quit CDD to avoid a spanking. She urged husbands to do a thorough job with punishment spankings, continuing until the wife was repentant and no longer resisted the pain.[41] She also recognized that some husbands were reluctant to give maintenance spankings, since this kind of discipline was not a response to wrongdoing; its function was to reinforce the wife's submissive nature. But Kelly argued that wives instinctively responded to assertive husbands. "God created women to want to feel a man's strength and authority," she explained to wives. "It makes her feel more secure and protected. Plus, it gives him an 'edge' or 'persona' of power that makes him very attractive to you."[42] The spanking itself was not the turn-on, Kelley asserted; rather, the experience of the husband and wife acting out their God-given roles of initiator and receiver was what made spanking an intimate and exciting act of love. "Many women," she contended, had "a deep seated need to 'feel' their husband's authority on a regular basis."[43]

To illustrate that need, a woman at Kelley's site described a spanking like this: "I am no longer in control, & I love that! . . . Isn't it amazing that I have never felt more loved or cherished than I do in this moment right now. The pain is mounting & the spanks are swift; I am not sure it will ever end. When he feels I have seen my errors, he picks me up & draws me to his chest. I can do nothing but cry. In this moment, I am his! . . . What better man could God have made for me? NONE!"[44]

Kelley concluded, "There are probably few things that punctuate our most basic roles in marriage more than the dominance and submission of a discipline session." That is why "CDD marriages are among the best in the world. Couples . . . report greater intimacy, special closeness, increased trust, and fantastic sex lives."[45] Biblical manhood and womanhood, in short, balanced pain and pleasure. For Kelley, God's plan for romance rested upon a wife's willingness to submit not simply to her husband's leadership but also to his forceful physical chastisement. In the world of CDD, a husband without a paddle—or at least a spatula—was not a man at all.

Romance Is My Passion

For spanking devotees, Kelley's website was the CDD equivalent of an online Disney World. And as flashy as the lingerie shop was, visitors who sampled Kelley's fictional depictions of female submission and male domination invariably emerged with violent graphic images seared on their brains. Whether readers were aroused or outraged, they had to concede that Kelley took a backseat to no one when it came to depicting spankings rife with indelible brutality and suffering. Her female characters were difficult to tame, but their fathers and husbands knew how to apply the rod. And the paddle. And the belt. And the switch. And the razor strop.

Moreover, Kelley's fiction output was simply astonishing. Her offerings in January of 2007 included fourteen CDD spanking romance novels and short story anthologies. Kelley set her plots in antiquity, the Middle Ages, the nineteenth century, and in contemporary America, with several in her native Appalachia. Two featured racial themes, with *Dream in Black and White* chronicling a retired South African NFL player taming his diminutive white fiancée with an elephant-hide *sjambok* whip,[46] while *Captive Dreams* chronicled the adventures of an escaped octoroon slave and the southern disciplinarian who thought she was a white woman when he married her.[47] Kelley rated each title according to spanking intensity (mild, moderate, or severe) and provided plot synopses such as "over 50,000 words of punishment spanking fiction involving men who strive to instill values into their family by the use of the rod" and "In part 4, Jill-Ann remembers why she hates a belt, and in part 5, Alyssa learns to hate one as well. ***Contains spanking of teenage girl."[48]

Kelley acknowledged that she found CDD erotic and that the punishment spanking scenes in her fiction were a turn-on.[49] But alluring as spanking scenes might be, Kelley insisted that her fiction focused primarily on relationships, not sex. "Romance is my passion," she explained. "I love to create stories with strong heroes teaching and leading their feminine heroines as set up in the Bible. Men were never meant to be the wimps the world and the church have taught them to be." Kelley actively sought writers for her website and her online Lulu store who could write about "Biblical manhood and womanhood . . . from a CDD viewpoint."

Kelley argued that the key to good CDD fiction was finding a balance between love and discipline. Her alpha male heroes had what she called that "edge" or "persona" of power that allowed them to conquer women and bend them to their will. They said things to women like "You just don't understand, do you? . . . All that prissing around, shaking your butt, and your feminist crap . . . we just don't cotton to that here. . . . I don't want to go through this crap every day of my life with a woman determined to have her way and refusing to do a thing I say."[50]

In Kelley's stories, when a woman learned to accept the submissive role God had ordained for her, she became more compliant.[51] Inevitably, however, the woman would soon thereafter fail her man, by disobeying him, lying to him, or doing something he deemed dangerous. The beating she received would be brutal—consider this scene, in which a young woman under her brother's care was disciplined by his best friend Cameron for riding a city bus alone at night:

"Cameron!" she squealed. "Don't do this! Please!"

He drew back his arm and brought the belt down hard across the front of her thighs, jerking a scream from her lips. "Bend over the bed now!"

Shoshana leaned over the bed and grabbed a pillow, already sobbing with fear and pain. He wasted no time in bringing the leather down again across her bottom. She squeaked in agony. Almost before she could catch her breath, the leather wrapped around her thighs, and then her lower buttocks with a snap. Her mouth opened in a silent scream as she lost her breath. She'd never been spanked so hard in her life. . . . Her bottom and thighs were on fire and she could barely breath.

She couldn't stand it. She rolled over onto her back, her eyes pleading with him to stop while she cried uncontrollably. He hesitated only a moment before he stroked the front of her thighs. Again she screamed. She'd never been in so much pain.

"Turn back over, Shoshana," he ordered as he spanked her thighs again. "You're making things worse for yourself."

"Please," she begged, her hands shielding the front of her thighs. "Please!"

"Turn back over!" he ordered.

She rolled onto her stomach with a sob, the front of her thighs burning as well as the back. "You're killing me!" Her words ended on a scream as he resumed his spanking of her hind parts.

"Pleeaase stop! I can't stand it!"[52]

Spankings generally lasted until the woman could no longer protest because she was drowning in tears.[53] At this point, if the couple were married, they would have sex. Typically, that was the husband's idea, and the wife was not always a willing participant. In a short story called "The Women's Rebellion," a wife named Emily begged her husband Jake to show mercy from a relentless belt whipping. After thirty-seven strokes, he paused and told her to lie in bed on her stomach. "Please, no," she wept, to which he replied, "Then turn back around and we'll finish your whipping." Emily reluctantly laid on the bed and, completely overpowered, submitted to anal sex.[54] Another story related a husband's preference for rough sex after light spankings,[55] while yet another noted a husband's insistence on sex after spankings even though his wife was not aroused.[56]

Kelley advised wives that since their bodies belonged to their husbands they should never refuse their husbands' sexual advances, and she claimed to follow that counsel in her own marriage.[57] But she also admitted that her "fascination with punishment spankings" was strictly fantasy. "I would be terrified if my husband spanked me as long and hard as the heroes in my books," she confessed.[58] Kelley and her husband focused on play spankings, which she described as "much better than the dreaded punishment spanking and quite possibly just as effective." Watching her husband exercise his authority, even in play, was a win-win situation, Kelley said, because it "greatly increased my sexual awareness of him as a man" and improved their relationship in and out of the bedroom.[59]

Kelley's personal experience of CDD was emphatically tamer than that of her fictional characters. Among the CDD practitioners who visited her website or the Yahoo CDD site, Kelley's experiences and views of CDD were often moderate.[60] Nor did her fiction offer "silent spankings" using capsaicin cream, a practice that the Yahoo group approved.[61] As far as Kelley was concerned, spankings that did not involve a spirited assault on a woman's nether (and occasionally other) regions were pointless. For Kelley, a spanking was a morality play—a physical enactment of God's pronouncement in Genesis 3:16 that a woman would desire her husband, who would rule over her. No woman in Kelley's personal or fictional universe would be impressed by a man who applied hot pepper cream to her buttocks. Real men enforced their will through the strength of their arms. And real women loved and lusted after them for it, just as God had ordained in Eden.

As It Was in the Beginning
I Need More Caveman from Him

It is one thing for fictional characters to inflict spankings that in real life would cause immense physical damage and another for flesh-and-blood women and men to negotiate CDD relationships. This is where Internet communities provide advice, support, and critiques. The Yahoo CDD group is one of the oldest and largest CDD sites, dating back to March 2003. As of April 23, 2012, it had 2,296 current members and had accumulated 88,166 total messages.[62] Members who are active at the Yahoo group typically belong to other CDD groups as well and may also have their own blogs. Overlap between the Yahoo group and the forum at Kelley's site is considerable.[63] Moreover, it is not unusual for a member or a couple to pursue discussion on the same topic at several sites simultaneously. And some articles and links show up repeatedly on a variety of sites.[64] Bolstered by this rich contextualization, messages at the Yahoo group afford insight into a core group of couples and discussion topics over a number of years.

When people ruminated on how they came to practice CDD, they invariably cited Scripture. Genesis 1–3 functioned as the entry portal for CDD couples, with discussion focusing on three texts. The first was Genesis 1:27-28, where God created human beings male and female in the divine image and gave them dominion over the earth. Very rarely someone argued that this text suggested an original gender equality, but the common wisdom was that at best men and women were spiritual but not social equals in the beginning.[65] CDD practitioners believed that their second preferred text, Genesis 2:20-22, confirmed this primordial gender hierarchy by depicting the woman as a secondary creation designed to be the man's helper. And they concluded that when the first man failed to supervise his wife properly, God instituted DD in Genesis 3:16 to ensure that women and men enacted the roles for which God created them. "Your desire shall be for your husband, and he shall rule over you," God decreed. Originally, men were natural leaders and women were natural followers. But in a fallen world, people rebelled against the created order. The purpose of CDD was to train men to be dominating and women to obey them. Or, in other words, the point was to teach biblical manhood and womanhood.

CDD men suggested that being ruled was a good thing, especially for women. "I find more freedom when there are rules to govern me," Messianic Rabbi explained. "That's the way that G-d made us. Women, according to Genesis chapter three, have a greater need for that. When they can totally let go, then they can totally win."[66] Others cautioned that even though a wife must submit utterly to her husband, he should remember that she "is not a servant, doormat, slave, or anything along those lines. She is the completion of God's design of His image."[67] Some men stressed the subordinate status of women and demanded that their partners abase themselves; for these couples, discipline and domination were the most important aspects of CDD. Other men saw themselves as servant leaders and, while they did not hesitate to use vigorous physical discipline, for them being an HOH meant working endlessly to shepherd their partners into mature biblical womanhood. Many CDD practitioners—both male and female—shuttled back and forth between those two poles.

CDD wives routinely extolled their husbands' willingness to take them in hand. Mrs. Bulldog asserted that "God showed me that He placed man over woman," described her husband as an "Alpha Male," and credited his willingness to discipline her as the key to her becoming the submissive woman God "created me to be." Sometimes, she confessed, it was difficult for Bulldog "to correct me, but he knows it is what needs to happen so I can trust his leadership and boundaries."[68] It was not unheard of for wives to ask their husbands to discipline them more rigorously. As Heather acknowledged, "I want/crave/ need more guidance, more submission, more caveman from him." Heather worried that perhaps she was taking too much pleasure from being dominated. "Why do I crave this?" Heather wondered. "Why does my heart skip a beat when I am told to go to our room, and assume the position?"[69] Nikita14576 provided a ready answer. "It is easy . . . you find the answer in Genesis," she assured Heather. "'Your desire shall be for your husband and he shall rule over you.' . . . [God] created us to be in submission to our husbands."[70]

The Yahoo group did not require members to practice or even approve of CDD, but posters who suggested that no one should take an ancient text like Genesis seriously got told off quickly. Belinda made just such a case: "God didn[']t ordain these 'rules,'" she asserted, "a bunch of old men did thousands of years ago, and you fools are living your lives around them." Apostlebdm responded, "You are a rebel—a witch—who is going to Hell. Like the demons you serve, you are also trying to take as many souls with you. . . . It is our job to rebuke your puke & I have." Lilibeth did not defend Belinda, but said she could understand Belinda's misguided beliefs, since they were as old as humanity itself. "They started in Eden with Eve," Lilibeth declared, and "we all know that worked out well for all of us! . . . I would prefer to be submissive, even spanked (and I am) rather than follow" in Eve's footsteps.[71] In the CDD world, where gender hierarchy was constitutive of biblical manhood and womanhood, Eve was every woman's constant companion, sounding the siren call of equality and seeking to overturn the righteous rule of men.

Once people decided to practice CDD, they had to deal with the reality that most everyone else thought they were at best deluded and at worst dangerous. Even as she was becoming famous for her advocacy of CDD, Leah Kelley refused to tell her friends outside the movement what kind of fiction she wrote, fearing their disapproval and ridicule. No one was more active on the CDD discussion boards than Bulldog, author of the two-volume *Order of Marriage and Christian Domestic Discipline*, but he hid behind his pseudonym when he published books and articles. When he and his wife appeared on Australian television to discuss CDD, they requested that their faces be blurred so that no one would recognize them.[72] Fearing opposition or even police intervention, typically couples did not tell the rest of their family about their involvement in CDD. Parents worried about how to hide noisy spankings from their children—run the vacuum cleaner, radio, or television in the background were common suggestions—and practitioners engaged in intense conversations on the discussion boards about how to find quiet spanking implements. Loopy johnnies were popular recommendations, as were wooden spoons, dowel rods, mini blind rods, birch bundles, and plastic spatulas.[73] If absolute silence was necessary—such as when staying overnight with relatives or in public when discipline simply could not wait until later—couples could always apply capsaicin cream or patches to the woman's posterior.[74]

Not all CDD women craved spankings as Heather did; some were terrified of physical discipline. Deanna told of a Tuesday night belt whipping administered by her angry fiancé for being "loud and rude." On Wednesday, she and her fiancé went shopping, and he purchased three more belts.[75] On Thursday he spanked her for joining the Yahoo CDD group to complain about Tuesday's spanking. He also announced he would be instituting thrice-weekly maintenance sessions beginning on Friday evening.[76] Then on Friday morning he used one of the new belts on Deanna to begin maintenance early. In the afternoon he popped home to give Deanna a "Discipline Strap" and ordered her to don a short sundress and await his return at 8:45–9:00 in the evening. Deanna emailed her group while waiting, begging people to reply before 8:00 if they could. The strap, she reported, was "longer than a ruler, must be at least 2 in[ches] wide if not more and [I] couldn't tell you how thick." She confessed she was panicking: "I am terrified, the strap looked brutal, I have tears in my eyes now thinking about it." She asked the group: would it bruise her, or hurt

worse than a belt? And how many strokes could she expect to get for a maintenance spanking? "I am still sore from the 3 spankings I all ready [*sic*] received
this week," she agonized.[77]

Deanna's story played out predictably. Her HOH used the Discipline Strap
despite her pleas, and members applauded his diligence. Corinne assured
Deanna that "this lifestyle is truly a gift,"[78] Paul asked Deanna if she had managed to work up heartfelt remorse for her rudeness yet,[79] and Monica promised
to pray for Deanna and her HOH as Deanna learned "to accept and submit to
his guidance and discipline."[80] A number of members conceded that communication between the two could be improved, but the bottom line, as Jane
put it, was this: "In a DD relationship you should realise [*sic*] that his decision
regarding your behavior and punishment is not something to be negotiated, it
is final." Moreover, Jane admonished, "you may find this hard [to believe] but
you will learn to love and respect him for it."[81]

No other conclusion was possible. In the world of CDD, the woman must
admire her HOH for acting decisively, even if she disagrees with him. This is
particularly true when he disciplines her. If she cannot submit willingly, their
relationship is doomed. To survive, much less thrive, CDD women must have
transformative experiences like aj38320's, who marveled after a week of severe
discipline that she "never thought a spanking could feel like a religious experience . . . but it can!!!!!!!" She continued,

> i feel like my life is a new page. he has decided on daily maintenance until i can sub-
> mit with joy in all things. and while i really don't relish the idea of anything touching
> the soreness for a while, if it can make me feel what I feel right now it will be worth it.
> my bottom may have some bruises, but my spirit has been healed.[82]

EmmyGV's experience was also instructive. Tired of the endless rounds of
chastisement, she announced to her dumbstruck husband that she no longer
needed physical discipline. So her husband followed the only course available
to him as a responsible HOH. As Emmy wrote later, he "forced me over his
knee anyway and gave me a very severe spanking." The results were salutary. "I
was shocked," Emmy conceded, "but I also felt a sense of peace because it was
him in control, not me. . . . Afterwards I felt such a huge respect for him [']cause
I knew it took such a strenght [*sic*] of him to do that."[83] In successful CDD marriages, wives like Emmy learned to regard spanking as loving attention, and
they came to see their husbands' diligence in applying physical discipline as
a theological virtue. Domination and submission, after all, were what biblical
manhood and womanhood was all about.

Oh, Paddle! Take Me Away!

At the other end of the spectrum, some CDD women found physical discipline erotic. The over-the-top punishment spankings in CDD fiction provided gratifying fantasies for such women, and for those who craved the real thing, the myriad forms of CDD spankings offered physical and emotional release. But adherents had to take care not to reduce spanking to a mere fetish or sexual craving; CDD was a legitimate lifestyle for them because they regarded it as divinely mandated, not because it was fun. This was where the biblical underpinnings of CDD were critical. If God created women to lust after domineering men, then the blazing sexual appetites these Christian women associated with physical discipline were gifts from God. So extravagant were their desires to be disciplined that these women credited spanking with extraordinary benefits. From the first physical punishment, CDD women praised spanking for releasing their guilt, for dissipating their stress, for providing immediate intimacy with their partners, for making them orgasmic, and for instantaneously improving family dynamics. At times, it seemed that there was nothing a good spanking could not do. As one wife blogged,

> After the spanking, and even during for that matter, I felt myself regaining composure and peace of mind, my breathing slowed down and my spirits perked up—by the time he was finished I actually didn't want to get off his lap, I had become so peaceful and relaxed. It was true catharsis, pure and simple.... If I was ever in a commercial it wouldn't be for Calgon ... mine would be, "Oh, paddle! Take me away."[84]

Rapturous as spankings could be, CDD women were painfully aware that outsiders assumed they were victims of abuse. As a result, CDD women went to great lengths to deny that spankings constituted domestic violence.[85] Message boards abounded with wives' testimonials to the joys of CDD. In post after post, wives relished the intimacy physical discipline brought to their marriages, and they thanked their husbands for caring enough to correct them. They also expressed pity for households in which "real" domestic abuse occurred—homes where husbands neglected their wives and did not bother to take them in hand. And wives complained that they were not publicly free to express what they "need/want, because the world says that this lifestyle is abusive." In affirming the goodness of CDD, some wives were willing to accept phenomenal amounts of physical punishment as appropriate. As Kai explained,

> Speaking for me personally, because I do believe in male headship, any discipline, spanking or otherwise, he would choose to give me—whether I consented at the

time or not—would be very much within his right to administer. It could even be a very severe spanking as long as it didn't become a BEATING. There is a difference, and much/most of that has to do with intent. I think most wives, once they are done receiving their spanking and have had time to calm down and think about things, can tell the difference. For me abuse is when he very obviously is out of control... punching, pulling hair, choking, throwing her across the room and into walls etc.... This is how I draw the line.[86]

Such a claim was unlikely to convince anyone outside of the world of CDD that it renounced domestic violence, and even practitioners could find such language over the top. Occasionally punishments were so gruesome that group members complained, which invariably prompted moderators or other members to defend an HOH's right to decide how best to apply discipline in his own home. In 2007 ongoing battles between a couple named Jim and Teri embroiled members for months at the Yahoo CDD group. Teri provided lyrical accounts of the daily discipline sessions that sent her into sexual ecstasy but forced her to postpone getting a mammogram because a hospital gown would reveal to medical staff just how bruised she was. Meanwhile, her husband Jim came to the conclusion that Teri was a cheat and a liar who was using his labor with his paddles (wooden and Lexan), leather strap, belt, and loopy johnny only for her own enjoyment.[87]

As the soap opera picked up steam, Jim became convinced Teri was in love with another man, so he grounded her for weeks at a time and required her to spend hours on her hands and knees scrubbing tile floors. Jim was enraged, and he did not hide his feelings from the group: "She is everything to me," he explained, "and I just want to hurt her right now."[88] For some group members, that was just too much. Sarah protested that people were confusing CDD with BDSM.[89] Joanne declared that CDD was sick. "After reading Teri's recent post about her taste of a disciplinary spanking," she reported, " I have serious doubts about the validity of the CDD lifestyle and those that feel it's okay to beat someone in that way and still call it a spanking or to brush it off as 'to each their own.' ... There is spanking and then there is something else. I'm not sure I'm up to being here any longer."[90] And Mr. John Havelin disclosed that he "had a confession to make." Even though he had a "very pronounced spanking gene," he explained, reading the saga of Teri and Jim had convinced him to seek a marriage of virtual equality. Under no circumstances, he insisted, could he imagine inflicting the kind of "harsh punishments" on his future wife that Teri had endured.[91]

That renunciation of the male privilege inherent to biblical manhood was startling and possibly unprecedented. Nevertheless, both the moderators and Leah Kelley reminded everyone that the discussion board was intended to be a safe space for CDD practitioners. No one in the group should have to apologize for discussing discipline, no matter how severe.[92] And Teri continued to insist that "I don't want you to think that Jim abuses me or uses CDD to be a wife beater. I don't think a spanking, even a hard spanking is a violent act." For his part, Jim was convinced that the "poor women" in the group were just oversensitive.[93] And so the group had reached an impasse. With the moderators defending a husband's right to discipline as severely as he chose, they had essentially defined domestic violence out of existence. Some members had no doubt Jim was committing it, but unless Jim acknowledged that his discipline had become abusive, no authority in the Yahoo group would question him.

Overzealous discipline thus posed serious questions for the Yahoo group, but it was not a central concern. Women were much more likely to complain about partners who neglected to apply discipline consistently and energetically. This failure struck at the heart of what it meant to be a man (dominant) or a woman (submissive), and it could make wives develop contempt for their spouses. Joinedbygod9 posed this question to the group: "Does anyone else on here feel unimportant when your H says he is going to do something but then puts it off[?]" She explained, "I don't want to wear the pants in the family. I want to follow more than anyone could ever know." But her husband just was not stepping up. When joinedbygod9 had originally suggested that they practice CDD, she thought that "bringing CDD to our marriage was a way to keep us in our roles decided by God." Instead, it had just raised her expectations. "Now," she sighed, "I am afraid that wanting CDD and wanting more for my marriage, may end up in a divorce," for "all it has done has made me not believe in my H anymore."[94]

Clearly, some men did not have what it takes to be an HOH. It was a role that went against the grain for men who were not naturally dominant or turned on by spanking.[95] It also required a huge level of commitment. Women who thrived in DD relationships wanted to be monitored closely and held accountable for their shortcomings. For these women, spankings demonstrated not only that their HOH cared about them but also that he wanted to help them grow in submission.[96] Such women felt relief at placing themselves in the control of a trusted HOH, and spankings offered benefits for both partners. The

HOH could feel gratified by the exercise of dominance and by his partner's willing submission to discipline. And spanked women experienced a sense of absolution as well as the kind of release and contentment normally associated with gratifying sexual activity.[97]

While some men were too timid or uninterested to be good HOHs, other men in the Yahoo group would have been happy to give women like joined-bygod9 the attention they craved—and far more. William, for example, had enthusiastically recommended anal plugs, figging, and "nipple discipline" for Teri when she was in need of correction. And a number of wives reported that their husbands subjected them to anal procedures involving ginger root, peppermint oil, painfully inserted fingers, and rosebud plugs. Some men tied their partner's hands during spankings. Other men required their partners to shave their pubic hair. Others did not permit them to wear clothing at home or underwear at any time. Some men required their partners to drop to their knees to administer oral sex on demand. Many women were not permitted to refuse demands for sex, and some were not allowed to experience orgasms. Others were weighed weekly and spanked if they were five pounds off their target weight. Still others were required to complete complicated rituals of physical and sexual submission.

And then there were husbands like "Babygirl's Boss." Boss spanked Babygirl every time she texted or called him Jamey (his name) instead of "Daddy." And Boss thought nothing of inflicting a thirty-five-minute spanking, followed by another fifteen minutes, laying it on as "hard as I could spank, without Punching." Using a riding crop, belt, leather paddle, or even his hand, Boss administered up to 280 swats in a session, following the scientific method of swinging away until Babygirl got "the anger out of her eyes." And he lamented that his biggest problem was that "i stop too soon." To continue the corrective discipline, Boss made Babygirl sleep at the end of the bed or on the couch. However, as he pointed out, he never prevented Babygirl from leaving the house if she wanted to go out, because, after all, "she is my wife not my dog."[98] Indeed.

Other than the respectful advice offered from one HOH to another at CDD websites, there were few if any checks on men in CDD relationships. A CDD wife craved an alpha male, not a wimp; but if she was unlucky, she could end up with a brute. Deanna's case was instructive here. She survived her fiancé's assaults with the Discipline Strap. But after their marriage, he grew increasingly violent, at one point beating and raping Deanna. She finally kicked her husband out of the house, and they entered joint and individual counseling. Deanna went on to become one of the few people in the Yahoo group who urged women not to submit to physical abuse. By April 9 of 2012, Deanna proclaimed herself "happy and proud" that she and her husband were back together and that she was ready to give birth to their second child.[99]

On April 23, 2012—thirteen days after the baby was born—Deanna posted a message asking if anyone else in the Yahoo group had ever endured a belt whipping to the hands. Her HOH had just administered one to her and had threatened to imprison her in the bedroom if she resisted. The only reason he had refrained from beating her body was that they had agreed that spankings were unsafe until she returned to her physician for her six-week checkup. None of the six people who responded to Deanna's post criticized her husband, and three advised her that if she were only more submissive to him, these things would not happen to her.[100]

This reaction was a predictable result of a theology that required utter submission from women and absolute domination from men. Those attributes, moreover, were constitutive of the gender roles routinely celebrated in evangelical Christianity. CDD merely revealed the dimension of coercion inherent in biblical manhood and womanhood.[101] If, as evangelicals argued, God created men to dominate women and promised to hold men accountable if they failed at that task, it was hardly surprising that physical violence proved to be a useful or even celebrated tool. As one member of the Yahoo group observed, in answer to a post asking people how they had discovered CDD, "I found out about CDD when I typed in 'Biblical womanhood' into the google search engine."[102] For women like Deanna, there was nothing Edenic about reenacting the story of Adam and Eve. Sadly, Deanna's desire *was* for her husband, and he DID rule over her—with a vengeance.

Disco Stu and Princess Angel
A Day in the Life

Other stories had happier endings. One of the best-known couples in the CDD world was Disco Stu and his wife Princess Angel. They started CDD in 2009 after many tumultuous years of marriage punctuated by tantrums and frequent bouts of screaming. Since Angel hated being spanked, both of them were amazed when CDD increased their intimacy, encouraged Disco Stu to be more attentive to Angel, and curtailed their fighting. Disco Stu became a devotee of CDD, enthusiastically contributing to more online groups than would seem possible. He threw himself into it, announcing that he and Angel were taking off the "training wheels" and graduating from "CDD-lite."[103] He listened when moderate voices in the movement advised him to slow down and demand less of Angel and when they criticized him for arguing that CDD wives owed their husbands sexual services on demand. He also explored the hard-core side of CDD, joining a group called Alpha Males and Their Submissive Women (AMATSW). There he discussed adding anal plugs and enemas to Angel's schedule of discipline, and he expressed approval when one of the AMATSW men announced that he regularly gave bare-bottomed discipline spankings to his wife and two adult daughters in front of the entire family, including his two teenaged sons.[104]

Angel, meanwhile, struggled with submission. She was accustomed to Disco Stu being absent for months at a time on military deployments, and at one point declared herself an "AMAZON WOMAN" capable of running the house and taking care of their son by herself.[105] Angel confessed she was scared of losing herself as a CDD submissive wife at the same time that she was thrilled to receive so much loving attention from Stu. "There were years," she said, "that he rarely looked at me nor talked to me." Now things were better: "Stu is more dedicated than ever and really listening and beginning to understand me."[106]

For his part, Disco Stu spoke admiringly of his wife's competence and struggled to show Angel his gratitude for submitting to him as her HOH. He made her breakfast in bed every morning before work, held her hand whenever they were in public, took her on a weekly date, and accepted her dictum that she did not owe him sexual favors on demand. He studied Scripture so that he could be the family spiritual leader, and he made Sunday mornings a shrine to CDD. The day began with a discipline spanking if Angel was in arrears. If she was not, Stu made love to Angel while she was on her hands and knees in front of a mirror. Angel was excessively modest, and she hated watching herself have sex, particularly in a style she considered wanton and degrading. Stu required her to announce each orgasm to God, and Angel found that humiliating too. Then it was off to church, where they snuggled together contentedly. The goal throughout the morning was for Angel to feel her submission to Disco Stu.[107]

Stu took pains to lecture Angel when he gave her disciplinary spankings so that she would associate his voice with his authority as HOH. His work bore fruit they never anticipated. One March Sunday in 2010, Stu was so pleased and humbled by her submissiveness that he stood before the entire congregation to let people know that Angel was making him a better husband simply by encouraging him to be a leader.[108]

On a Sunday soon after that, Angel and Stu were in a church class together, and Stu was reading and explicating Scripture. Angel suddenly shivered and grasped his hand tightly. "My voice and presence, talking in authority and being a spiritual leader had affected her as a woman," Stu later reflected. "It gave me pause to think that I could affect her at such a primal and profound level. I hadn't touched her intimately and hadn't done anything blatantly erotic." Nor had he needed to—simply being a masterful HOH was arousing in itself. "That I was leading her spiritually, being a strong HOH made her have a response to what her husband was doing," Stu marveled. "She had had a small sexual climax just listening to me be the spiritual head of the family."[109] Clearly Stu had mastered his command voice.

Disco Stu and Princess Angel had many rough times ahead of them, which Stu would document online in his customary painstaking fashion. But on that 2010 March Sunday, he and Angel had fulfilled the promise of CDD, finding intimacy and ecstasy in acting out the biblical roles of Adam, the alpha male created by God for leadership, and Eve, the woman designed to be his submissive partner. A year later, looking back on nineteen years of marriage, Angel would say that they had never been so happy and that she finally understood that God had created woman to encourage and assist her HOH. "God took out one rib bone to make the help mate[,] the woman, the Eve to help the man for all the years on the earth," she explained. "So I . . . help him like Eve helped Adam and call on God when I am tempted to eat that apple by sinning and arguing and being lazy."[110] Angel also dreamed that when her son married he would not need CDD. "Some people have awesome marriages without it, and I admire that," she confessed. "Unfortunately, I need the spankings in my life."[111]

Disco Stu had earlier reached the same conclusion. "I am trapped perhaps in CDD with her," he reflected. "She cannot escape because she has embraced submission as a lifestyle. I cannot escape because Lyn will not allow that emotional commitment she has always hungered for to be reduced or lost." As Stu looked back on his marriage before CDD, he did not like the person he had been then. That man, he said, had considered himself strong and masterful, but he had actually been "deluded and did not understand or appreciate the jewel he possessed or how special a submitting wife is and how humble she can make him feel."[112]

Angel's willingness to endure maintenance spankings simply because Stu asked her to had allowed her to breach the "thick masculine walls" Stu said he had erected to protect himself emotionally. He had imagined himself safe in his metaphorical fortress of solitude, and then, surprisingly, one day he found Angel there with him, "setting up a picnic blanket of sorts in my courtyard quite casually. She seems comfortable and determined to be there," he noted. "She doesn't want the old Stu back and I don't quite know where he has run off to anyway." As he looked ahead, Stu knew that Angel was facing a difficult future. There would be "more spankings . . . and more maintenance," he fretted. "I NEED to counterbalance all that pain and suffering with tenderness and affection, consistently. Any request she make[s] I find I move quickly to meet that need. Partly it is because she asks so little and submits so much."[113]

Perhaps without even realizing it, Disco Stu had left the world of biblical manhood and womanhood behind. One of the many disquieting dynamics of CDD theology and fiction is how they reduce the complex relationship between man and woman to an endless game of Whac-A-Mole. Throughout a woman's life, her male partner repeatedly clubs her back into her proper place: submissive and obedient, just as Eve was to Adam before the fall. Except that the CDD woman never quite gets there. Even when vigorous spankings restore a wife to submission, she remains east of Eden; her rebellious nature has only been chastened, not redeemed. CDD incorporates maintenance spankings because the female's primary sin against biblical womanhood is not her errant deeds; it is her very nature—fallen, rebellious, eager to overthrow man from his God-given throne.

It is striking that CDD practitioners never relate chastised women's physical suffering to Christian traditions of penance. In that context, suffering can be transforming, connected to larger stories of asceticism, spiritual pilgrimage, and salvation. Even more telling is the failure to link the pain CDD women undergo to the image of agony basic to the Christian story: the cross. In revealing the mystery of redemptive suffering, Jesus' crucifixion is the central reality of Christianity. Because Jesus willingly endured torment on behalf of others, Christians believe that the love displayed on the cross has the power to renew and recreate the children of Eden. The Apostle Paul referred to Jesus as the new Adam, the man of heaven, the correction and fulfillment of the original Adam, the man made from dust. "Just as we have borne the image of the man of dust," Paul promised, "we will also bear the image of the man of heaven." Or to put it another way, "If anyone is in Christ, there is a new creation: everything old has passed away; see, everything has become new!"[114]

Uniquely in the CDD community, Angel and Stu's journey calls upon these traditions and images to extol the significance of woman's suffering. By her husband's own account, Angel's willingness to submit to physical discipline was the very virtue that created the new Stu, freeing him from emotional isolation and uniting the two of them in life-altering communion. In submitting to Stu's physical discipline, Angel was functioning for him as a Christ figure. Alone among his peers, Stu recognized that he owed his revitalized marriage and the privilege of being an HOH to his wife's willing suffering on his behalf. And he honored her sacrifice.

Any theology that ties male redemption to female suffering is problematic, all the more so when that suffering involves physical abuse. Most of us are never going to think wife spanking or the subordination of women to men is a good thing. But this version of CDD is not preoccupied with Lexan paddles or obsessed with punishment spankings that render women broken and violated.[115] Nor does it produce lurid fiction inviting readers to indulge in misogynistic fantasies of divinely ordained rape, enslavement, and torture. And, unlike evangelical definitions of biblical manhood and womanhood, it treasures a woman's voluntary sacrifice on behalf of a loved one as an exquisite gift that can create new and better ways of being male and female. Here, there are hints of genuine transformation, where the possibility of a new creation unmasks the endless exaltation of male dominance for the vainglorious enterprise it is. This version of CDD looks forward to the day when husbands no longer spank wives.

It's also *much* easier on the spatulas.

~ RECYCLING EDEN ~

The story fascinated all sorts of people
for all sorts of reasons. . . .

Some thought the story funny and laughed at its retelling
subtly changing it here and there
to produce the desired results.
But, humor isn't always about entertainment.
And jokes about Adam and Eve
are jokes about us all.

Others were drawn to the story's ideas
like "temptation" and "taboo."
Marketing strategists saw power in temptation and taboo
power that could be turned into money.
Eve the temptress and the forbidden fruit were their inspiration.
They used them ruthlessly to tempt others
into buying their goods.

—L.S. & V.Z.

4

~

LAUGHING AT ADAM AND EVE
Humor and Gender Stereotypes

Then the Lord God said, "It is not good that the man should be alone;
I will make him a helper as his partner."

—Genesis 2:18

Readers of the Bible often extract "religious" meaning from its verses. They strive to implement in their own lives the truths they find in the Bible precisely because for them, the Bible is *Scripture—sacred writing*. In a sense, they attempt to recreate in their own lives the values and principles found in the Bible because they view the Bible as the authoritative word of God. But there is another intersection between the Bible and culture that is more "secular."[1] These appropriations utilize the myths and symbols found in the Bible precisely because they are powerful as recognizable *cultural* artifacts. This is especially true in popular culture mediums like songs, films, television, video games, comics, advertising, jokes, and so on.[2] This type of commodification and commercialization often recycles biblical stories instead of attempting to recreate them. When appropriations like this happen, however, they divorce the story's themes and characters from their original religious context and function. The result is a product that may have little resemblance, or even stand in opposition to, the "Scripture" recognized in that culture as authoritative.

Genesis 2–3 is a good story. And good stories are capable of being told and retold in a number of different ways. Both the story and the symbols found in Genesis 2–3—Eve, the Garden, Adam, the snake, and God—are "multivocal."

They mean different things to different people in different time periods. The medium in which they are recontextualized also plays an important part in determining how they are reimaged and interpreted.[3] Humor, for example, is only one of a myriad of areas that utilize Genesis 2–3's symbolism.[4]

Stories of origins are never *just* about the past. Contemporary readers appeal to Genesis 2–3, for example, to explain *present-day* realities such as what it means to be a "man" and a "woman." Since relationships and sex are central to what it means to be "human," it should not come as a surprise that Adam and Eve are the prime targets of jokes dealing with these topics. Indeed, as the prototype male and female in Western religions, their story becomes a natural platform for such jokes.[5] But in spite of the frequently heard comment—"it's only a joke"—jokes are not simply about entertainment.[6] Humor can both support and advance the status quo or be a subversive form of resistance.[7] The jokes in this chapter all focus on gender and use Genesis 2–3 as a platform for their humor. And depending on their content, they forward gender inequalities (sexist humor),[8] challenge them (feminist humor),[9] or integrate aspects of both (post-feminist humor).[10] Thus humor about Adam and Eve not only reflects society's attitudes and assumptions about gendered relationships (whether they focus on women, men, or both), but can also work to challenge and change them. On one level, jokes about Adam/man and Eve/woman not only comment on relationships, but also reflect the conflicts that exist between men and women in contemporary society.

Internet Humor, Gender, and the Garden

Humor about sex and relationships is not new. However, in the past few decades a new *venue* for this humor has emerged—the Internet.[11] Before the Internet, the reception of jokes depended on oral or media delivery (e.g., radio and television), or on the publication of joke collections. With the advent of the Internet, both the production and distribution of jokes have entered a new age.[12] Now, Internet users have become active in the production of humor while their intended audience has literally gone global. Internet humor is also accessible with an ease that is astonishing.[13] Some meta-characteristics of Internet humor involve digital capabilities that make possible the combination of communication morphologies (e.g., script and sound, etc.), digital capacity to store and deliver materials from a variety of sources, and access to a global audience.[14]

One of the most prevalent topics of Internet humor is sex and gender.[15] When analyzing this type of humor, frequently used categories are sexist humor, feminist humor, and post-feminist humor. Whereas sexist humor is understood to be an "old" type of humor, feminist humor is believed to have been prevalent in the 1960s and 1970s, while post-feminist humor is thought to represent contemporary culture.[16] Sometimes this last category is understood to be an "updating" of the feminist movement, while others see it as a cultural backlash against feminism.[17]

Humor—both visual and verbal—comes in a variety of different genres. Some are "old" genres (e.g., jokes), while others represent "new" Internet genres (e.g., photoshopped pictures). The Adam and Eve humor in this chapter is verbal and represents, primarily, the genre of "joke." Simply put, a joke is a short story with a punch line.[18] Although some comedians have voiced their opinion that jokes are a "dead" medium,[19] humor scholars have argued that the Internet has resulted in a resurgence of the genre.[20]

Although structurally simple, jokes are a complex form of discourse. They work only if they resonate with an experience or an interest of the listener.[21] In a "non-ordinary way" they raise questions and deal with them. Often they walk a fine line between funny and offensive.[22] Indeed jokes allow insult and disrespect to be conveyed in a deniable form.[23] Theorists have noted this somewhat "hostile" aspect of certain jokes.[24]

The selection of the verbal humor analyzed in this study was performed according to specific criteria: it had to deal with gender/sexual issues, it had to use the Genesis 2–3 story as its platform, and it had to be located on the Internet. On the one hand, because these jokes deal with sex and gender (universal human issues) they have the potential of being more "global" in their outreach than other joke themes. On the other hand, there is also a "local" sense to these jokes because they deal with religious characters (Adam and Eve) who are situated in *Western* religious traditions.

The jokes in this study represent a sample from both joke sites and sites having only one joke. Very quickly it became apparent that the search was reaching a "saturation" point where sites began using the same jokes. Some of these jokes, however, were only *structurally* similar. A single joke can be retold in a variety of different ways. The words, characters, and settings can all change, but the basic structure/logic remains the same.[25] The value of looking at some of these variants lies in how these changes affect the joke's impact and meaning. Analysis of all of the following jokes was performed through a close critical reading and content analysis that asked what messages (both explicit and implicit) are being communicated about gender in the joke.

Sexism and the Garden
Laughing at Eve

Sexist representations of women in jokes reflect cultural assumptions about women. Women are understood not only as "other," the binary opposite of men, but also as occupying a lower social position.[26] Elements of sexist humor are an emphasis on women's inferiority when compared to men, explicit or often implicit targeting of women, use of cultural stereotypes of women, and a belief in a social hierarchy based on male superiority.[27]

A common strategy sexist jokes employ is to reduce women to traditional stereotypes. Indeed, these jokes often depend on such stereotypes.[28] Women are often portrayed as being in the private sphere (e.g., housework, children, etc.) but not the public one. They are depicted as romantic, sensitive, dependent, emotional, and vulnerable. Sometimes they are imaged as sex objects with an emphasis on their appearance and sexual attractiveness. Frequently they are seen as either not interested in sex or as oversexual (both extremes). Stereotypes that are especially negative involve imaging women as stupid,[29] needy, illogical, talkative, and nagging.[30]

A good example of a sexist joke involving the first woman and man starts out with God creating man and then resting.[31] God then creates woman, which is followed by the punch line, "Since then, neither God nor man has rested. AMEN."[32] Although it clear that this joke references Genesis, it is not an accurate account of either of the stories in Genesis 1–3 (in neither story does God "rest" between the creation of man and woman). Nor does the joke specifically name the first man and woman—though culture appropriations of the creation accounts would normally label the first man, "Adam," and the first woman, "Eve." This omission reinforces the association of *first* man with *all* men and *first* woman with *all* women.

Since the actual cause of man's lack of rest is never made explicit, the reader is left with several options as to the stereotypes being inferred. On the one hand, it may evoke the stereotype of the nagging, irritating wife.[33] Or perhaps it is not just her endless chatter that is called to mind, but her "to-do list" (the "honey-do" phenomena), while the man (and God) wants nothing more than to simply rest. Either way, this joke implies that life for man and God would have been simpler (or at least more restful) without the woman. Perhaps some might say that this joke is tame—a type of benign amusement. But given the history of imaging God as male in Western culture, this joke aligns two "male" characters against the first woman. By doing so it establishes an uneven power distribution between males and females.

Another sexist joke involving Genesis 2–3 begins with a needy Eve in the Garden who is feeling a bit of "relational angst" about her marriage to Adam. When she finally confronts Adam and asks the question "Do you love me?" Adam replies, "Of course dear," and then he mutters to himself "Do I have a choice?"[34] In this joke, Adam and Eve are married, and a somewhat pathetic Eve seeks reassurance that she is loved. The joke's setting plays off of the common comedic themes of woman as "dependent, emotional, needy, [and] talkative."[35] That Adam's response is basically insincere is revealed by the words muttered under his breath ("Do I have a choice?"). Adam's response calls to mind the stereotype of the sorely tested husband who agrees with his wife in public but in private feels quite differently. Indeed, a common theme of sexist jokes involving marriage is men's dissatisfaction with their sex lives.[36] By setting this joke within the frame of "marriage," it allows the joke to comment, not just on the first couple's relationship, but on the institution of marriage as well. A common image of marriage in jokes is that of a "battlefield" between the sexes,[37] where the "terrible wife" stereotype is prevalent,[38] though in this joke Eve appears more annoying than terrifying.

In another version of this joke, Adam asks Eve quite directly, "Do I have a Choice?"[39] Eve is still imaged as needy, but there is no mention of marriage with Adam. This omission changes the thrust of the joke. Now the implicit stereotype is of women who seek commitment from men who are unwilling to commit. Moreover, instead of being affirmative, Adam's answer is pragmatic and strikes a somewhat sarcastic note. What is muttered in private in the previous joke now becomes a public response. For some listeners, Adam's answer may reinforce the stereotype that males are basically insensitive when it comes to women's feelings. Indeed, the reader is left to wonder in this joke whether Adam would still choose to be with Eve if he had a choice.

One final version of this same joke characterizes Adam as quite acerbic. When asked if he loves Eve, there is no attempt to be devious or sarcastic. He simply says: "NO I DON'T!" A tearful Eve (imaged by a crying emoticon) asks, "Then why did you make love to me?" Adam's rude reply is simply: "HELLOOOOO! does it look like I have a f***ing choice?"[40] In this last version, Adam's thoughts and emotions are made graphically clear. In this joke, it is Adam's response that stands in stark contrast to the others. This Adam *is* emotional, but it is the emotion of *anger* not tenderness. He is verbally abusive and yells (see all CAPS) that he, in fact, *does not* love Eve. Adam is confronted with a crying (a very emotional and old stereotype of women) Eve, who asks why he recently "made love" with her. His cold and harsh answer is simply that there was no one else from which to choose. Moreover, his use of the term "f***ing" plays into the stereotype of men having rough, coarse speech habits. Eve/woman appears in this joke as not only needy but also clueless ("HEL-LOOOOO"). While this joke adds to women's imperfections (they are over-emotional and clueless when it comes to men), the joke also (inadvertently?) functions as a cautionary tale for all woman. Just because a man sleeps with you, do not assume he does it out of "love." After all—you just may be the only woman around at the time.

The fact that Eve was the only woman in the Garden emerges again in another joke—this time to emphasize Eve's irrationality. Arriving home late one night, Adam is confronted by an angry Eve who yells at him and accuses him of being out with another woman. Adam calls her "silly" and reminds her that she is the *only* woman around. Adam then goes to sleep only to be woken up by a poking, prodding Eve. When he asks what she is doing, she replies: "I'm counting your ribs."

In this joke, Eve is—once again—the image of the insecure woman. She is also irrational—after all, there *are* no other women in the Garden. That Eve persists in counting Adam's ribs shows how little she accepts his previous dismissal of her fears and insecurities. On one level, the joke resonates with a male audience who often feel they are unjustly accused of infidelity. On another level, however, female listeners may sympathize with Eve because they believe that men who stay out late at night may well be unfaithful to the woman who waits at home.

Whereas the jokes analyzed thus far are rather short, one final example of a longer sexist joke is one that actually involves sex—or the lack thereof:

> After a few days on the new Earth, the Lord called to Adam and said, "It is time for you and Eve to begin the process of populating the earth, so I want you to kiss her."
> Adam answered, "Yes, Lord, but what is a 'kiss'?"

> The Lord gave a brief description to Adam, who took Eve by the hand and took her to a nearby bush. A few minutes later, Adam emerged and said, "Thank you Lord, that was enjoyable."

> And the Lord replied, "Now, I'd like you to caress Eve."
> And Adam said, "What is a 'caress'?"

> So, the Lord again gave Adam a brief description and Adam went behind the bush with Eve. Quite a few minutes later, Adam returned, smiling, and said, "Lord, that was even better than the kiss."

> And the Lord said, "Now, I want you to make love to Eve."
>   And Adam asked, "What is 'make love', Lord?"

> So, the Lord again gave Adam directions and Adam went again to Eve behind the bush, but this time he re-appeared in two seconds.
>   And Adam said, "Lord, what is a 'headache'?"[41]

Although in Genesis 2 the man and woman appear to be created as adults, in this joke they lack both experience and knowledge. They are totally ignorant of even the most rudimentary aspects of sexual contact.[42] Adam does not know what a kiss or a caress is—although when he performs both he finds them "enjoyable" and cause him to "smile." This joke is structured on the rule of three. Three times God commands Adam to engage in some type of sexual activity (kiss . . . caress . . . make love). The punch line can be found after God's third command when Adam (two seconds later) returns to God with a question: "Lord, what is a 'headache'?"

After the joke's first line, Eve is offstage ("behind the bush") and never is given a voice. We do not, for example, know whether the caress and kiss were as enjoyable to her as they were to Adam. What we do know, by the joke's punch line, is that she is unwilling to make love with Adam and uses the iconic excuse of a "headache." The joke perpetuates the stereotype woman as "undersexed" or less interested in sex than men. In it, woman is a sex object who exists solely to populate the earth, be receptive to Adam's sexual needs, and always be available. That she does not comply evokes the contemporary issue that emerges in relationships when women just say "no."[43]

Feminism and the Garden
Laughing at Adam

Not all jokes target first woman/Eve—there are those that make Adam their central focus. Some of these fall into the category of "feminist" humor. Characteristics of feminist humor are that it challenges gender inequalities, often targets men, and focuses on gender.[44] Historically, jokes have been perceived as masculine constructions in which perspectives tended to be male. Recently, however, jokes told at the expense of men have reportedly become more common in industrialized countries.[45] Their emergence is often credited to the contemporary feminist movement.[46] On the one hand, feminist humor attempts to equalize the power distribution in contemporary society. As such, it challenges the status quo. Although such jokes evoke a sense of solidarity among their female audience, they often achieve this by reinforcing old stereotypes about men, resulting in a kind of reverse discrimination.[47]

Like the jokes that target Eve, jokes that target Adam/man employ stereotypes—this time of men—to achieve their goals. Men are thought to function well in the public sphere but poorly in the private sphere (e.g., housekeeping, rearing children). They are rational, individualistic, and independent but find it difficult to express emotions and to display weaknesses. Men are imaged as self-centered, aggressive, insensitive, hypersexual, violent, and stubborn and are basically stupid (e.g., childish, think with their penises, etc.).[48] Interestingly, these stereotypes are frequently the opposite of those held of women. For example, men are not emotional while women are too emotional, and men are not good in maintaining relationships, while women are, and so on.

The first example of feminist humor about Adam is "funny list" humor. It enumerates the ten reasons why God made Eve. Reasons 10–3 are based on what is seen as stereotypical characteristics of men (the implied stereotypes in italics after each reason were added):

10. God was worried that Adam would frequently become lost in the Garden because he would not ask for directions. [*Men won't admit they are lost and ask for directions*]
9. God knew that one day Adam would require someone to locate and hand him the remote. [*Men are slovenly housekeepers*]
8. God knew Adam would never go out and buy himself a new fig leaf when his wore out and would therefore need Eve to buy one for him. [*Men are useless at shopping—either they can't or won't shop*]
7. God knew Adam would never be able to make a doctor's, dentist, or haircut appointment for himself. [*Men need a keeper—won't go to a doctor when sick*]
6. God knew Adam would never remember which night to put the garbage on the curb. [*Men's task is to take out the garbage*]
5. God knew if the world was to be populated, men would never be able to handle the pain and discomfort of childbearing. [*Men are wimps when it comes to pain*]
4. As the Keeper of the Garden, Adam would never remember where he left his tools. [*Men are slovenly housekeepers*]

   3. Apparently, Adam needed someone to blame his troubles on when God caught him hiding in the Garden. [*Men are irresponsible*]

   2. As the Bible says, It is not good for man to be alone!

   1. When God finished the creation of Adam, He stepped back, scratched his head, and said, "I can do better than that!"[49]

Reasons 10–3 give the "backstory" to God's statement in Genesis 2:18 (that it is not good for man to be alone). While the biblical text never explains *why* it is not good, the joke elaborates on this omission. Indeed, reason 2 actually summarizes Genesis 2:18. Ostensibly the joke *could* end with reason 2—but it does not. The joke's punch line is found in reason 1 when God steps back and says, "I can do better than that." The joke challenges readings of the biblical story that would argue for men's superiority and women's subordination based on their order of creation. In this joke God creates Eve—not just because Adam is lonely but because Adam is rather flawed. The downside of this particular joke, however, is that the reasons given for why Adam "needs" Eve mirror cultural stereotypes of women (e.g., women are good shoppers, etc.).

Throughout the history of Genesis 2–3's interpretation, people have questioned how Eve's creation should be understood. Most of the time, they assume that her secondary *creation* implies her secondary *status*. Moreover, since she is created to assuage man's loneliness, her very creation is seen as a derivation. In the "Why God Created Eve" list just analyzed, that assumption is challenged by presenting Adam as so flawed that a second creation is necessary. This idea is repeated in a cluster of shorter jokes that dot the Internet. Usually the first line of these jokes poses a question that the second line answers. Examples include "What did God say after he created man?" (Second line: "I can do better than this, so he created woman.")[50] and "What did God say after creating Eve? (Second line: "Practice make perfect.").[51] Not all jokes of this type, however, are short two-liners. Another example of this kind of joke starts with a question but incorporates a series of answers: "Why did God create Adam first?" Answer: "1. Practice makes perfect. 2. Give us someone to bitch at immediately. 3. There's a first draft with anything. 4. To see what needed to be fixed and then make the proper changes. 5. First is the worst . . . Second is the best! 6. To be funny."[52]

Another way to address the issue of the order of creation and how it relates to gender is simply to change the story. For example, one joke begins by announcing that the biblical account is wrong—that actually Eve was created before Adam. When questioned by God as to how she is doing, Eve responds that she really likes the Garden and animals—but hates her three breasts. Apparently the middle one pushes the other two out and they get caught on branches. God defends himself by saying, "Hey, it was my first shot at this, you know. I gave the animals what, six? So I just figured half, but I see that you are right. I'll fix that up right away!" Thus he rips the third breast out and throws it into the bushes. Three weeks later God returns and again asks Eve how she is doing. Eve then calls attention to another mistake made by God. She does not have a mate (like the animals do) and she is lonely. Once again God readily admits his oversight. God promises Eve a mate taken from her body. The punch line concludes the joke: "Now, let's see. . . . Where did I leave that useless tit?"

The setting for the above joke reverses the order of creation found in Genesis 2 by having the woman created first—albeit with three breasts. The joke is composed of two movements. The first has Eve quite taken with the sensual aspects of the Garden (sunsets and sunrises) but emphatically *not* taken with her three breasts. God's characterization in the joke is less than transcendent. God speaks colloquially ("How's it going, Eve?") and apparently has no other reason for giving Eve three breasts than the fact that he "just figured" three would be right for Eve. The second part of the joke takes place three weeks after God's impromptu surgery on Eve. Once again, God is characterized as a rather bumbling deity. In a role reversal, now man is made from a body part of woman. But by describing that part as "useless" the joke invites the listener to wonder if this new creation can be more useful than the part from which it originates. By having Eve created first, however, the joke reinforces the importance of the being first in the order of creation.

Most people are familiar with the "good news/bad news" joke type. Jokes using this structure are a comedy trope that usually generates humor based on contrast. In one such joke, God informs Adam that God has both good news and bad news for him. The good news is that God has two organs for Adam— a brain and a penis. The brain will allow Adam to be very intelligent, enable him to create new things and help him have intelligent conversations with Eve. The penis will allow Adam to reproduce (and populate the earth) while making Eve happy by giving her children. Adam is pleased and really does not see how there could be any "bad news." The joke's punch line comes with God's last words to Adam: "the bad news is that when I created you I only gave you enough blood to operate one of these organs at a time."

God's response in the above joke reveals the "bad news"—either man can be intelligent, but live a rather sterile existence, or can be fruitful without the leveling influence of reason and intelligence. The joke seeks to explain a stereotype often ascribed to men—that they are often led by their penises and not their brains. In jokes, male genitalia are often featured as the primary instruments in men's decision making.[53] It is interesting to note, however, that the joke focuses on reproduction rather than pleasure as the penis' primary function. Ironically, when men are depicted as thinking with their penises rather than their brains, having children may be the farthest thing from their minds.

A different "penis" joke is set right after creation. This joke begins with God's announcement that he has two things leftover from his creation of Adam and Eve. God then proceeds to give the first man and woman a choice as to which item they want. The first item (a "thingy that allows its owner to pee while standing up") is obviously a penis. But before God can identify the second item, Adam interrupts. Adam is depicted as childish and immature—like "a little boy"—and demands that God give it to *him*. If Adam is depicted as immature, Eve's depiction is just the opposite. She smiles (indulgently? patronizingly?) and tells God to let Adam have it. Neither Adam nor Eve knows what the second item is until its identity is revealed in the joke's punch line: "'Well, here's the other thing, it's all yours.' 'What's it called?' said Eve. 'A brain,' replied God."[54]

The punch line identifies this joke as a type of "stupidity" joke that presents Adam as essentially stupid and Eve as superior to Adam. Eve has no "penis envy" in this joke—quite the contrary. In some ways this joke is reminiscent of the "good news/bad news" joke previously analyzed. In that joke Adam had both penis and brain, but not enough blood to operate them both at the same time. In this joke Adam gets a penis but no brain. This reinforces the stereotype that men are bereft of reason and often at the mercy of their sexual organs. Women, on the other hand, are depicted as in control and, as a consequence, smarter.

Another version of this joke uses this same structure but tweaks the content.[55] While the joke is structurally the same as the previous one, Adam's characterization as childlike is even more accented:

> Adam popped a cork. Jumped up and begged, "Oh, give that to me! I'd love to be able to do that!
>> It seems the sort of thing a Man should do.

Oh please, oh please, oh please, let me have that ability. I'd be so great!

When I'm working in the garden or naming the animals, I could just let it rip, I'd be so cool.

Oh please God let it be me who you give that gift to, let me stand and pee, oh please..."

On and on he went like an excited little boy (who had to pee).[56]

But the most significant change in this version is in its punch line—God's words to Eve are simply: "What's left here? Oh yes, multiple orgasms."[57] Unlike the joke in which Eve is given a brain and is essentially superior to Adam intellectually, this version highlights her essential *sexual* superiority. The listener knows that while males have to recuperate after climaxing, women can go on to experience multiple orgasms. In the end, these jokes depict woman as superior to man, whether in having a brain or the ability to have multiple orgasms,. The irony of the joke, of course, is that Adam could have had the "superior" gifts had he not interrupted God with his childish greed.

Post-Feminism and Paradise

A third type of Adam and Eve Joke actually contains elements critical of both Adam/man and Eve/woman. This type of joke is sometimes called "post-feminist" humor.[58] The definition of post-feminist humor is a debated and ambiguous area. Among the characteristics attributed to this category, however, are two that are helpful in analyzing Adam and Eve jokes: (1) they contain both feminist and antifeminist ideas and (2) they emphasize the differences between men and women.[59] This last characteristic is sometimes called the "Mars and Venus" phenomena.[60]

The first example of post-feminist humor focuses on why God made Eve:

Adam and God were walking in the garden one day and Adam said to God, "God, why did you make Eve so beautiful?"

God answered, "So you'd like her, Adam."

They walked on. . . . And Adam said, "God, why did you give her such lovely lips?"

And God said, "So you'd like her, Adam."

They walked on. . . . And Adam said, "God why did you give her such a beautiful figure?"

And God said, "So you'd like her Adam."

And they walked on. . . . Then Adam said, "God, why did you give her such a little brain?"

And God said, "So she'd like you, Adam!"[61]

This joke is a "stupidity" joke. In answer to Adam's question concerning why God made Eve so beautiful, the joke is structured on the rule of four. Four times Adam inquires as to God's motivations for making Eve. The first three questions highlight Eve's physical qualities. By focusing on her physical attributes, the joke sexually objectifies Eve by basically reducing her to attractive body parts.[62] She is "beautiful . . . has lovely lips and . . . a beautiful figure." Since God creates her in this way so that Adam will "like" her, it reinforces the stereotype that men are attracted primarily to women's physical attributes. If Eve had been ugly, it is implied, Adam might not have "liked" her—a grim prospect for the future of the human race. The fourth question and its response function as the punch line for the joke. While it could be argued that the first three of Adam's questions imply complimentary observations about Eve's body, the last stands in stark contrast. Shifting from Eve's physical attributes to her mental/intellectual ones, Adam asks why God gave Eve "such a little brain." Eve may be beautiful, but she, it is implied, is stupid and inferior to Adam when it comes to intelligence. Of course Adam is not much better in this joke. In an ironic reversal, the punch line explains that God created Eve thus so that *she* could like *him*. We have not been told much about Adam up to this point, other than he is curious as to why God made Eve. The joke's punch line implies that only a stupid Eve would like Adam—if she had a bigger brain (was smarter) she would know better.

Another version of the "Why God Made Eve" joke type, once again, emphasizes Eve's "less-than" attributes. This joke's structure is similar to the previous one with a few differences in content. In this joke, Adam begins by telling God "how much the woman means to him and how blessed he feels to have her." Her attributes in this joke—while still physical and complimentary—are also different from those mentioned in the previous joke: "so beautiful . . . skin so soft . . . smell so good." Moreover, now God indicates that Eve's creation is such that Adam will desire intimacy with her: "you will . . . look at her . . . touch her . . . be near her." Adam's relationship with Eve in this joke is reduced to physical intimacy rather than the "love" mentioned previously. Now, in the fourth question, Adam bluntly asks God why he made Eve "so stupid"; God's response? "So she would love you." The implication inherent in the previous joke's reference to a "small brain" has now been made concrete.

One last version of this joke type is quite blunt in pointing out Eve's imperfections. In this form of the joke, the initial question comes from God, not

Adam. In it, Eve—though never mentioned by name except by the narrator—is referred to as Adam's possession ("How is your woman?"). This joke attributes no complimentary physical qualities to the woman—not one. There is only one question rather than the four seen in the previous jokes of this type, but its main point is the same—the woman has been made "stupid and ignorant" so that she will love Adam. Once again this observation does no favor to Adam, who apparently cannot attract a smart woman.[63]

An intriguing post-feminist joke can be found in the "I have a Problem, Lord" joke type.

> Adam was walking around the Garden of Eden feeling very lonely, so God asked Adam, "What is wrong with you?"
>
> Adam said he didn't have anyone to talk to.
>
> God said, "I was going to give you a companion and it would be a woman. This person will cook for you and wash your clothes. She will always agree with every decision you make. She will bear your children and never ask you to get up in the middle of the night to take care of them. She will not nag you, and will always be the first to admit she was wrong when you've had a disagreement. She will never have a headache, and will freely give you love and compassion whenever needed."
>
> Adam asked God, "What would a woman like this cost me??"
>
> God said, "An arm and a leg."
>
> Adam asked, "What can I get for just a rib???"
>
> And now you know . . . the rest of the story.[64]

Although the above joke is based on Genesis 2, it makes significant changes to the story. In the joke, Adam complains to God that he is lonely, but in Genesis 2 it is God who says it is not good for humans to be alone (2:18a). In the joke, God responds immediately by agreeing to make Adam a companion, but in Genesis 2 God creates animals before creating woman. While Genesis 2 describes woman only as a helper and partner, the joke goes into detail as to what this might imply. The portrayal that follows describes her function in the stereotypical and traditional roles of housewife and sex object. She is a "good housewife" because she cooks, washes clothes, always agrees with him, will bear his children, and never ask for help. She will never nag, will always say she is wrong in arguments with him. She will let him have free rein—never asking about where he has been or who he has been with. In short, she will be a passive, obedient, hardworking wife. But that is not all—she will always be available for sex on demand whenever he wants it.

The description of woman as ideal passive housewife and always available sex object is a familiar cultural stereotype of a "perfect" companion vis-à-vis gendered notions of femininity from a male point of view. Since this joke is talking about the *first* woman, the description given by God to Adam in this joke ostensibly presents the intended prototype for *all* women. Of course, women are no more like this prototype now than they were in antiquity. Thus, the joke addresses why this is so in its closing lines. Following God's offer, Adam judiciously asks what such a companion will cost him. God responds, "An arm and a leg." This answer is crucial for it indicates that she is not only costly, but perhaps overpriced.

The joke ends with Adam's last reply, the punch line of the joke: "What can I get for just a rib?" The punch line implies that the companion Adam gets is "less than" the one God would have given him. Thus, in the end, this joke denigrates both Adam and Eve, Adam because contemporary relational problems can be attributed to his own stinginess and Eve because she is not what God had originally intended as Adam's companion. The humor (and irony) in the punch line is that Adam, not Eve, is at fault for this.

Another version of this joke contains a similar structure but with three significant changes in content.[65] When God asks Adam what is wrong, he replies, in part, "The sheep and I do not speak the same language." This comment carries with it the hint of Adam's dissatisfaction with animals as mates.[66] Interestingly, this is a nod to an actual aspect of the biblical story. It is animals that are created immediately after God's pronouncement that it is not good for humans to be alone, not woman. A second significant change is found in the woman's description. Instead of housewife and sex object, we now have a woman who has what could be considered strong characteristics were they not given for the sole purpose of serving Adam and making him the center of her existence. She is intelligent ("so intelligent that she can figure out what you want before you want it"), sensitive and caring ("so sensitive and caring that she will know your every mood and how to make you happy"), beautiful, and empathetic ("She will unquestioningly care for your every need and desire. She will be the perfect companion for you"). The final significant change is found in the joke's closing lines. When asked how much the woman will cost him, God replies to Adam, "She'll cost you your right arm . . . your right leg . . . an eye and an ear . . . and . . . your left testicle." While the joke adds "an eye and an ear" to the woman's price, it is "your left testicle" that is most provocative. In this joke, the price of such a woman is partial castration. Thus, the implication is that that strong women come at a price—a price that embodies the fearful image of woman as castrator.[67]

Another joke is similar in structure to the above joke but significantly changes its content by changing its human speaker:

> One day in the Garden of Eden, Eve calls out to God . . . "Lord, I have a problem."
> "What's the problem, Eve?"
> "Lord, I know you've created me and provided this beautiful garden, and all of these wonderful animals, and that hilarious comedic snake, but I'm just not happy."
> "Why is that, Eve?" came the reply from above.
> "Lord, I am lonely. And I'm sick to death of apples."
> "Well, Eve, in that case, I have a solution. I shall create a man for you."
> "What's a man, Lord?"
> "This man will be a flawed creature, with aggressive tendencies, an enormous ego and an inability to empathize or listen to you properly. All in all, he'll give you a hard time. But he'll be bigger, faster, and more muscular than you. He'll also need your advice to think properly. He'll be really good at fighting and kicking a ball about, hunting fleet-footed ruminants, and not altogether bad in the sack."
> "Sounds good to me," says Eve, with an ironically raised eyebrow. "What's the catch, Lord?"
> "Yeah, well . . . you can have him on one condition."
> "What's that, Lord?"
> "You'll have to let him believe that I made him first."[68]

Although this joke has the same structure as those just analyzed, it reverses the identity of the human speaker—it is now Eve, not Adam, who complains to God. God's description of "man" employs the stereotypical ways *men's* faults and strengths are often discussed. This joke highlights stereotypes about *men* not women. Men are useless in relationships ("he'll give you a hard time"), ignore women's feelings ("inability to emphasize with you"), violent and aggressive ("aggressive tendencies . . . good at fighting"), and self-absorbed (have "an enormous ego" and have an "inability to . . . listen to you properly"). The description starts with man's flaws and then moves to the more positive aspects of having a man. Eve immediately suspects "a catch." God responds by admitting that she's right, and the joke moves to the punch line: "You'll have to let him believe that I made him first."

Once again, like the previous jokes that challenge traditional assumptions of her "derivative nature" and her subordination to men based on her "second-ary" status in creation, this joke suggests it was Eve, not Adam, who was created first. While this proclamation undercuts those arguments, it does so by making man secondary and the dupe of a conspiracy between woman and God. Also, one cannot help but wonder if Eve is actually so "superior" in this joke. If she were smart, she would have rejected such a flawed companion destined to give her such a "hard time."

Another version of this joke, with Eve as speaker, highlights men's faults more than their positive attributes. In this joke, the issue is not so much man's physical differences but his emotional differences and the problems this will imply for male/female communication. The list of negative aspects outnumbers the list of positive ones:

> He will desire to please you and to be with you.
> But I have to warn you, he won't be perfect.
> He'll have a difficult time understanding your feelings,
> will tend to think only of himself if allowed to,
> and will stay out late with his bowling buddies.[69]

Though in this joke Eve assures God that she can "handle" this flawed creation, once again one wonders whether Eve got the best of the deal. Whereas the jokes that were analyzed in which Adam was created first have Adam getting a "lesser" version of woman because of his stinginess, the jokes in which Eve was created first have an Eve who cannot say God failed to warn her.

One last version of this joke exaggerates the man's deficiencies:

> This man will be a flawed creature, with many bad traits. He'll lie, cheat and be vainglorious; all in all, he'll give you a hard time. But . . . he'll be bigger, faster, and will like to hunt and kill things. He will look silly when he's aroused, but since you've been complaining, I'll create him in such a way that he will satisfy your physical needs. He will be witless and will revel in childish things like fighting and kicking a ball about. He won't be too smart, so he'll also need your advice to think properly.[70]

In this version, man's positive attributes are so reduced that he becomes little more than a sex object ("he'll satisfy your physical needs") and a provider ("he'll . . . like to hunt and kill things"). Such imaging presents Adam as uncultured and primitive.[71] Once again, his bad traits outnumber his good ones. He may satisfy woman's physical needs, but he will also "lie" and "cheat."

The most significant content change in this version, however, comes in its punch line: "So you'll have to let him believe that I made him first. Just remember, it's our little secret. . . . You know, woman to woman." Suggesting that God is a woman is subversive of centuries of imaging that portrays God as male. Subversive humor often uses humor as a safe venue to introduce an idea that would, in another context, be unacceptable.[72] In this joke, the Garden is not a males-only club anymore. By making God female, it could be argued, the joke elevates all females. On the other hand, the conspiracy described in this joke—between a female God and the first female—says little in favor of an even playing field between men and women. Indeed, while listeners might be encouraged to rethink their ideas about gender and God, the joke has now made the Garden into a women's club.

Laughing and Leaving the Garden

All of the jokes analyzed deal with one of three aspects of the Genesis 2–3 story: Genesis 2:18 (the statement that it is not good for man to be alone), the order of creation—who was created first and second and the significance of this order and speculation as to *how* God intended males and females to function in relationships. The jokes also assume that the Genesis account of creation can be a useful springboard to say something about male and female relationships in the contemporary world.

Humor functions to "affirm, reinforce or even challenge" contemporary attitudes toward gender.[73] On the one hand, there are some jokes that depend on traditional stereotypes to "connect" to the joke's audiences and, in the process, affirm patriarchal hierarchy. Other jokes, however, interject a "surprise" element that challenges that hierarchy. When using Genesis 2–3 to do this, however, joke tellers felt free to add to or change the biblical story. For example, jokes that challenge patriarchal hierarchy explain God's motivation for creating Eve/woman (and in doing so either critique Adam/man or present Eve/woman as superior) or actually change the order of creation and have Eve created first.

Genesis 2–3, as a story of origins, depicts relationships as they were originally intended by God. In it, Adam/man and Eve/woman are in harmony with God, with their ecosphere, and—most important—with each other. But humans throughout history have never lived in that idyllic Garden. Harmony has never been a basic characteristic of human relationships (gendered or otherwise). As we have seen in this brief survey, contemporary humor—as a "nonordinary" response to real-life situations—attempts to go back to the Garden either to support existing power structures and stereotypes or to challenge them. Such recycling attempts are less interested in the story as "Scripture" and more interested in how it can be used to shape current culture. In doing so they remind us that stories of origins are never simply about the *past*, nor is humor always about *entertainment*.

AND YOU THOUGHT THE FRUIT WAS TEMPTING?
Adam, Eve, and Advertising

And the Lord God commanded the man, "You may freely eat of every tree of the garden; but of the tree of the knowledge of good and evil you shall not eat, for in the day that you eat of it you shall die."

—Genesis 2:16-17

Now the serpent was more crafty than any other wild animal that the Lord God had made. He said to the woman, "Did God say, 'You shall not eat from any tree in the garden'?" The woman said to the serpent, "We may eat of the fruit of the trees in the garden; but God said, 'You shall not eat of the fruit of the tree that is in the middle of the garden, nor shall you touch it, or you shall die.'" But the serpent said to the woman, "You will not die; for God knows that when you eat of it your eyes will be opened, and you will be like God, knowing good and evil." So when the woman saw that the tree was good for food, and that it was a delight to the eyes, and that the tree was to be desired to make one wise, she took of its fruit and ate; and she also gave some to her husband, who was with her, and he ate.

—Genesis 3:1-6

Another medium that utilizes the myths and symbols found in the Bible—not because they are normative but because they recognizable *cultural* artifacts—is advertising. Once again, this type of commodification and commercialization recycles Genesis 2–3 instead of trying to recreate it. Advertising itself is a type of myth making.[1] Not surprisingly, contemporary advertising—which integrates cultural images with marketing strategies—finds in the symbolism of Genesis 2–3 a veritable Garden of Eden for its own interests.[2] In doing so, however, it divorces Genesis 2–3's symbols from their scriptural moorings and uses them for commercial purposes. These purposes are a far cry from the Scripture's original meaning and function. The Adam and Eve you encounter in advertising are symbols co-opted from Genesis to be used in an entirely different cultural system—the marketplace.[3] As a result, they often have only a tangential relationship to Genesis 2–3.

Since "persuasion" is a key principle in advertising, marketers find in Genesis 2–3 a *story of origins* for marketing as well as *a resource for marketing* their products. Two themes found in the Garden story are especially useful in marketing are attraction/temptation and sin/taboo. Just as the first male and female "gave in" to temptation, so viewers/readers of ads are encouraged to do likewise (and buy the product being advertised). But marketers are not bound to the canonical form of the story and can change story elements to suit their own purposes. Sometimes, for example, an ad might tweak the story line so that Eve does not eat the forbidden fruit or Adam says "no" to Eve when she offers it to him.

But aside from simply selling a product or advocating some type of action, ads often have more implicit messages that they telegraph to readers/viewers. While it is true that culture provides the materials from which ad agencies craft their ads, advertising is itself a form of discourse with culture.[4] Viewers may well reject the claims that ads make about their products but then turn around and accept the ad's symbolism and the values it assumes without much question. This is especially true when it comes to gender.[5] Since many of the ads employing Garden of Eden symbols focus on Eve, not Adam, the ads often signal messages about women's essential nature and their bodies.[6] These messages frequently underscore traditional stereotypes of women (like that of the sensual Eve/temptress) and men (like that of Adam/man, the innocent victim of Eve/woman's wiles). In doing so they reinforce, almost unconsciously, the ideas that while woman were created "for" man, it was woman who "tempted" Adam/man. In ads, temptation is not only emphasized but glamorized with the woman as the great temptress and the forbidden fruit as the ultimate goal.

Temptation, Genesis 2–3, and the Art of Persuasion

In Genesis 3:5-6, the serpent insists that Eve will not die if she eats the forbidden fruit. Instead, her eyes will be opened and she will be like God. After seeing that the fruit of the tree is desirable, both aesthetically and intellectually, the woman takes the fruit and eats. She then gives it her husband, who is with her, and he also eats. The text is silent as to *why* her husband eats, although later, in verse 17, God mentions to the man that since he has *listened to the voice of* (his) *wife, and* (has) *eaten of the tree* God is now going to punish him. Since there is no actual act of persuasion by Eve directly described in Genesis 3, ancient readers "filled in" the gaps by proposing a variety of inducements that Eve must have used on Adam.[7] The idea that somehow Eve "persuaded" Adam to eat the forbidden fruit is key to the advertisements' recontextualized symbols.

While Genesis 2–3 is often seen as an explanation for a number of things—marriage and children, sexual attraction, weeds, snakes' slithering on the ground, the pain of childbirth, the sweat of farm work, and the subordination of women to men—readers do not usually see in these chapters what some contemporary marketing experts see: *the origins of sales and marketing.* One advertising agency, for example, defines Adam and Eve as follows:

> History's earliest upscale demographic "couple." At one time, it is believed, they owned the rights to the planet's entire agricultural output, but disagreements with the original rights holder led to a sudden economic downturn.
>
> Also noteworthy in advertising history because they were active participants in the first known marketing campaign, which utilized antiquity's original groundbreaking campaign slogan: "Go ahead, one bite won't kill ya!"[8]

It is easy to see why people identify the serpent as the first salesperson and Eve as the first customer. In the serpent we have the epitome of a tempter figure. He is crafty. He promotes an action (the eating of the fruit) in its best possible light. He emphasizes the advantage of eating while minimizing any of its undesirable effects. In fact, what the snake does sounds a lot like a good marketing campaign. Such an association makes the motif of temptation simply another way of describing a great sales technique.[9]

Of course not all contemporary readers of Genesis 2–3 find the serpent alone in doing some persuading. Frequently Eve is depicted as being a type of tempter as well. Indeed, since Eve is the archetypical temptress in Western culture, it is not surprising that marketers make use of this archetype.[10] Some marketers actually collapse the distance between Eve and Snake and image them as close collaborators in the action of selling/persuasion.[11]

Marketers also find in Genesis 2–3 specific guidance on sales and marketing.[12] In giving advice to prospective sales and marketing personnel, one marketer went so far as to extract "lessons" from the serpent's actions in Genesis 3:

> So let's review the selling environment for the serpent; no compelling reason to purchase, no purchasing authority at the local level (we can assume God's

commandment was the guiding principal), not a very big market (although 2 out of 2 would be considered 100% market share) and decision making shared between two people.[13]

And what "lessons" did the snake's example teach aspiring salespeople?

Get your customer to start talking. Deal with arguments one at a time. Portray a compelling image post purchase. Get the customer engaged in a trial.[14]

Perhaps it was only a matter of time that some entrepreneurs cemented the relationship between Genesis 2–3 and advertising by starting an ad agency named "Adam & Eve." It opened on January 21, 2008,[15] and by 2010 the London-based agency was winning awards.[16] The agency even went so far as to name its communication planning and media buying service "Eden."[17] Interestingly, the company did not choose the stereotypical human male/Adam and female/Eve for as their company logo, but instead chose two animals. On top and to the right of the words "adam & eve" is the colored-in outline of a lion (male?), while the animal on the left is more diminutive and appears to be a deer (female?).[18] In the contemporary world, these animals represent predator and prey. Since in the logo they stand in close proximity to each other (almost as a couple), the two are imaged as having no fear of the other. Such imaging emphasizes the *absence* of a predatory relationship and thus evokes the image of harmony in the Garden. Whether or not this is a statement on gendered relationships is difficult to discern since the relationship could also indicate company (lion?) and client (deer?) as well.

Tempting Buyers
Products That Persuade

Genesis 2–3's influence on the marketing industry is not limited to the *act* of sales, however, but also affects the *products* being sold. Of particular interest are those products that *function persuasively* as well as *employ persuasion* in their advertising campaigns. There is a type of advertising actually called "persuasive advertising." Unlike ads that seek to be informative and give consumers data about their products, persuasive advertising appeals to emotions and cultural assumptions.[19]

In 1996 German designer Wolfgang Joop introduced his All About Eve scent. The scent was described as "inspired by Eve and the original seduction," and both its packaging (apple-shaped bottle)[20] and its product title exploited Genesis 2–3. In one ad, for example, the product's name "All About Eve" is in the top-right corner. To its left, a picture of a blond woman in a black top that shows a little cleavage dominates the entire left half of the ad. Her mouth is slightly opened with her hand raised and thumb/index finger resting on her lip. She gazes provocatively at the viewer. The visual impact of these images, taken together, results in a highly sexualized message about what Eve/woman is "all about." The perfume bottle is on the bottom right. Underneath it is the word "Joop."[21]

In an online sales pitch, All About Eve is described as "a homage to the origin of femininity" and is "confident yet accessible, playful and independent, expressing subtle sensuality."[22] This description characterizes Eve, the scent's namesake, as the woman who defined femininity and who is subtly sensual. It also telegraphs to its readers that what was true for Eve ought to be true for contemporary women as well. Moreover, because the scent is "recommended for office wear,"[23] one can surmise that subtle sensuality is seen in this pitch as an important aid to women as they enter the work world.[24]

Two years after Joop's launch of "All About Eve," Christian Dior announced its "Hypnotic Poison" campaign (1998). Although Eve was not mentioned explicitly in the perfume's title, one ad clearly used common images linked with Genesis 3: a woman, a snake, and a red apple-shaped perfume bottle. In the ad the woman (Monica Belluccii) is laying down with her upper body propped up with an elbow. She is wearing a purple and black outfit that is set against the ad's purple background. A purple and black snake is entwined around her with its head pointing to the perfume bottle in her hand. This collapse of the distance between the woman and snake fosters the image of both as collaborators, sharing a common goal.[25] Indeed, one viewer, after looking at the ad, posted this on her website:

> I had the weirdest feeling that Monica was the snake. . . . That somehow, even if the snake is somewhere around her shoulders, it looks just like it's one with her. Maybe it's because of the purple dress she wears. Did you have the same feeling?[26]

The woman gazes out to the viewer with a mesmerizing facial expression that alludes to the perfume's title, "Hypnotic Poison."[27] Since snakes are sometimes venomous, the juxtaposition of the two images evokes the association of poisonous snake/poisonous woman. But the ad does not include an "Adam." This makes the object of her seduction a bit ambiguous. On one level, it is true that the ad presents the idea of customers buying the perfume in order to attract/seduce the love object of their choice. But on another level, the "Adam" that the ad is trying to seduce is none other than the viewer—the prospective buyer. If the ad can "persuade" the viewer to buy its product, then its act of "temptation" is successful.

Another perfume, launched by Coty in 2006, is a by-product of an ad campaign, for the popular TV series *Desperate Housewives*. The scent, billed in a print ad as a "new seductive fragrance," comes in a box with a picture of the biblical Garden story.[28] But while the ad's purpose is perfume sales, the majority of its space is devoted to the program's five characters as they lie on a bed of apples. Instead of one apple, we now have a proliferation of apples. Since the apple is the focal point of cultural depictions of temptation, then it follows that temptation itself is increased in this picture. Moreover, instead of one Eve look-alike, we now have five women lying on their backs in a circle. All are attired in black dresses with varying degrees of seductively dipping necklines, their hair spread out in an alluring manner. Once again, the models look out at the viewer. They partook of the forbidden fruit and do not look worse for it. Thus, potential customers too can benefit from the "forbidden fruit" (the perfume). Notice here that the idea of "forbidden fruit" is limited to "allure/sexual attraction" and divorced from any sense of the later punishment found in the biblical account. As such, it becomes taboo without consequences.

Television advertisements also make use of the image of Eve the "seductive temptress" that these perfume ads utilized. The contemporary television program *Weeds*, which debuted in 2005, used Eve to market its product while at the same time saying something about the tempting nature of the program's characters and plotlines.[29] One print ad for *Weeds* features a woman (actress Mary Louise Parker) whose body is positioned sideways to the audience with her face gazing out at the audience. Like Eve (before she disobeyed), she appears in the ad "naked but not ashamed." The nudity and the seductive over-the-shoulder gaze telegraph a message, not only about Eve but about women in general. Once again, the close proximity of the snake draped over the model's shoulders presents an intimate relationship between woman and snake. As the snake in Genesis 3 is imaged as "tempter," so this proximity identifies Eve/woman as tempter as well. Tucked behind the model's ear is a marijuana leaf (Parker's character is a widowed suburban housewife who sells marijuana to support her family). While there is no apple in this ad, the leaf functions as its analogue. But unlike the iconic apple, the leaf carries with it cultural taboos that are recognized by the viewing audience. After all, in today's health-conscious contemporary society, there is nothing "forbidden" about eating an apple—quite the contrary. The same cannot be said for marijuana. As long as marijuana remains illegal in the United States (except for medical purposes) the ad presents the viewer with a truly "forbidden" item to replace the more traditional fruit. Both Parker and the program she advertises are tempting. Another ad reminded its readers that Monday nights on Showtime (when the program aired) are tempting and to "give in to temptation."[30] Once again, in the absence of an Adam figure, the reading audience substitutes as the focus of this temptation.

While *Weeds* utilized Genesis 2–3's symbols in its promo ads, a more routine use was made by another television show, *Desperate Housewives*, that first aired in October 2004. ABC'S website describes *Desperate Housewives* as "a primetime soap with a truly contemporary take on the 'happily ever after.'" The series "takes a darkly comedic look at suburbia, where the secret lives of housewives aren't always what they seem."[31] As a viewer described one of the program's promos,

> The setting is a dreamlike, slightly menacing, suburban Garden of Eden. . . . "Juicy," the sultry women of the show sing, one after the next, while plucking rosy apples from trees, bathing in them and cutting them open to watch blood ooze out—as clocks run backwards on the wall and wispy clouds fly by overhead. "Tempting, isn't it?" says the onscreen copy at the end.[32]

Images of Eve also formed the setting for the show's opening episode, which began with a picture inspired by Lucas Cranach the Elder's *Adam and Eve* (1526). An ad agency describes the opening scenes as beginning

> with a famous Renaissance painting of Adam and Eve animated by yU + co artists in the manner of a pop-up children's book. In a Monte Python-esque moment, Eve lowers the boom on her disagreeable hubby with an *apple* the size of a Volkswagen.[33]

On their website, the artistic designers of the program's opening images (yU + co) describe their intent behind such imagery:

> In this Emmy-nominated show open we offered a wickedly funny take on the history of female angst. Iconic imagery is used to convey the anguish of the feminine mind, displaying how women from Eve to the present have chafed under their marital status. The designers' aim goes beyond typical television show opens, which merely introduce the characters and setting. Here familiar historical artwork and icons are employed—and humorously violated—to evoke the show's quirky spirit and playful flaunting of women's traditional role in society.[34]

Their explanation is intriguing. One presumes that the "traditional role" of women they are "flaunting" is that of housewife and obedient/loyal partner.

While the biblical Eve has no emotions imputed to her in the story, the same cannot be said of the program's Eve, whose anger is illustrated—in the opening scene of every episode—by her lowering the apple on her unsuspecting spouse. As Eve's "anguish" is the result of "chafing" under her marital status—the same is being said of women in marriages everywhere. Indeed the artists claim that "women from Eve to the present" share this relational problem. Thus the artists feel free to "violate" both the story and its iconography by imbuing women (and the show) with a "quirky spirit." And if the women of this show are like Eve—the men also resemble their predecessor Adam. As ABC's website explains to viewers,

> Welcome to *Desperate Housewives*. Just take a look at Susan Mayer (Teri Hatcher), the sweet girl next door who finally got everything she ever wanted. Or did she? And there's Lynette Scavo (Felicity Huffman), she was once a high-powered executive but then four . . . no, make that five, kids got in the way. How can she handle it? What about Bree Hodge (Marcia Cross)? That prim and proper homemaker used to be the best caterer in town. Now I hear she's on the outs with her partners and . . . with another man. And, of course, there's Gabrielle Solis (Eva Longoria Parker), the sultry former runway model who's now running after two children. She's still as wicked as ever. Did I mention that glamorous socialite Renee Perry (Vanessa Williams) is moving in at the end of the block? Just wait 'til they get a load of her.
>
> It's always hot on Wisteria Lane. These women have it all: friendship, fun, love, sex, excitement, danger, and the men . . . well, the men don't stand a chance.[35]

The use of the temptation theme in these perfume and television ad campaigns, with Adam/consumer as victim, should not come as a surprise given the long history of imaging Eve as a tempter figure. What *is* surprising, given its track record for "shock advertising," is the way that Benetton depicted Adam and Eve in its 1988 "United Superstars of Benetton" ad campaign.[36] Benetton is an Italian fashion company whose products are described by one student business columnist as "Italian design for the masses . . . Armani at Banana Republic prices."[37] To understand fully the significance of their use of Adam and Eve imagery, however, one has to delve for a moment into Benetton's advertising philosophy and history.

Founded in Italy in 1955, Benetton opened its first store for the "exclusive marketing of apparel" in 1969.[38] Its radical departure from traditional advertising, however, began with the hiring of the award-winning fashion and advertising photographer Oliviero Toscani in 1982. During his years with Benetton (his last campaign was in 2000), Toscani produced a variety of controversial graphic ad campaigns, often linked to the product (clothing) only by the name of the company or its slogan. Instead of focusing on the company's *product*, Toscani's ads made socially conscious statements about the company's values and ethics.[39] He is quoted as saying, "I am not here to sell pullovers, but to promote an image. . . . Benetton's advertising draws public attention to universal themes like racial integration, the protection of the environment, AIDS."[40]

By 1984 Benetton ads highlighted "all the colors of the world" using children of different ethnic groups as their models. From this emphasis came the "United Colors of Benetton" slogan.[41] The topic of race relations, however, took a leap forward in 1989 with the launching of Benetton's "Contrasts in Black & White" ad campaign. One controversial ad showed a black woman nursing a white baby. The shot started at the top of the woman's chest and ended at her waist.[42] The woman's red sweater threw into relief the stark darkness of her skin against the baby's whiteness. This ad received severe criticism because it reminded people in the United States and the United Kingdom of the "times of slavery when black women breast-fed white babies."[43]

Benetton's ad campaigns did not limit their focus to racism. Other political and social issues received attention as well. One 1992 ad depicted a dying AIDS activist and victim (David Kirby) with his family at his bedside.[44] This theme was further developed in Benetton's 1997 ad highlighting the red AIDS-prevention ribbon on the crotch of two models' underwear.[45] Another ad depicted the ecological horror of an oiled bird on the shores of the Persian Gulf (1992),[46] while a 2000 ad featured real pictures of death row inmates, putting a "real" face on the controversial issue of capital punishment.[47] Nor did Benetton shy away from dealing with controversial religious issues. This is graphically seen by the Benetton ad featuring an Israeli and a Palestinian boy that addressed religious/political issues. Another example is the 1991 ad dealing with religion and sexuality that featured an Italian priest clothed in black kissing a white-clad nun.[48] Both of these ads belong to a period in Benetton's advertising history labeled by Benetton as its "cycle of difference" campaigns in which visual opposites were used to make a point. As Benetton explains,

> All of these conflicts were based on taboos, on the impossibility of co-existence, on a difference that separates rather than unites. By acknowledging these differences and prohibitions, the brand appeared more involved. It took sides, rather than presenting a simple "objective" portrayal of the world; it made a commitment to foster the cohabitation of opposites, to break down barriers and ensure dialogue. Benetton had a plan: to integrate opposites, to unite differences under a single flag, the flag of its own logo.[49]

From this quick overview it is quite clear that throughout Toscani's association with Benetton, the company's advertising strategies reflected a willingness to push the boundaries of social acceptability in the service of social reform (and sales).

With this proclivity for "shock advertising," the way they chose to image Adam and Eve (1988 "United Superstars" campaign) is absolutely astonishing.[50] Like the ads featuring the Israeli and Palestinian boys and the priest and nun kissing, the Adam and Eve ad belongs to the "cycle of difference" period in Benetton's ad campaign history. But unlike those ads, this ad merely reaffirms stereotypes rather than challenging them. Both Adam and Eve are clothed in jeans. The woman (Eve) has a self-satisfied smirk on her face. Her denim top is open to show a bit of cleavage, and she is wearing a suggestively unbuttoned and partly unzipped pair of jeans. She stands in stark contrast to the rather innocent, somber-faced man (Adam) who appears next to her (bare-chested but with pants zipped) and takes the apple from her hand. Thus, rather than challenging stereotypes (as he did with the sexual stereotype of the priest and nun or the political stereotype of the Israeli and Palestinian), when it came to interpretations of Genesis 2–3 and the social construction of gender, Toscani chose to fall back on the tired cliché of Eve as temptress and Adam as innocent victim.

Ironic Twists to the Temptation Theme

In addition to marketers who use the temptation/persuasion theme in Genesis 2–3 to describe the *process of marketing* and the *products they market*, there are ad campaigns that *subvert* rather than merely repeating the Genesis story. Three ads—for Liberty Mutual, Twix, and Faberge—change the traditional story line of Genesis 2–3. Nevertheless, all three wind up promoting the stereotypical gender images of Eve/women that are often a part of Genesis 2–3's interpretation.

In 2005 Liberty Mutual ran a series of commercials that rewrote the outcomes of their parent story lines. In one ad, for example, the inhabitants of Troy are frankly skeptical of Greeks bearing gifts and turn away that wooden horse. Another ad fantasizes about what might have happened if Eve had simply said no to the snake.[51] As one viewer describes the commercial,

> The "Adam and Eve" spot opens in the Garden of Eden. The serpent appears to tempt Eve with an apple that contains "all the knowledge of the universe." Eve figures out what the snake is up to and predicts how her world will change if she eats the apple. She tells the serpent that she and Adam will be kicked out of paradise and have to wear clothes, and start worrying about "tax brackets and counting carbs."[52]

Another viewer adds,

> In this :60 spot, Eve, not wanting to wear clothes or count carbs, hurls the apple
> back at the snake. Sound design was crucial for comedic timing, which includes the
> satisfying *twock* of the apple hitting Satan it its human-like head.[53]

On the surface, this ad had the possibility of reworking Eve's traditional characterization. After all, *this* time Eve *did not* give into the snake's temptation.
Moreover, by throwing the apple back at the snake, there might be seen a
sense of a feisty "payback" on Eve's part. Interestingly, in the ad the snake has
a human head—a *male* human head. This is quite refreshing given the history
of iconographic interpretation that often images the serpent—when imaged as
human—as having a *female* human head.[54] In spite of these changes to Genesis
2–3's story line, however, the purpose of the ad apparently was *not* to image the
biblical Eve in a more positive/heroic light. The voice-over in the commercial
makes its selling point: "Hindsight is easy, it's thinking ahead that's hard."[55]
The implication is that if only the biblical Eve had done what the ad's Eve did—
thought ahead—things would indeed be different for the entire human race.
Thus the wise consumer is the one who "thinks ahead" by employing Liberty
Mutual and thus avoiding "the accidents and pitfalls that historically have
bedeviled mankind."[56]

Or consider another "what-if" scenario. Suppose Eve took the fruit from
the snake but decided to keep it for herself. Such was the premise of a Twix ad
from Mars, Inc. Twix is a caramel cookie candy covered in chocolate. Each
package contains two bars. On the surface it would appear that it is a product
made with sharing in mind—no messy splitting, no dripping caramel—all one
has to do is open the packaging and give one to a friend (after all, parents tell
their children *to share*). But one ad for Twix disagrees.[57] The ad is divided into
two sections. The top half has a blue hand set against a yellow background
holding an unbitten apple with the words "ÉVE SHARED THAT APPLE
AND LOOK WHAT HAPPENED." The bottom half of the ad has a blue
hand holding a wrapped Twix bar set against a red background with the words
"DON'T YOU MAKE THE SAME MISTAKE!" At the bottom of the ad, set
against a black background, is a package of Twix with the words "two for me,
none for you." In this ad the fruit of Genesis 2–3 is identified as an apple (no
surprise there) and paralleled with a Twix package. According to the ad's message, Eve's mistake was not the act of *eating* the fruit. If eating the fruit had been
a mistake, the ad's parallel visual construction would imply that eating Twix
would be a mistake (a message definitely not intended by the ad's authors). The

ad's message is rather that the biblical Eve made a mistake by *sharing* the fruit with Adam. The ad's Eve—seen only in the ad as a hand triumphantly holding up an unbitten apple—rectifies this mistake by keeping the fruit to herself. True to Twix's brand theme (Two for me. None for you), the act of temptation is wrong not because it is morally reprehensible but because it is dumb. Why share when you can have the whole candy for yourself? In this ad it is not Eve's moral nature that is in question but her intellect.

Unlike Liberty Mutual's ad where an Eve resisted temptation and the Twix Ad where she simply kept the fruit for herself, Faberge's 1998 ad campaign for its fragrance "Impulse" contains a man/Adam resistant to woman/Eve's tempting charms.[58] In the TV commercial two rather good-looking men are walking along the street. Approaching them is a young woman with a bag of groceries. The young men accidentally bump into her and her groceries go flying. One of the men bends down to help her. She looks at him and her expression changes from anger to interest. They exchange looks while picking up the groceries and then both reach for an apple at the same time. Their hands touch, and his hand closes on hers. She smiles at him sweetly. They lift the apple together while she licks and bites her lower lip. He picks up a condom package titled "Passion: Ultra Lite," and she looks a bit embarrassed. The other man taps him on the shoulder and he rises to go. She looks surprised and disappointed. We see his back retreating while she looks puzzled. She then looks around her and sees two men talking intimately nearby and a poodle in a studded collar and leather jacket. She then smiles and hits her forehead with her hand. The viewer then sees the product, a body spray named "Impulse" with its slogan—"Men can't help acting on Impulse."[59]

The ad depicts the woman/Eve in the traditional role of temptress, albeit a bit clueless of man/Adam's sexual orientation. This archetype of woman/temptress/Eve is further emphasized by the lyrics of the ad's background music:

> Shock, shock, horror, horror
> Shock, shock, horror, horror
> I'll shout myself hoarse for your supernatural force
> The female of the species is more deadly than the male.[60]

This ad aired for the first time on British TV on May 18, 1998, and was scheduled to air subsequently in Europe, Latin America, the Pacific, and southern Africa.[61] It is, some would argue, the first "gay" ad to air on British television.[62] While "Adam and Eve not Steve" would become a bumper sticker in the

United States, Faberge's ad campaign suggested to its viewers that it was Steve not Eve who sometimes won the struggle for Adam's affections. Of course, the fact that Adam was even tempted by Eve is the selling point of the ad. Although he ultimately resists that temptation, the ad nevertheless makes its point. If Impulse can get a gay man to notice a woman, just think what it can do to a heterosexual one. In making its point, however, the ad once again utilizes the image of woman as a seductive temptress—a temptress who *almost* succeeded in making a man forget his own sexual preferences.

All three of the above ads radically change the story line of Genesis 2–3. Instead of presenting Eve/woman in a more positive light, however, all reinforce traditional stereotypes about women. After all,

If Eve would have thought before she acted we'd all be better off (Liberty Mutual).

Eve was stupid to share when she could have had the entire fruit for herself (Twix).

Even a gay guy is not immune to the sinister charm of women (Impulse).

Taboo
Knowledge as the Forbidden Fruit

In Genesis 2:16-17, God warns the first man that he may "freely eat of every tree of the garden; but of the tree of the knowledge of good and evil you shall not eat, for in the day that you eat of it you shall die." Later generations of readers, influenced by Western iconographical traditions, would identify this fruit as an apple.[63] In the story, however, it was not the *type* of fruit that was its allure but its *forbidden* status. Indeed "forbidden fruit" would become a catchphrase in literature associated with anything that is desirable in spite of (or perhaps because of) its taboo status. Since there is nothing like forbidding something to make it more attractive, it is no wonder that the metaphor of *forbidden fruit* is another way in which marketing cashed in on Genesis 2–3. Although the focus of these ads is on the allure of forbidden actions, some still managed to denigrate Eve/woman in their portrayals.

In Genesis 2:17 the prohibited tree is called the "tree of knowledge of good and evil." Since the Hebrew term for knowledge (*yadah*) *can* refer to "intellectual knowledge," it is not hard to see how this interpretation paved the way the computer industry's use of Genesis 2–3. Perhaps the most popular image that comes to mind when you put together *computers* + *knowledge* + *Genesis* 2–3 is the logo for Apple Computer. Ironically, however, Apple's original logo was not originally a Genesis spin-off at all. Ronald Wayne, cofounder of the company, designed the original logo—an ink drawing of Isaac Newton sitting under an apple tree reading a book.[64]

It had "Apple Computer Co." on a fabric banner with a quote of William Wordsworth running around the ad's edge: "Newton . . . A mind forever voyaging through strange seas of thought . . . alone."[65] Visually it was complicated, and the lettering was almost unreadable unless the picture was fairly large. Moreover, the Preliminary Apple BASIC User's Manual issued by the company simply had an *unbitten* apple on its cover.[66] In that same year, art designer Rob Janoff was asked to design a new Apple logo. The new logo had an apple with a bite taken out and the colors of the rainbow in the wrong order.[67] When asked about the company's logo, Apple executive Jean Louis Gassée replied,

> One of the deep mysteries to me is our logo, the symbol of lust and knowledge, bitten into, all crossed with the colors of the rainbow in the wrong order. You couldn't dream of a more appropriate logo: lust, knowledge, hope, and anarchy.[68]

The new logo evoked comparisons with Genesis 2–3 as evidenced by a 1979 ad for a writing contest sponsored by Apple. The ad pictured a naked Adam (holding a strategically placed computer) standing by a tree with a snake. The ad's copy announced, "We're looking for the most original use of an Apple since Adam." It asked readers, "What in the name of Adam do people do with Apple computers? You tell us."[69]

Apple is only one of the of several technology companies to capitalize on Genesis and its motif of "forbidden knowledge." COLECO (Connecticut Leather Company) manufactured a computer called ADAM (June 1983) that was later discontinued (January 1985).[70] One might suspect that the ADAM's connection to Genesis 2–3 is a bit of stretch. There was, however, a precursor to COLECO ADAM. It was produced by LOMAC (Logical Machine Corporation) in 1976 and was also named ADAM (and yes, LOMAC brought a lawsuit against COLECO about the name).[71] LOMAC's ADAM came with its own desk, printer, hard disk, and chair. It proudly displayed the name "ADAM" as well as the image of a fig leaf.[72] Unlike COLECO's ADAM, with LOMAC's ADAM we have a name *and* a fig leaf—but there is no mention of Eve. Some ads hinted at an Eve, however, by imaging a woman sitting in front of a keyboard. In an early ad, the woman is imaged in a somewhat dowdy dress that covers everything but her face and hands.[73] But a quite different picture of Eve/woman is found on the front page of one of LOMAC's brochures. Here you have a L-shaped desk with a computer on one side and a printer on the other. The background is outdoors with grass and flowering bushes (a garden?) with a drop-down white text box in the upper-left-hand corner. The text box has a fig leaf and the words "ADAM the creative computer." Sitting on a chair behind the keyboard is a naked woman slightly turned around and gazing at the reader. While her left hand is on the keyboard, her right hand holds an apple, from which she is taking a bite.[74]

When COLECO and LOMAC chose to name their product "ADAM"— whether consciously or not—they identified Adam/man with "logic/reason" and drew on an ancient interpretation of Genesis 2–3. Moreover when the manual for the LOMAC ADAM came out with a naked Eve behind a keyboard eating an apple, the picture underscored the gender stereotypes of Adam/man/logic and Eve/woman/senses. While in ancient thought both logic and the senses were necessary, it was always the task of logic to keep the senses in line. Thus, it should not come as a surprise that, when it came to "knowledge/computer" as the "forbidden fruit," the technology industry either named their product "ADAM" (ADAM/COLECO, ADAM/LOMAC) or used Adam in their advertising and ultimately imaged their logo after the Garden's fruit (Apple). When Eve finally appeared with an apple in the LOMAC manual cover, the image presented was not the "logical" but the "sensual."

In spite of information technology's identification with Genesis 2–3, it is really hard to think of computers as "forbidden" or "taboo." The same cannot be said for other products associated with Eden's "forbidden fruit"—like gambling, alcohol, and tobacco.

Gambling in the Garden

Q—Where did the first gambling take place?
A—In the Garden of Eden.[75]

While the connection between gambling and Genesis 2–3 may not be immediately evident to most people, there *are* those who see Adam and Eve as the first "gamblers."[76] If eating the fruit of the Garden was a gamble, however, one could argue that it turned out quite different from how the snake promised. And therein lies the problem. As much as gambling advertisements promote "responsible" gambling, there is still the allure of the forbidden surrounding gambling, and it is all too easy to give into the temptation of gambling with more money that one can afford. One Internet site, devoted to helping those people addicted to gambling, even begins with this observation: "People have probably been gambling ever since Eve first bet Adam that one bite wouldn't hurt—and we've all been paying off that bet ever since!"[77] With this in mind, perhaps it is not so surprising that the gambling industry also finds Genesis 2–3 useful in marketing gambling products (online slot machines) and gambling venues (online casinos).

Two slot machines that utilize Genesis 2–3 are the Garden of Eden and Forbidden Fruit. The Garden of Eden, for example, has symbols on its reel that include an apple and a snake (an angel is the jackpot symbol). One game review describes it like this:

> This . . . slot machine offers online slots players a trip through the Garden of Eden. With Adam on the right, and Eve on the left, and a tempting pay line in between them, what do you imagine these two are wandering the reels in search of? Why, the forbidden fruit of course! It seems after all these centuries have passed, Eve is still not done tempting Adam with its taste. Find it, and you just might find this online slot machine's jackpot![78]

The all-too-familiar stereotype of Eve as temptress surfaces once again in this game review. Moreover, Eve/woman is imaged as tempting Adam/man down through the centuries. Only this time gambling is the "forbidden fruit" that she uses to tempt "Adam with its taste." Some reviews, however, were uncomfortable with this online machine's blatant use of biblical imagery:

> Garden of Eden is a unique theme slot machine that plays pretty well. It has a good jackpot and paytable for this type of machine, and a consistent theme that works well (if you can get over the concept of biblical themes in gambling).[79]

Another online slot machine—Forbidden Fruit—also draws on the Garden story. If you bet the maximum, the machine's top jackpot is one thousand coins and can be won by having three apples appear on the machine.[80] Of course, if online slots are not your preferred form of gambling, you can try Adameve: The Genesis of Poker (an online poker site)[81] or visit the Adameve Online Casino.[82] Both have a logo that is a spade with a bite out of it.

America's first casino king[83]—Richard Albert Cansfield"[84]—once said, "They gambled in the Garden of Eden, and they will again if there's another one."[85] Apparently, for some, the Internet has become a virtual Garden of Eden with the forbidden fruit of gambling just waiting to be plucked. In the biblical story both Adam and Eve were warned and presumably knew better than to eat the fruit. The same can be said for customers who play online slot machines and visit gaming venues. The allure and promise of the forbidden, however, are as potent today as centuries ago when the Garden story was written. In this garden, however, the "sin" frequently results in addiction, not expulsion from the Garden.

Eden and Alcohol

Of all the products that utilize Adam, Eve, and Eden's "forbidden fruit" in their marketing campaigns, none do it quite as well as those found in the alcohol and sex industries. Ironically, the association of alcohol as "forbidden fruit" is far from new. In antiquity, when the fruit of the Garden was identified as grapes,[86] the "sin" of the Garden became drunkenness.[87] And since in this version Eve made the wine that resulted in Adam's drunkenness, this presents another way that Adam was victimized by Eve.

In the contemporary world of marketing, the "forbidden fruit"—with its taboo status—has been a "fruitful" way to advertise beer, wine, and hard liquors. Marketers of alcohol basically appropriate the Genesis 2–3 story in two ways—either they simply use the story as part of their ad campaigns or they name their product after the Garden story and employ its symbolism in their titles and labels. Either way, the result is the same—the biblical account of temptation and sin becomes associated with alcohol consumption and its promotion. Once again, the possibility of addiction becomes the surrogate of expulsion from the Garden.

Two examples of companies that simply use the story's symbols in various ad campaigns are Absolut (Absolut Merlet) and Smirnoff (Green Apple Vodka). In one Absolut ad, for example, the figures of Adam and Eve twine around a statue of a vodka bottle with an apple and a snake.[88] The location of the Adam and Eve figures—at either side of the bottle's top—presents an interesting association. Here the analogue to eating the "forbidden fruit" seems to be opening the bottle and drinking it.

An ad that also employed "forbidden fruit" imagery is one by Smirnoff for their Green Apple Vodka.[89] The ad is interesting because it tweaks the usual presentation of the Garden story. In the ad we have a tree with green apples hanging from its branches. Eve is pictured to the right of the tree and is in the process of picking an apple while she gazes down at a sitting Adam. Adam is looking away from Eve and gazing soulfully at the snake, which is twined around the tree. The snake, whose face is strikingly female, has lips and looks as if it is about ready to kiss Adam. Moreover, given the suspicious lump in its torso, the snake appears to have ingested one of the apples. These changes to the Genesis story line are prompted, one suspects, by the ad copy in the bottom right hand corner: "A New Twist on an Old Story." Instead of Eve and the snake entering into a dialogue (the old story), it is Adam and the snake who are drawn to each other (the new twist). But since the snake is imaged as female, these changes in the story line once again emphasize the female as a seductress and temptress—although this time it is the snake, not Eve, who does the tempting.

Another type of appropriation of Genesis 2–3 occurs when companies actually name their products after the Garden. Examples of this are Forbidden Fruit Wines,[90] Forbidden Fruit Apple Ale,[91] and Forbidden Fruit Liqueur.[92] Another example of this type of appropriation is "Verboden Vrucht" (forbidden fruit) by Hoegaarden (Belgium). Its label, with Adam giving Eve a glass of beer,[93] even forms the wall fresco in a Toronto bar.[94] Michael Jackson (the beer critic, not the singer) reports a problem the beer had in clearing U.S. customs:

> Forbidden Fruit's label is modeled on Ruben's painting Adam and Eve. When the brewery tried to export to the US, the beer was banned because the couple are nude. "This is not pornography," protested the brewery, "it is a great work of art from our country."
>
> "Yes," replied the American Bureau of Alcohol, Tobacco and Firearms, "but Adam should be handing her an apple—not a beer."[95]

Whether the alleged incident happened or is mere legend, it draws attention to the juxtaposition of beer with the nudity of the label. It is not unusual to find alcohol ads implying sexuality or sexual opportunity.[96] Using this beer's label as a background for a bar, for example, certainly makes this connection.

Another company that capitalizes on the taboo associations between Genesis 2–3 and alcohol is the New York company "Original Sin," which markets an apple product—hard cider.

> Originated in Eden, revived in New York. Original Sin derives from the myth about Adam and Eve, the oldest story of temptation and attraction between males and females. As the story revolves around the apple, it's a perfect fit for an apple cider.[97]

While both the bottle and the company's posters make ample use of Genesis 2–3 symbols (snakes curling around bottles,[98] snakes curling around nude woman with a strategically placed leaf),[99] this product and its ad campaign actually go a step beyond those taken by many alcohol ads. By naming its product "Original Sin" after the theological concept associated with Augustine of Hippo, the company makes use of the later theological association of sin with Genesis 2–3. For Augustine, sin and sexual desire were related.[100] Unlike Augustine, who saw original sin as a sad fact of human existence, Original Sin's owners embrace the notion of sinning (and hence buying their cider) as a pleasure to be sought after. Indeed, the company's website informs its viewers, "We hope you visit some of the great locations stocking our product, and please let others know how refreshing and pleasurable Sin can be."[101] If sin is as pleasurable as the website promises, it is no wonder that the product's posters proclaim "Live Good and Sin Hard," with the added imperative to "Sin Here." Interestingly, of the twenty-nine posters in the company's online store, twenty-seven feature seductively posed and scantily clad women, one features an inflatable bottle, and one has a male with wings (presumably Satan).[102] The shop also offers one style of T-shirt. Both the men's and women's versions have the same picture— on a red background, a woman outlined in black in a bikini is leaping up with an outstretched arm holding an apple. The woman has horns.[103]

But perhaps the best example of a product that integrates alcohol, passion, and sexual promise with Genesis 2–3 is Adam and Eve Ale produced by Great Sex Brewing Company in California. Its logo incorporates a snake curled around an unbitten apple, and its label has a picture of Adam and Eve in the Garden. Both logo and label proclaim, "Brewed with Love, Consumed with Passion." Both reflect the popular identification of sex as the forbidden fruit of Genesis 2–3.[104]

The problem in the Garden, or so the founders of this brewery would have us believe, was Adam and Eve's dissatisfactory sex life, or thus says this rewriting of Genesis 2–3 found on the beer's label:

> IN THE BEGINNING . . .
> Adam & Eve were unfulfilled. Hence, an arduous journey for complete satisfaction delivered them to the "Gemütliche Brothers.™" With divine conviction the brothers conceived "Great Sex Brewing." So, it came to pass . . . An ethereal nectar was created that pleases all of the senses!!!
> Come to the garden and enjoy.[105]

Drinking the brewery's product—Adam and Eve Ale—apparently promises to rectify sexual dissatisfaction. Indeed one of GSB's bumper stickers advises you to "Honk if you love Great Sex."[106] To the right of these words is the company's logo—the snake of Genesis twined around an apple. It is a somewhat ironic claim considering the effect that increased amounts of alcohol has on sexual performance.

Tobacco and Taboo

Unlike gambling, which is problematic if done irresponsibly, and alcohol, which is unhealthy if used to excess, tobacco products are clearly unhealthy, associated with a variety of illnesses, and have no real redeeming qualities. Often the marketing of these products runs into opposition, not by users but by those who view the advertising of dangerous products as unacceptable.[107] Thus when tobacco manufacturers use Genesis 2–3 imagery in their products' advertisements, the "forbidden fruit" metaphor is especially useful.

Although tobacco companies have not made use of Genesis 2–3 in any way commensurate with that of the alcohol industry, there is one appropriation that is especially interesting: Eve cigarettes. Eve cigarettes are made by the Liggett tobacco company. They were introduced in 1971 as a response to R. J. Reynolds' 1968 Virginia Slims.[108]

Virginia Slims' marketing slogan—You've Come a Long Way Baby— stressed women's independence, liberation, and empowerment. Not accidentally, these were values promoted by the second wave of feminism in the 1960s. For example, a two-page 1972 print ad detailed the movement of women's fashions while also drawing attention to the women's suffrage movement. On the left page are five women whose attire (dresses and hats), from left to right, displays the changing style of women's fashions. Behind the third woman from the left a right to vote sign appears in the background. On the opposite page is a woman in a pants suit with her hair pulled back. In between the five women and the contemporary woman are the words "You've come a long way, baby." Two packs of cigarettes are in the lower-right-hand corner of the ad, with the product name "Virginia Slims" immediately on top.[109] A later 1985 ad even offered a special deck of cards (men were the jokers) to anyone who bought two packs of cigarettes.[110] Both ads targeted female smokers. Both aimed at getting viewers to identify positively with the product ("You've come a long way, baby") without saying much about the actual product and what it would do to the smoker. Indeed, imaging smoking as a sign of women's independence and autonomy allowed young women to view smoking as a sign of breaking with tradition.[111]

But not all women fit the niche market of the profeminist Virginia Slims. For those more interested in their "femininity" and appearance there was "Eve." It was marketed as a beautiful cigarette for a beautiful woman, and its original 1971 packaging contained flowers and a woman in a garden. The copy in the lower left of the ad said,

> The newest way to express your love of pretty things. That's Eve. The first truly feminine cigarette. With pretty filter tip. Pretty pack. Rich, yet gentle flavor. For the lady with taste. Also with menthol.[112]

Although the package's symbolism did not include a temptation scene with an apple or snake, it did promote the beauty ideal and a sense of women's vanity over their looks and thus developed another theme found in Genesis 3. In Genesis 3:3 we are told that the woman saw that the tree was good for food—that it was a delight to the eyes. Thus while Eve was tempted by her senses, later interpreters would see Eve herself as representing the sensual. Moreover, that sensuality would be seen to stand behind Adam's downfall. The ancient writer Tertullian, for example, advised women on their appropriate dress by referring to Genesis 3:

> I think, rather, that you would have dressed in mourning garments and even neglected your exterior, acting the part of mourning and repentant Eve in order to expiate more fully by all sorts of penitential garb that which women derives from Eve—the ignominy, I mean, of original sin and the odium of being the cause of the fall of the human race. "In sorrow and anxiety, you will bring forth, O woman, and you are subject to your husband, and he is your master." Do you not believe that you are (each) an Eve?[113]

For Tertullian, all women were like Eve. The advertisers of Eve cigarettes agreed—the ad copy for a number of ads declared, "There's a little Eve in every woman."[114]

While some of these ads depicted women in normal clothing, others presented a more sexualized image. One ad in particular had a woman leaning back while she gazed at the reader.[115] The model in this ad is healthy looking and beautiful, which nullifies any fear of smoking that one might entertain. Indeed, the ad and others like it imply that beautiful women smoke beautiful cigarettes. According to one survey, women's brands and marketing targeting women resulted in an increase in women smokers.[116] But both the arrangement of the model's body as well as her alluring gaze in the ad also telegraphed the idea of seductive sensuality. In this ad we once again we have Eve as seductress—a trait that this ad sees inherent in every woman.

Liggett intended the cigarettes themselves as an "Eve" to other women. One of the first slogans coined by Liggett was "Women have been feminine since Eve, now cigarettes are feminine."[117] While the cigarette started out 100 millimeters long, it was soon lengthened to 120 millimeters, some suggest to better image the ideal of slimness.[118] As Eve's femininity was understood to have tempted/seduced Adam, Liggett's cigarettes, with their flowers and (later) butterflies, were designed to tempt/seduce Eve's daughters. According to a study published in the *Journal of the American Medical Association* and quoted in the *New York Times*—they were successful:

> The study linked advertising campaigns for Virginia Slims, Silva Thins and Eve cigarettes, all of which were aimed at women, with striking increases in the start

of smoking by young girls. During a six-year period from 1967 to 1973, when sales of women's cigarettes skyrocketed, there was a 110 percent increase in the rate of 12-year-old girls who started smoking, a 55 percent increase among 13-year-olds, a 70 percent increase among 14-year-olds, a 75 percent increase among 15-year-olds, a 55 percent increase among 16-year-olds and a 35 percent increase among 17-year-old girls.[119]

Advertising is a form of public discourse. Each day we are bombarded with a multitude of images. Some we remember, most we forget. When advertising calls on scriptural symbols like Eve, Adam, and the Garden of Eden, it often advances old interpretive frameworks as backdrops for their sales pitch and thus reinforces these selfsame images. Even a forward-looking, socially conscious company like Benetton continued to promote the tired stereotype of Eve the temptress and Adam the innocent victim. Now if Eve were just a character in some ancient fictive work, we might be able to overlook this, or at least view it as insignificant in the long run. But Eve, throughout her history of interpretation, has never really stood for just herself. Eve is seen as all women everywhere. As advertising presents images of Eve that tempt and seduce, these messages are telegraphed to viewers as essential traits of all women. Moreover, as the image of the "forbidden fruit" is associated with gambling, alcohol, and tobacco consumption, the Garden imagery becomes a doorway to addiction rather than paradise—with Eve/woman paving the way. These ideas, rather old in themselves, are kept alive in contemporary advertising.

Virginia Slims ads boasted that women had come "a long way"—and they have. But when it comes to imaging Genesis 2–3 and women in advertising, it appears that some things just do not change.

ECSTASY IN EDEN
The Sexploitation of Adam and Eve

Then the man said, "This at last is bone of my bones and flesh of my flesh; this one
shall be called Woman, for out of Man this one was taken." Therefore a man leaves
his father and his mother and clings to his wife, and they become one flesh. And the
man and his wife were both naked, and were not ashamed.

—Genesis 2:23-24

Then the eyes of both were opened, and they knew that they were naked; and they
sewed fig leaves together and made loincloths for themselves.

—Genesis 3:7

As we have seen, the idea of "forbidden fruit" is a well-used metaphor in the
world of marketing, especially when it comes to "taboo" products. It tanta-
lizes consumers into buying both alcohol and tobacco products, in addition to
engaging in other addictive pursuits (e.g., gambling). But there is another area
of "forbidden" activity that recycles the symbolism of Genesis 2–3 and that
can lead to another type of addiction—sex.

For millions of people who regularly cruise the Internet, Adam and Eve
is synonymous with the adult entertainment industry. Little did ancient sto-
rytellers imagine that the story they preserved would someday become a platform for pornography. Nor would they have guessed that Adam and Eve, the
main characters in their story, would be used to satisfy customers' sexual fantasies. Yet that is exactly what has happened. How this happened is an intriguing journey that begins in antiquity. While some ancient readers saw sex in

the Garden as a positive act, others identified it as the forbidden fruit and had a more negative response. Contemporary readers are heirs to this association of sex in the Garden and encounter the idea in a number of different cultural media. Perhaps one of the more striking venues is Philip D. Harvey's *Adam & Eve* stores and Internet services.

No one disputes that Adam and Eve had sex. But they *are* split in deciding whether it was a good or bad thing.[1] Since sexual congress is at the heart of physical intimacy, deciding on whether or not sex is a good action or a result of humans' sinful nature is important. How you resolve this issue has ramifications for how Eve/woman is imaged. For example, in a host of popular culture venues, Eve/woman is imaged as a sensual creature whose sexuality is a prime weapon in her relational arsenal. This essentially works against any egalitarian notion of male-female relationships and views intimacy as manipulation—*women's* manipulation of men.

Harvey's *Adam & Eve* stores were designed to present a more positive image of sex. Whether he succeeded or, in the end, simply repackaged old stereotypes about Eve/women is an ongoing debate in the twenty-first century.

Garden-Variety Sex in Antiquity

Now to be fair, even ancient readers suspected that Adam and Eve did more than simply "eat fruit" in the Garden. The problem was no one in antiquity could agree on just *what* they did and what were the *consequences* of their actions. For some, words like *naked* and *knowing*—not to mention strategically placed leaves—were blatant indicators of a sexual event. But whether this was a *good* thing or *bad* thing depended on the interpreter.

For the rabbis, sex between Adam and Eve was more than good—it was divinely *mandated*. After all, the command to procreate and fill the earth in Genesis 1:28 could hardly be fulfilled by Adam and Eve "holding hands." Some writers thought that Adam and Eve's initial marriage and coupling took place in the Garden long *before* God gave them *any* prohibitions—so sex could not have been connected with their initial disobedience. They envisioned the day of creation having twelve hours. At the eighth hour two people (Adam and Eve) went to bed and later four people (Adam, Eve, Cain, and Abel) got up. It was not until the ninth hour that God gave them the prohibition and the tenth hour—long after the first family was in place—that Adam and Eve sinned.[2] This, by the way, made sense given the wording of the later punishment of women in Genesis 3:16: "I will *increase* your pain in childbearing." Indeed, not only did Adam and Eve have sex in the Garden, but some rabbis even suggested that they became "sex educators" for the rest of creation.[3]

A few writers in antiquity actually argued that Eve and Adam had a variety of sexual partners. Adam, for example, was said to have slept with all the animals before achieving satisfaction with the woman (whom he then recognized as "bone of his bone").[4] As for Eve, it was reported that she actually slept with the serpent.[5] One writer elaborates on this idea by suggesting that the serpent was the fallen angel Sammael and that their union resulted in a son—Cain.[6]

Other sources argued that it was only *after* Adam and Eve left the Garden that they had other sexual partners. According to this view, the 130-year gap between the births of Cain and Seth can be seen as evidence of Adam and Eve's waning desire for each other and their resulting separation (they get back together with the birth of Seth). During this 130-year separation Adam and Eve were sexually active—just not with each other. Adam lay with female demons and Eve with male ones.[7] Another tradition has Adam linking up with his ex-wife Lilith during this 130 years, producing demons, spirits, and imps by the thousands.[8] According to tradition, Lilith left Adam in the first place because Adam refused to let her "be on top" during intercourse.[9] The writers are silent as to whether or not this changed during this 130-year reunion.

Not everyone, however, agreed that sex in the Garden was a good thing. Some thought that the physical expression of sex was either the *original* disobedience or a *consequence* of that first disobedience.[10] Proponents of this latter position argued that Adam and Eve were virgins in the Garden and that only *after* their disobedience they got married and engaged in sex. But even if sex was not the original disobedience, it was not necessarily a good thing. As one ancient Christian writer argued, the command in Genesis 1:28 to procreate

> is fulfilled after Paradise, and nakedness, and the fig leaves that betoken the lasciviousness (*pruriginem*) of marriage. . . . Eve was a virgin in Paradise. After the garments of skins her married life began.[11]

Sex, Adam, and Eve in the Twentieth and Twenty-First Centuries

As writers in antiquity disagreed as to whether sex had positive or negative origins, so contemporary writers still debate the issue. For example, in 1995 the publishing house Hodge and Braddoct published a dictionary titled *And Adam Knew Eve: A Dictionary of Sex in the Bible*. Its cover image was a picture of Adam and Eve in the Garden. In the entry on "Adam and Eve," it is clear that the writer defends a more positive reading of sex and Genesis 2–3:

> Perhaps Genesis makes no mention of Adam and Eve making love in the Garden of Eden because it is taken for granted. . . . In the noncanonical book of Jubilees (3:6), Adam and Eve have sexual relations as soon as God introduces them. It is literally love at first sight. . . . Sex, in any case, has nothing to do with Adam and Eve's Fall from grace in Genesis. Their sin is one of disobedience. . . . Eve, tempted by the serpent to partake of the fruit, gets blamed by Adam ("she gave me of the tree," Adam tells God, "and I did eat," as if Eve had a choice but poor Adam didn't).[12]

Of course *And Adam Knew Eve* deals with sex in antiquity, so perhaps it is fitting that the couple responsible for the first sexual act is highlighted in its title and cover. But this association is found in contemporary secular sources as well. Take, for instance, the April 1984 *Time* magazine cover that featured the image of a comedic Adam and Eve—looking a bit startled or frightened—sitting on either side of an apple tree with apples cascading over them. The title of the article is found underneath the *Time* title: "Sex in the '80s: The Revolution Is Over."[13]

This cultural association of sex with the Garden of Eden and Adam and Eve found in antiquity is replayed countless times in the world of contemporary advertising. While it is frequently seen in the sexual/seductive way in which products use the Garden to sell nonsexual products, it also is present in the marketing of sex products.

One example of a nonsexual product that uses sex and the Garden in its marketing strategy is the pomegranate drink POM. A 2010 commercial for POM Wonderful utilizes the imagery of a garden, a snake, and a naked woman. A voice-over proclaims,

> Some scholars believe it wasn't an apple, but a ruby-red, antioxidant-rich pomegranate, with which Eve tempted Adam. And only POM Wonderful has the juice of four whole pomegranates and is backed by modern science. Powerful then. POM Wonderful now.[14]

Although the voice-over makes reference to scholarly opinion that the fruit of the Garden might have been a pomegranate, it is the commercial's visuals that really capture the attention of the viewer. A sultry Eve is stretched out, lying naked on her side in the Garden. Just to the left of her outstretched right arm is a bottle of POM Wonderful. As the voice-over is heard, a snake slowly wraps itself around the naked body of the Eve/woman. Although there is no Adam in this visual, there is intimate contact between the snake and Eve—a slim but curvy Eve. Once again, Eve/woman uses her sexuality to tempt the viewer.

Another use of nudity/sex and Eve/Garden imagery is found in a rather odd advertisement sponsored by PETA (People for the Ethical Treatment of

Animals). The ad features a nude Angela Simmons with snake-like ivy running around her naked body. She gazes out toward the audience with an apple in her hand. The copy reads, "Eating Meat Is a Sin: Go Vegetarian."[15]

PETA's use of sex in this ad borders on gratuitous. Simmons'/Eve's seductive body and gaze have nothing to do with what PETA is trying to persuade its audience to undertake—vegetarianism. While it is true that in Genesis 1 the first woman and man are vegetarians (as are all the animals), this prohibition is never implied in the Genesis 2–3 story in which Eve is found. Moreover, since the apple is a later identification of the "forbidden fruit" of the Garden, the ad implicitly advocates eating it—which will later, in fact, be understood as the first "sin." The irony is that the ad—if seen in light of Genesis 1–3—advocates abstinence from one sin in favor of another. Of course, a key issue in this ad is the ethical use of "sex sells" marketing strategies to save animals, while the ad campaign, in fact, objectifies women in the process.[16]

A more understandable way in which marketers use sex and Genesis 2–3 is in the sales of sex-related products. A good example of an advertisement that presents a natural "fit" with Genesis 2–3's symbols is a 2003 print ad for Durex condoms.[17] The ad, mimicking a Peter Paul Rubens painting (1597), has a nude Adam and Eve in the Garden wearing strategically placed leaves on their genitals. Adam is imaged almost cajoling Eve (a turnabout from the idea of Eve tempting Adam). Since the product is condoms, the viewer assumes that his act of persuasion is aimed at sexual consummation—understood here as the Garden's forbidden fruit. Of course, with the ad copy at the bottom right (Durex Condoms—Fits Any Size) one cannot help but note the disproportionate size of the ad's fig leaves (Adam's is much larger). The original artwork by Rubens has both leaves about the same size.[18] Unlike the imagery in many ads, here Adam/man appears as the sexual aggressor. But since condoms are a male product and the ad is designed for a male audience, it is perhaps understandable that the picture chosen for this ad was one in which Adam/male appears more in control.

Another sex-related product that utilized the Garden of Eden's imagery is Pfizer's Viagra. Pfizer released five print ads titled "Jardim" (garden) in October 2007. One imaged a man and a woman (pictured from their knees down) standing in grass with a round blue object on the ground in the ad's lower-left-hand corner. In the lower-right-hand corner is the copy "powered by Pfizer" with the word "Pfizer" in a blue oval. Although there is what appears to be a low-hanging branch in the upper-right-hand corner, there is little to associate this entire image with the Garden of Eden.[19] This changes in the next three ads. In one ad the couple are standing to the left of a tree. Scattered around them on the ground are blue pieces of "fruit" about the size of apples. The woman is holding the fruit while the man is cupping her hand with his.[20] A second ad has the man sitting on a rock slightly to the right of the tree in the background. The woman is standing, howbeit bending over, with a blue fruit in her hand as if she is offering it to him.[21] The third ad has both man and woman sitting in front of the tree. Their eyes are closed and they are nuzzling each other while the woman hands the blue fruit to the man. The only copy in all three ads (located either at the top or lower right of the picture) is the words "Powered by Pfizer." Again, the word Pfizer is encased in a blue oval. Since Pfizer markets a blue oval Viagra pill, the fruit of the ads is none other than Viagra, and we are now, without question, in the Garden of Eden.[22] Unlike many ads that make use of the Garden imagery, however, these ads present Eve and Adam fully clad in contemporary clothing. This cements the association between Eve/Adam and contemporary woman/man. The images retain the traditional blame placed on Eve/woman, however, by having her in control of the pill/fruit. In the fifth ad, however, there is no Adam/man. There is simply Eve/woman holding out a blue fruit/pill.[23] Thus the idea of sex/temptation/Eve that is implicit in the imagery of four of the ads is made explicit in a fifth ad, when Eve/woman boldly offers the fruit to the viewer. The body language and the seductive visages of the characters in all of the ads make the "forbidden fruit" metaphor almost superfluous. After all, technically, it is not eating the fruit that is at issue here, but how *long* you can make the feast *last*.

Not everyone, however, thought that Adam was necessary for Eve's sexual satisfaction. In half of a framed picture, a 2005 Swiss ad features a nude woman with an apple in her hand and a tree in the background. The ragged edge on the left of the picture of Eve suggests that the frame originally held a picture of Adam and Eve that has now been torn in two.[24] This suggestion is validated when one looks at a print of Lucas Cranach the Elder's 1531 painting of Adam and Eve (apparently the template for the ad).[25] The resulting picture in the ad is one of Eve standing alone in the Garden without Adam. But since the ad is for Sensuelle—a purveyor of women's sex toys—the copy on the ad's top, when translated, makes sense of the ad's solitary Eve: "For women, who can do it on their own."[26] In this ad, sex/orgasm is a solitary pleasure, not dependent on Adam.

While the ad just analyzed focuses on female autoeroticism, another ad suggested that it was Adam who did not really need Eve.[27] While Green Apple

Vodka is not a sex-related product, its ad does tweak the notion of sex in the Garden in a quite different direction. Smirnoff's parent company, Diageo, launched a television and print campaign that featured "twisted" packaging for a group of flavor infused vodka. The United States launch campaign to the GLBT community featured an ad depicting a Garden of Eden in which Eve was noticeably absent. Instead, a nude Adam with strategically placed leaf, is touching an apple hanging overhead and gazing at a snake entwined in the tree. To the left, another nude man (with leaf) looks speculatively at Adam. The copy at the bottom reads, "The Original Sin Just Got a Little More Tempting." At the bottom left is a message in small print, "Please drink responsibly," that is in keeping with Diageo's policy of social consciousness in advertising.[28] In this ad, sex is identified as "the original sin," much like we have seen in other ads that equate sex with the forbidden fruit. But while the Sensuelle ad implied that women could have sexual pleasure without men, it did not equate autoeroticism as the original sin. The same cannot be said of the Smirnoff ad. This ad implies that sex was the original sin. But since we are talking about two men, this message has implications for contemporary discussions of sexual orientation. No doubt, this was *not* the message Smirnoff intended to convey to its GLBT audience.

The assumption behind all of these examples is that sex is intrinsically linked with the Garden and Adam and Eve (or simply Eve or Adam/"Steve"). Another type of appropriation, however, links sex in a more comprehensive way with Eden—the sale of erotica.

Eden and Erotica

Today, Googling "Eve's Garden" will produce links to a variety of businesses. Some are restaurants while others deal with plants and garden implements. If you look closely, however, you will find a company located in New York City that operates both a store and an online catalogue for erotica.

Eve's Garden was founded in 1974 by the feminist Dell Williams. Its website describes it as "the world's first mail-order catalogue and sexuality boutique designed for the unique needs of women." Eve's Garden does not cater to the "bachelorette," nor does it specialize in "gag gifts." Instead, it seeks to meet the needs of the "discerning female consumer seeking to expand and celebrate her sexuality and enhance her sexual experiences."[29]

Williams is a women's rights activist who is listed in the Who's Who of Sexual Academics and Leaders. She recently donated her papers to Cornell

University's Department for Feminist, Gender, and Sexuality Studies. The impetus to open Eve's Garden began after Williams was humiliated when she went into a store to buy a vibrator. She combined her interests in politics and feminism to create "a safe, private and supportive way for women to purchase vibrators, educational materials and sexual aids without feelings of shame or self-consciousness."[30]

The logo for Eve's Garden consists of the words "eve's" and "garden" in lowercase letters separated by a red apple. Clearly this positions the company within the symbolism of Genesis 2–3. This imagery is repeated on the cover of Williams' 2005 book, with a naked woman holding an apple sandwiched between the book's title (*Revolution in the Garden*) and its subtitle (*Memoirs of the Gardenkeeper*). A partial picture of a large apple occupies the lower-right-hand corner.[31] In chapter 2 ("The Power of Naming Things"), Williams explains how she arrived at the title of her company:

> Since the time of the Old Testament, it has been a matter of policy that woman is inherently defective. Our nature is base, our minds are weak, our bodies are shameful. Is it any wonder that our sense of ourselves is diminished, or that so many of us have conformed so concretely to male models of social and economic and political structures to say nothing of the male model of sexual pleasure?
>
> How efficient debasement is when you want to keep a group of people unstable, unsure, in line!
>
> "Eve," I thought that day at my desk, "I'm going to reclaim your garden. And I'm going to invite every other woman I can possibly reach to come back home into paradise with you." . . .
>
> Our version of "Eve" is a transformation from a fallen, shamed woman to a strong, powerful woman proud of her strength, sensitivity, and sexuality.[32]

In addition to founding Eve's Garden, Williams became an interfaith minister and continued to participate in women's rights activities, including having a part in a West Side production of Eve Ensler's *Vagina Monologues*.[33] In a letter written by Gloria Steinham and presented to Williams at its final performance, Steinham said,

> For those of you who don't know, long before Babeland and *Sex in the City* and V day, Dell founded Eve's Garden, a modest shop in Midtown with a radical goal—giving women sexual autonomy. In this culture we are still struggling to explain that pornography is not erotica . . . pornography is not about sexuality but about power.[34]

Eve's Garden, however, is a small business compared to the giant pornographic empire founded by Phil Harvey. In spite of the general cultural pervasiveness that we have seen thus far combining the Genesis 2–3 symbolism and sex, *no one, no one* has done more to solidify this connection in our contemporary consumer culture than Philip D. Harvey, founder of Adam & Eve. Whether his usage of the symbolism results in a more positive imaging of Eve/woman and sex or a pornographic objectification of them remains to be seen.

Phil Harvey and the Origins of Adam & Eve

In 1961 Harvey graduated from Harvard with a BA in Slavic languages and literature. After serving in the army he joined CARE,[35] and for the next five years he worked with their food distribution programs in Bombay and New Delhi. Ultimately he became deputy director of CARE in India.[36] Harvey remembers feeling frustrated with this work because CARE's food distribution programs were unable to keep pace with India's rapidly growing population. He once remarked in an interview:

> We worked tirelessly to feed children and every year their numbers swelled as we realized that our end of year results got poorer and poorer due to the increase in the number of children. I finally gave in to the idea that it was perhaps not very thoughtful to send only food to the needy.[37]

For Harvey, the answer to the misery and ineffectiveness he saw lay in better family planning programs. All this motivated him to enroll at the University of North Carolina at Chapel Hill, where in 1970 he earned an MA in family planning administration from the university's School of Public Health.[38] When at UNC he teamed up with an English doctor, Tim Black, and submitted a thesis project based on the idea of "social marketing"—the concept of using commercial means to encourage people to do things that are good for them. As part of his thesis he got permission from the university to experiment with the mail-order sale of condoms.[39]

In 1970 Harvey and Black started the first mail-order condom business in the United States. It was an action that was technically problematic since the Comstock Law, which classified condoms as obscene, prohibited mail orders.[40] Harvey and Black's ads targeted college and university campuses. One ad showed an outline of a couple sitting with the man's arm around the woman's shoulders. Its copy said, "What will you get her this Christmas—pregnant?"[41] In 1971 Adam & Eve sent out its first mail-order catalogue.[42]

Eventually, the profits from Harvey's condom selling went to fund a nonprofit organization—Population Services International (PSI). Today PSI describes itself as "a global health organization dedicated to improving the health of people in the developing world by focusing on serious challenges like a lack of family planning, HIV/AIDS, barriers to maternal health, and the greatest threats to children under five, including malaria, diarrhea, pneumonia and malnutrition."[43]

PSI's mission is "to measurably improve the health of poor and vulnerable people in the developing world, principally through social marketing of family planning and health products and services, and health communications. Social marketing engages private sector resources and uses private sector techniques to encourage healthy behavior and make markets work for the poor."[44] Its website proudly proclaims the company's values, including "making markets work for the poor; measuring impact; speed, efficiency, and outcomes over process; decentralization and empowerment; and long-term commitment to the people we serve."[45] Later, in 1989, Harvey founded DKT International, named after D. K. Tyagi, one of India's first crusaders for family planning. Its goal was to provide low-cost family planning. Eventually DKT would provide people with much-needed information about HIV/AIDS as well. Its list of donors includes foundations and countries, one of which is the U.S. Agency for International Development. Today DKT's website reports,

> Since 1989, the nonprofit organization DKT International has been promoting family planning and HIV/AIDS prevention through social marketing. DKT has 19 programs in 18 countries and in 2011 provided and sold 650 million condoms, more than 72 million cycles of oral contraceptives, and over 14 million injectable contraceptives, 1 million IUDs, and 12 million misoprostol pills. Last year, DKT efforts prevented 7 million pregnancies, 11,000 maternal deaths, and 1.4 million abortions.[46]

Ten years after the founding of DKT, Harvey published his book *Let Every Child Be Wanted: How Social Marketing Is Revolutionizing Contraceptive Use around the World* (1999). It earned Harvey the nickname of "guru of social marketing."[47] On reviewing the book, former President Jimmy Carter said,

> Phil Harvey's book, *Let Every Child Be Wanted*, describes a highly effective way of making affordable contraceptives available to even very low-income couples in Africa, Asia, and Latin America. It contributes in a lively and interesting way to our understanding of foreign assistance programs, particularly those for family planning and AIDS prevention.[48]

One might wonder what all this has to do with Genesis 2–3 and sex. Or, as one reviewer asked his readers in his article's byline, "How can a vibrator in Topeka help halt the spread of AIDS in Hanoi?"[49] Well, Harvey's condom-selling mail-order business became the precursor of not only PSI and DKT but also Adam & Eve—the flagship company of Phil Harvey Enterprises (PHE), currently centered in Hillsborough, North Carolina.[50] And Adam & Eve went on to become the largest and most successful seller of sex toys and erotic/pornographic merchandise in the United States—the proceeds of which partially go to fund Harvey's philanthropic projects.[51]

To be fair, Harvey tried to branch out beyond mail-order condoms by selling a number of benign items like belt buckles and model airplanes. Nothing really took off, however, until he offered a few pieces of women's lingerie. One news report quotes Harvey as saying, "We got nothing but a big yawn until we put in something with erotic appeal. Then sales [went] through the roof."[52]

At the beginning, when sexually explicit videos started to appear in Adam & Eve catalogues, the items chosen were in sync with the company's goals of better reproductive health. Films, with copulating couples coached by sex therapists, aimed at giving permission to people to look at healthy depictions of sex—people who would not normally look at pornographic materials. But by the mid-1980s, Adam & Eve's materials included bondage magazines. In his own words, Harvey admitted, "To be blunt, I just didn't pay enough attention to the kinds of portrayals that began finding their way into our inventory."[53] The U.S. government agreed. The Justice Department charged Harvey with breaking obscenity laws that prohibited the distribution of obscene materials through the mail. A May 1986 raid on the corporate offices procured evidence that was later produced in court. So began an eight-year period of legal attacks against Harvey, which he documented in his book *The Government vs. Erotica: The Siege of Adam & Eve* (2001). Ultimately, juries acquitted Adam & Eve and Harvey of the felonies with which they were charged.

Adam & Eve and the Adult Sex Industry

In 1996 Adam & Eve launched a virtual catalogue on adameve.com, the online division of Adam & Eve.[54] In that same year the company began Adam & Eve Productions (prior to this, it had invested in other companies' films).[55] In 2000 Adam & Eve launched www.adamevod.com, a video-on-demand site providing customers with streaming adult videos on their computer.[56]

Adam & Eve's first nationwide adult TV commercial aired in 2002.[57] In 2004 Amazon proudly announced that over twelve hundred products from Adam & Eve would now be available at Amazon.com. This would bring an "exciting blend of enjoyment and edgy shopping that customers of Amazon.com have not had access to before."[58] In 2005 Adam & Eve teamed up with Reality-X Productions to announce the premiere of *Reality-X: The Search* for *Adam & Eve*.[59] *Reality-X* was a reality show, the purpose of which was to find the sexiest couple in America. Adam & Eve also started branching out by franchising branded stores. And in 2009, Adam & Eve started offering online adult DVD rentals. This allowed customers instant access to adult movies instead of waiting for them to be mailed.[60]

Today, according to its website, Adam & Eve has a loyal following of nearly ten million catalog and Internet customers.[61] Its catalog has items ranging from apparel to DVDs to its own signature line of products. Condom sales now account for only a small portion of gross sales.

The growth of Adam & Eve reflects the mainstreaming of pornography in America today. As *Wall Street Journal*'s "Business World" columnist Holman W. Jenkins Jr. notes, "Porn has moved out of a few segregated public spaces, the seedy book shops and triple-X theaters, and become ubiquitous on the web, on cable, in neighborhood video shops."[62] According to Adam & Eve's Fact Sheet, about 75 percent of its catalogue customers are male and 25 percent are female. A slightly higher number of its online customers are female.[63] To entice even more women, Adam & Eve introduced home "Temptations Parties"—a bit like Tupperware nights, only selling vibrators.[64]

In 2011 Adam & Eve celebrated its fortieth anniversary. Its fortieth anniversary website displayed seven women in various types of lingerie posing suggestively for the camera—there were no men.[65]

Ecstasy in Eden
Stores and Sex Toys

Currently there are over forty Adam & Eve stores across America, with plans under way for forty more.[66] They are not the seedy triple-X stores usually associated with the adult entertainment industry.[67] The basic layout of every store is almost predictable. The front section features clothing, costumes, lingerie, massage aids, books, as well as a variety of novelty items. The cash register and checkout stations are also here. Behind all that is a section in the back that can be visited only by persons who are at least eighteen years old. This is where you will find sex toys and performance enhancers, ranging from bondage and discipline items to vibrators and inflatable dolls. Some would argue that by making sex toys and aids accessible in safe, even "classy" venues, Adam & Eve performs a valuable service. Indeed, the company explains that the concept behind its stores is "to accommodate the needs and desires of more women and couples seeking to explore erotica in a safe, comfortable, and friendly environment."[68]

If you perused the shelves of Adam & Eve or viewed their online catalogue, you would find objects that allude to the story of Genesis 2–3 and its interpretation. For instance, the company offers the following products for sale: *Eve's Pussy*, a full-scale working model of a female labia and vagina, with the tagline "Welcome to Paradise"; *Eden Waterproof Paradise Vibrator*, from the Adam & Eve Signature Toys collection, bearing the label "Eden" and urging customers to "[e]xplore your deepest fantasies in a hidden paradise"; *Adam's Pleasure Skin Cock* promising to be the "Dick of Your Dreams"; and *Eden Snake of Paradise*, an Eden dildo that utilizes the Garden's snake, whose online description reads, "Invite this snake into your garden and you'll be happy you did."

Adam & Eve
Sex Positive?

Phillip D. Harvey is a social entrepreneur *and* porn magnate—the founder of two NGOs (PHE and DKT) and of Adam & Eve. While he notes the irony involved in blending pornography with charitable activities, he is not ashamed of Adam & Eve. For Harvey, his companies serve similar purposes. Each allows clients control over their sexual behavior. In DKT the control is over pregnancy, in Adam & Eve the control is over pleasure.

Harvey insists that all of his company's materials and activities are geared to be "sex-positive." The company's website proclaims,

> Adam & Eve also encourages consenting adults to think "sex positive" and be aware that they have the right and opportunity to enjoy safe sexual experiences within their own personal boundaries. To that end, Adam & Eve works on three different areas: Inform adults about issues, trends and cultural influences on the sexual experience. Advocate sexual honesty while encouraging adults to exercise their political influence to maintain their freedom. Entertain adults while helping them to view sex as a healthy, normal and positive experience that can be enjoyed within the privacy of one's own home.[69]

Phil Harvey is a proponent of what is called the "sex-positive" movement. In chapter 2 of his book *Government vs. Erotica*, he asks, "Is Pornography Harmful?" Harvey then cites Lloyd G. Sinclair, a sex therapist and sex educator who is certified by AASECT (American Association of Sexuality Educators, Counselors and Therapists). According to Harvey, Sinclair—who is also an Adam & Eve colleague—claims that nonviolent adult pornography is "harmless, benign, and useful."[70] In the "Issues of Harm" section in chapter 2, Harvey further argues that even though we know that cigarettes and alcohol are harmful we permit these—yet no one has died of pornography. Given this fact, he finds it "difficult to understand the outlawing of explicit sexual depiction which, on the basis of a massive body of evidence, impose no harm on anyone at all."[71]

Phil Harvey is a libertarian. He believes people should be free to pursue and be responsible for their sexual activities and fantasies.[72] In his own words, "You shouldn't tell [people] what they should pay their babysitters or what kind of porn to watch."[73] For Harvey it is an issue of free speech. After all, "If we have come to accept the utilitarian (and other) value of free political and religious speech, what is our basis for continuing to suppress sexual speech?"[74] Indeed he argues that political tyrants "almost always do their best to suppress sexuality."[75] In other words, Harvey seems to think that what happens in the bedroom stays in the bedroom, with no harm done as long as it is consensual between adults. Indeed, he goes so far to suggest that the depictions of women in his erotic materials *empower* women rather than victimizing them.

But not all people agree with Harvey's views on the harmlessness of sexually explicit materials, nor do they feel that the objectification of women is a source of empowerment. With the onslaught of the Internet, pornography is now more available to consumers than at any other time in history. Its ubiquity makes it important, now more than ever, to examine the social and psychological costs it imposes on society. While Harvey cites studies and experts to support his position—that there is no proof that pornography is harmful—one could just as easily cite other experts and research findings that describe the harm caused by pornography.[76] Experts Mary Eberstadt and Mary Anne Layden argue the following: Consumption of pornography can harm women and children in particular. Pornography can harm people not immediately connected to consumers of pornography. Pornography can be addictive and thus has the potential to harm its consumers. Pornography consumption is philosophically and morally problematic. The fact that not everyone is harmed by pornography does not entail that pornography should not be regulated.[77]

One could also point out that Harvey's philosophy sometimes clashes with what his company actually sells. For example, the head of Adam & Eve's gay porn division once noticed that, of the visitors to the website who entered a search term, 88 percent of them entered a slang term for unprotected sex between males. The company's response was to begin selling such videos because they increased sales. When informed of this, Harvey reportedly pursed his lips and said, "That's a little depressing"[78]—a response falling far short of the one might expect of an HIV/AIDS educator and an avid provider of condoms to the third world.

Another interesting question is raised by a writer who visited and talked to Phil Harvey, Susan Montani, and Candida Royalle (former pornographic actress, producer/director of couples-oriented pornography). In the writer's own words,

> Sexuality, Phil tells me, when it's good, can be a way of asserting or a "way of submitting oneself to the power of another person. That has strong psychological components, not just enhancing intimacy but ratifying a love between two people. The bond is important in life. Sex ratifies the bond."
>
> When Harvey says this, I am struck by something Susan Montani and Candida Royalle said as we were talking in Montani's living room. Taboo is good, they said. "Doing something slightly taboo—don't you think when you do it, when you share that with a partner, it is like a special new link, a secretly shared thing?"
>
> "Porn is not a huge taboo anymore," Candida said, "but it is still a taboo and that helps it retain its sexiness."
>
> "So what happens," I asked, "when nothing is taboo?"[79]

Phil Harvey
The Sexploitation of Adam and Eve

It is not easy to see how Genesis 2–3 fits into Phil Harvey's philosophy until you realize his opinion about religion. In chapter 11 ("Sex and God") of *Government vs. Erotica*, Harvey begins with a blanket condemnation of organized religion: "There is much evidence to support the conclusion that organized religion has caused more mischief in the world that it has done good."[80] After an extremely superficial survey of outsider/insider mentality and its relationship to violence and intolerance in world religions, Harvey moves on to his primary target in this chapter—the Christian church. Citing Tertullian, Jerome, Augustine, Ambrose, and a host of other patristic writers, Harvey paints a bleak picture of Christian attitudes toward sex.[81] But Harvey likes the Hebrew Bible. According to Harvey, it is not the source of fear/denunciation of sex, it speaks of sex in a variety of ways—but mostly positive, it is silent on a variety of sexual areas, and it depicts sexual congress as a pleasure.[82] Not surprisingly, one of his favorite books is Song of Songs. It was the Jewish tradition, Harvey argues, that promoted sexual intimacy not Christianity. After all, in Judaism, Harvey argues, a husband is required by Torah to learn, know, and do what will give his wife sexual pleasure.[83] Given this attitude and the cultural pervasiveness of the association of sex and Genesis 2–3, it is perhaps no wonder that he chose the title "Adam & Eve" for his stores. One interviewer actually asked Harvey about his company's name. Interestingly, Harvey reports that he simply cannot remember:

> *Harvey:* This is a question that has come up, as you would expect, a number of times and neither Tim nor I could remember how it happened, how it got started. It goes right back to the beginning; he doesn't remember suggesting it, I don't remember suggesting it but somehow we put Adam & Eve on one of the first catalogs and couple of years later we registered the trademark and logo and that's where we've been ever since. I just don't know. I admit it's odd. The original man and original woman—I can see how the idea might have come up. We're after all talking about sex products and the original sexual relationship between Adam and Eve is the best known of almost any in our culture so that makes a certain amount of sense, but I just don't remember the circumstances.[84]

While there are a number of critiques that could be made of Harvey's stance on pornography, his appropriation Genesis 2–3 is also problematic. Regardless of how you view his stores, the end result is that Harvey has successfully turned "Adam" and "Eve" into consumer commodities and made their very names into his own "brand."

When a consumer culture appropriates a religious symbol, it often reorients its meanings.[85] Religious traditions, after all, have their home in institutions and practices that help relate those traditions to daily life. The same thing can be said of biblical characters and their scriptural context. When religious symbols become cultural commodities, two processes are involved— abstraction and reification.[86] The symbols are abstracted from the context from which their meanings are determined. The result of this process is that their "semantic mass" is greatly reduced.[87] This makes them more susceptible to manipulation and misappropriation. Such symbols can be put to uses unrelated, indeed contradictory, to their original meanings.[88] In the end, customer culture encourages a shallow engagement with religious symbols, not because popular culture is necessarily shallow but because consumers have been trained to treat consumption culture in a shallow manner.[89]

In Genesis 2–3, Adam and Eve are more than sexual objects and male– female relationships are more than exercises in sexual fantasies. "Bone of my bone and flesh of my flesh" (Gen 2:23) speaks of a close kinship between man and woman—a partnership not only in relationship (e.g., marriage) but in life's goals—the stewardship of creation. Harvey's stores reduce the richness of Genesis 2–3 to a brand about sex, regardless, in many instances, of the form it takes. Harvey's company knows the value of a brand. It enforces to the customer who you are and what you stand for.[90] In their marketing of Adam &

Eve franchises, they claim that their brand—Adam & Eve—is "the number 1 recognized name in the business" of selling erotica.[91]

Although Phil Harvey did not create the association of sex with Adam and Eve, he certainly exploited it. While the same might be said of other products that use Adam and Eve in their advertising, no one, no one has achieved the degree of commodification of Adam and Eve as has Phil Harvey. By making Adam & Eve a consumer commodity and the brand of his pornographic empire, Harvey has reduced Adam and Eve to mere sex symbols. And since Adam and Eve stand for all men and women, the relationship between male and female gets reduced to just sex.

As an experiment, I polled five colleagues in my Religious Studies Department and asked them what came into their minds when I said "Adam and Eve." While it is true that no one said "sex toy," one colleague (a theologian) did say "sex." But after he said it, he got a surprised and somewhat perplexed look on his face, as if he could not quite pin down WHY he had said it. And then his brow cleared and he started to explain,

> You know why I said that? Have you seen that billboard downtown? The one about that new store in Spokane? Adam & Eve? I saw another one the other day on my way to Missoula. It's funny, now whenever I hear the phrase "Adam & Eve" . . . I guess I just think about sex.[92]

The connection between sex and Genesis 2–3 surfaces in a number of different ways in popular culture. It is the butt of jokes and the topic of advertisements. There are those ads that manipulate the Garden's symbols so that they become little more than marking tools for either products (e.g., POM) or for a desired behavior (e.g., PETA/vegetarianism). Other ads—like those produced by companies that market sex-related products (condoms, Viagra, etc.)—result in a closer relationship between sex and story. Finally there are those appropriations that are actively involved in the adult entertainment industry. This last category—including Eve's Garden and Adam & Eve—represents case studies of what happens when a company takes on the name of the Garden's primary characters. But when the names Adam and Eve are reduced to a brand for pornography (as is the case with Adam & Eve), it illustrates just how far popular culture appropriations can travel on the road *away from* Genesis 2–3.

CONCLUSION

It would be nice to tell you,
That this story has a happy ending,
Except . . . it hasn't ended yet.

—L.S. & V.Z.

People can and have used the story of Adam and Eve to illustrate just about anything. Hoping to meet Prince Charming? Interested in a bit of wife spanking? Want to teach your daughters to renounce personal autonomy? How about having some great sex? Or putting all those feminazis in their place by celebrating men as prophets, priests, and kings? Christians interested in recreating the Garden have produced an endless array of blueprints.

In the same way, the secular world never runs out of ways to recycle Eden, whether by telling jokes, selling products, or accessing a cavalcade of other mediums and venues.[1] In teasing out the story of the first human beings, recreating and recycling efforts focus on a variety of questions, but one issue ineluctably emerges: gender. By explicit instruction (recreating) or by implication and inference (recycling), both appropriations deal with what it means to be a man and a woman. In recreations of Eden, attention typically focuses on power dynamics. Whatever else people want to know about life in paradise, they are eager to discover who is the boss. For recycling Eden, old stereotypes of men and women abound, but challenges to those stereotypes are present as well.

Another dynamic is also at work as readers consider ancient texts. When interpreters transplant Eden into modern settings, the biblical world and the contemporary world mix and mingle, so that each domain is changed by association with the other. For those interested in recycling Eden, accommodating the Bible to popular culture is not worrisome. Since they seek to use the Garden for their own purposes, these interpreters are not trying to be faithful to the biblical text. People who want to recreate Eden, on the other hand, have a huge stake in correctly depicting the biblical world. But they, just like secular readers, bring to the Bible cultural presuppositions that color their understandings of Genesis. And religious interpreters, no less than secular ones, have been known to use the Garden story for their own ends.

Recreating Eden

Most Americans find these rival Edens bewildering, and few people outside conservative Christian circles regard the arcane theological debates surrounding Genesis 1–3 as intelligible, much less stimulating. Given the passion that undergirds evangelical conversations about Eden, however, every American has a stake in recreations of the Garden. For Eden functions as a normative culture, and the crusading evangelicals determined to recapture it have no intention of excluding nonbelievers from their new social order. Indeed, the prospect of remaking *all* American mores and institutions in the image of the Garden is precisely what appeals most to these reformers.

Their visions include heady mixes of patriotism, capitalism, consumerism, and, most important of all, sexism. More than anything else, the so-called complementarian understanding of the creation seeks to put women in their places as submissive servants of men. Gender hierarchy is not an afterthought in this theology; rather, it *constitutes* this theology. And it envisions a world in which husbands routinely inflict violence upon wives, fathers regard daughters as personal possessions created to wait upon them, and women everywhere— in the home, in the church, and in the state—are to remain silent. For the goal of this version of Christian life is to celebrate manhood, whether by emphasizing the masculinity of God, stressing the innate connections between men and their Father God, removing women from the public sphere so that they cannot threaten men, or denying daughters and wives autonomy in the home. This version of Eden regards the eternal subordination of women to men as the best news Genesis 1–3 has to offer.

Americans committed to gender equality find the prospect of living in such a social order terrifying. And if conservative evangelicals examine this Eden carefully, they too will be horrified. For in seeking to transform American culture, they have also embraced it. Despite their devotion to Scripture and their desire to enact God's will on earth, they have allowed secular values to undergird and even define their understanding of Eden. This is a danger inherent in interacting with the larger culture in order to transform it. Culture invariably shapes us, and unless biblical interpreters rigorously monitor the ways in which they read Scripture, they will inevitably apprehend it through contemporary eyes, not ancient ones. In their zeal to recreate Eden, conservative evangelicals have explicated Scripture through cultural constructs that have nothing to do with the Bible and in doing so have become captives to those constructs.

The color pink, for example, is nowhere celebrated in Scripture. Neither is Prince Charming. Or Mary Kay lip gloss. Or Victorian high teas. Or the "penetrating power" of masculine preaching. Or sexperiment bed-ins. Or worship in bed. Or wife spanking. Or militant fecundity. Or online dating services. Or—most important—gender complementarity. It is surely possible to read Genesis 1–3 as subordinating women to men. (It is also possible to see the creation of man and woman in the divine image, with both given dominion over the earth, as an example of gender equality. But that is another matter.) Nevertheless, neither Genesis 1–3 nor the New Testament delineates a doctrine of gender complementarity in which man and woman share equally in the divine image but eternally observe functional distinctions that limit initiative and authority to man while defining woman as a secondary creation designed to submit quietly to male directives. "Complementarity" is not a word that even appears in Scripture, much less a doctrine that encapsulates the essence of biblical revelation. The same is true of the phrase "biblical manhood and womanhood."

But these are concepts that allow conservative evangelical theology to honor woman as a good creation at the same time that they reduce real-world women to domestic servitude. So fundamental is the insistence on male initiative and female submission that, when single evangelical men refuse to marry expeditiously, an organization like Marry Well will surreptitiously empower women like Candice Watters to instruct single men to man up, while simultaneously teaching single women how to manipulate men into proposing. Sometimes, no matter how much conservative evangelicals are willing to compromise on their bedrock insistence that women may not teach or have authority over men, it is impossible to reshape people in the image of biblical manhood and womanhood.

In the end, religion and culture permeate and influence one another. And reformers who insist upon the purity of their theology of gender and dominion need to cast far more vigilant eyes on the ways in which they have become shaped by—and captive to—the culture they seek to recreate in the image of the biblical Garden. The dream of returning to Eden is not likely to dissipate, nor will the plethora of ways to imagine Eden. One thing, however, is certain. Whoever has the power to define and recreate the Garden will indelibly impact American life. We all have a stake in that conversation.

Recycling Eden

We live in a world where you can laugh at the Garden of Eden with a friend, sit down and drink Original Sin, and then go to Adam & Eve to buy sex toys for an evening of fun and games. Not surprisingly, many might conclude that this is a different story than the one they were taught in Sunday school. But if they think that, they would be only partially correct. Secular appropriations of the Garden story in contemporary popular culture are both *like* and *unlike* their biblical inspiration. Since this is the case, let us examine some hermeneutical observations about the contemporary recycling of Eden in humor and advertising.

It is clear that the symbols, themes, and characters of the Eden story play a major role in contemporary popular culture. In this way, the Genesis 2–3 story is unique among stories found in the Hebrew Bible. There is, of course, the Moses/Exodus narrative that exemplifies the fight against oppression. And there is the David/Goliath account that showcases the plight and ultimate victory of the underdog, or the David/Bathsheba story that warns that even the most favored in God's eyes are accountable for their abuse of power. But even Moses and David are not as ubiquitous in popular culture as are Adam and Eve. As a story of origins, their story speaks to the essential issue of what it means to be male and female—a question that has not been resolved in the centuries that separate contemporary readers from the ancient writers who crafted the story.

While elements of Genesis 2–3 are found throughout popular culture, the story itself is rarely replicated in its entirety. Appropriations draw on *aspects* of the Garden story (symbols, themes, characters), but they do not seem to be interested in telling the *whole* story. There are at least two reasons why.

First, the *medium* of the appropriation may make a difference. The verbal jokes analyzed in this book, for example, make little use of the snake from Genesis 3. Verbal representations of Genesis 2–3, by their very nature, function differently from visual ones. So while the jokes analyzed made little mention of Eden's snake, the same is not true of the humor found in comics and cartoons. In these visual mediums , one is very likely to find a snake at least in the background so that the viewer can instantly recognize the symbolism of Genesis 3 (a man and a woman, a tree/apple tree, and a snake) without being told that the picture depicts the Garden story. Since copy is kept to a minimum in comics and cartoons, the visual dimension has to communicate to the viewer the comic/cartoon's context. In verbal jokes, however, this is not necessary, as the setting of the joke establishes context. There is no reason to include a snake in a joke if there is no function for it.

Another reason that the story is not replicated in its entirety involves the intended use of Genesis 2–3's story elements. A good example of this can be found in marketing's use of the "temptation/persuasion" theme. While this theme is present in Genesis 2–3, it is not the sole focus of the story. In the ads analyzed, however, time and time again persuasion imagery was used to sell products. In the case of perfume, persuasion actually became an implicit promise of what consumers could do to others if they bought the product. In Genesis 3, giving into temptation is a *bad* thing. But in ads utilizing this theme, giving into temptation (and buying a product) is a *good* thing. Given this reality, the negative consequences in Genesis 3's story are counterproductive to the intended use of the story in the ads, and it is not surprising that they are often absent.

Although cultural artifacts may be connected to Genesis 2–3 intertextually, they are not limited to the narrative. Much has been done recently by biblical scholars concerning intertextuality and the history of a text's reception. Such study examines the interplay between the impact biblical materials have on culture and the ways in which that culture encodes the text.[2] In secular popular culture appropriations, however, there is no hesitation in using the story elements and then changing them. Genesis 2–3 thus becomes more of toolbox of useful items rather than an urtext to which any loyalty is owed.[3]

When the Bible appears in popular culture artifacts, it does so by no longer functioning as Scripture. Scripture—or sacred writing—is a term that operates within a religious framework. Scripture carries within it the possibility that readers/listeners can be transformed by an encounter with the divine. But when popular culture uses biblical characters, it often does so by divorcing them from their religious context and function. A good example of this is the co-opting of the "taboo/forbidden fruit" theme by advertising. What starts out as a prohibition in the scriptural account (with rather disastrous consequences for the human race when it is broken) undergoes a complete transformation in advertising. Products that capitalize on this symbol do so by accentuating the desirability of that which is forbidden. Whether it is gambling, alcohol, tobacco, or sex, all are presented as desirable given their association with the "forbidden fruit," and consumers are *encouraged,* NOT *prohibited,* to partake. As mentioned before, however, such promises can be deceptive, as each of these activities/products carries the possibility of addiction.

The use of Genesis 2–3's symbolism in secular popular culture challenges the concept of a "fixed text." In today's world of multiple versions and paraphrases of the Bible, it is not easy to agree upon a definitive translation of Genesis 2–3. Nevertheless, the story does remain somewhat "fixed." Adam is created before Eve because it is not good for the first human to be alone. No matter how loosely a contemporary Bible presents the story, it is not likely to have Eve created first, as we saw in various jokes, or to present Eve's creation as necessary because Adam was such a flawed creation. Nor are most Bibles going to image a Garden where it is Steve not Eve who is Adam's counterpart, as we saw in the Smirnoff ad. The bottom line is that while it is helpful for jokesters and advertisers that listeners/viewers *recognize* that they are in the Garden story, there is no reason for the secular appropriation to faithfully represent the story.

The reaction to the above observations is liable to be mixed. On one hand, there are those who will be appalled at the appropriations found in this book and rush to defend the story's sacred origins. This reaction is frequently found when secular appropriations utilize religious symbols in ways that radically change their function. On the other hand, there are those who will find this kind of appropriation interesting—even exciting—because it draws more voices into the interpretive discourse that exists between sacred texts and culture. In the course of this exchange, both story and consumer are changed.[4]

While encountering the Bible in popular culture may be "fun," it also carries implications for the construction of gender. Adam and Eve as the first man and woman in the story world of Eden still inspire us to call on them, whether for a joke or to sell a product. As long as that remains true, the path back to the Garden will beckon us to follow.

NOTES

Introduction

1   ms. Bookjunkie, comments on "Christian Domestic Discipline: Old-Skool Romance Come to Life?" http://www.smartbitchestrashybooks.com/index.php/weblog/com ments/christian-domestic-discipline-old-skool-romance-come-to-life/; and response by bagel of everything to "Christian Domestic Discipline," http://rationreality.com/ 2007/08/20/christian-domestic-discipline/.

2   T. D. Jakes, "Plug into God's Power," in *Holy Bible: Woman Thou Art Loosed! Edition*, ed. T. D. Jakes (Nashville, Tenn.: Thomas Nelson, 1998), 4. In *Evangelical Identity and Gendered Family Life*, Kindle ed. (New Brunswick, N.J.: Rutgers University Press, 2003), Sally K. Gallagher also remarks upon how the body, in evangelical theology, "becomes a metaphor for profound and intentional differences in spiritual and psychological being." Arguing that evangelicals referenced the body as much as they did the Bible in arguing that God created men to lead and women to submit to them, Gallagher concludes that for evangelicals "the body intimates the reality of masculinity as initiation and femininity as nurturing response." See Kindle locations 2788, 2822.

3   A. Duane Litfin, "Evangelical Feminism: Why Traditionalists Reject It," *Bibliotheca Sacra* 136 (1979): 267. For a more detailed discussion, as well as a consideration of contemporary egalitarian readings of Genesis 1–3, see chap. 8 of Kristen E. Kvam, Linda S. Schearing, and Valarie H. Ziegler, eds., *Eve and Adam: Jewish, Christian, and Muslim Readings on Genesis and Gender* (Bloomington: Indiana University Press, 1999), 371–401, 419–64.

In *Evangelical Identity*, Gallagher provides an accomplished discussion of gender hierarchy and difference as "*the* central metaphor for the ontological world view" of evangelical Christianity. "Tinker with gender," she asserts, "and you unravel the whole." She also argues that very few ordinary evangelicals are "hard-core gender essentialists" and that most evangelical marriages, despite the rhetoric of "symbolic traditionalism," evidence a "pragmatic egalitarianism." Nevertheless, Gallagher contends, hard-core essentialists like James Dobson of Focus on the Family and Wayne Grudem of the Council on

Biblical Manhood and Womanhood have done such a good job of associating egalitarian evangelicals with theological liberalism, arguments for androgyny, and a low view of scriptural authority that the hierarchical position reigns supreme among conservative Christians. See Kindle locations 2746–65, 1589–1660, 1334–43, and 2699–2727.

4   As Gallagher comments at Kindle location 2846 of *Evangelical Identity*, "conservative evangelicals have the established institutions, networks, and rhetoric. The story of husbands' headship and authority is articulated in hundreds of books, through thousands of radio broadcasts, and in millions of pulpits in Sunday school classes every week all over the country. For the time being, their institutional strength sustains the language of symbolic traditionalism, even though the practice of most evangelicals is pragmatically egalitarian."

5   Timothy B. Bayly, "Father Hunger among a Lost Generation: The Pastor's Opportunity," in *Pastoral Leadership for Manhood and Womanhood*, ed. Wayne Grudem and Dennis Rainey, Kindle ed. (Wheaton, Ill.: Crossway Books, 2002), locations 1493–1502.

6   Tedd Tripp, "Embracing God's Plan for Authority," Council on Biblical Manhood and Womanhood, http://www.cbmw.org/Resources/Articles/Embracing-God-s-Plan-for -Authority/ (accessed May 10, 2012).

7   This argument echoes several strands of scholarship related to religion in American culture. Historians have long pointed to the rise of fundamentalism in the late nineteenth and early twentieth centuries as a pivotal moment in American religious history. As classically presented by George M. Marsden in his *Fundamentalism and American Culture: The Shaping of Twentieth-Century Evangelicalism, 1870–1925* (New York: Oxford University Press, 1980), fundamentalism was a product of American evangelicalism and thus originally part of the religious mainstream. By the 1920s, however, fundamentalists' cultural pessimism distinguished them from their fellow citizens, and fundamentalists became subject to ridicule both within and outside of American Christianity. Marsden argues that fundamentalists reacted by withdrawing from the larger culture.

Marsden's thesis has been enormously influential and has set the stage for current discussions of conservative evangelicalism. Scholars typically distinguish conservatives' present desire to transform American culture from the earlier impulse to separate themselves from it. We argue that it was not Christian identity alone or even primarily that guided either the current activism or the earlier retreat from society. Rather, both impulses rested upon a passionate commitment to a cultural construct: "traditional" (i.e., Victorian) gender roles that confined women to the domestic realm and valorized men as women's virile masters.

In *Ungodly Women: Gender and the First Wave of American Fundamentalism* (Minneapolis, Minn.: Fortress, 1990), Betty A. DeBerg revolutionized the study of fundamentalism by demonstrating that the subordination of women to men and the desire to limit women to the domestic realm were central to the fundamentalist impulse. From its beginnings in the nineteenth century to the conservative evangelicalism of the twenty-first century, this branch of Christianity has celebrated female submission to male authority and initiative as essential to and even constitutive of Christian faith. As DeBerg compellingly documents, fundamentalist debates about Scripture in the 1920s were not really about its authority—conservative Christians uniformly regarded the Bible as the word of God—but rather about using the Bible to legitimize patriarchal gender roles at a time when the larger culture was questioning them. Fundamentalist ministers, DeBerg contends, "attempted, first, to diminish women's influence and power by calling into question the legitimacy of women speaking and holding positions of authority within the church. Second, they replaced feminized Christianity with the language of virility, militarism, and Christian heroism" (76). Those very same dynamics are at work in twenty-first-century conservative evangelicalism, as we will show.

Conversations about the relationship between the church and the larger culture invariably owe a debt to H. Richard Niebuhr's *Christ and Culture* (New York: Harper, 1951). Niebuhr identified five typologies to describe that relationship: Christ of culture, Christ above culture, Christ transforming culture, Christ and culture in paradox, and Christ against culture. Christians who regard the larger culture as evil and seek to separate themselves from it belong to the Christ against culture typology. Christians who believe that the larger culture exhibits the theological virtues of Christianity exemplify the Christ of culture typology. And Christians who contend that the larger culture falls short of the perfection of the gospel but are confident that it can be reformed fall into the Christ transforming culture model.

The fundamentalist retreat from the larger society in the 1920s is representative of the Christ against culture model. The current conservative evangelical desire to recreate America in the image of a hierarchical Eden aspires to the Christ transforming culture typology. But, we are arguing, it more closely resembles the Christ of culture model, given the secular values and institutions these Christians have appropriated as foundational to their faith.

8   In *Christotainment: Selling Jesus through Popular Culture* (Boulder, Colo.: Westview, 2009), editors Shirley R. Steinberg and Joe L. Kincheloe dub this parallel evangelical culture "Christotainment." In chapters titled "Selling a New and Improved Jesus" and "Christian Soldier Jesus," Kincheloe provides an exemplary analysis of this movement, arguing that it is driven by a small group of dominionists who appeal to an idealized patriarchal past, present themselves as victims of the current political order, advance obedience as the ultimate theological virtue, and demonize groups such as feminists, gays and lesbians, Muslims, and secularists for depriving them of their patriarchal privileges. "The images of the alpha manly man and the submissive Christian woman are omnipresent" in this rhetoric, Kincheloe notes. "The quantity and fervor of these portrayals fit to perfection the needs of the recovery of patriarchy perceived to have been fatally weakened by the 'feminazi' movement" (1–21 and 23–50). The quotation is from p. 43.

9   The home page for the Council on Biblical Manhood and Womanhood (CBMW) explains that it was formed by pastors and scholars concerned about the "influence of feminism" who hoped to oppose the "growing movement of feminist egalitarianism." They hoped to persuade people that God had created husbands to head the household and wives to submit to them. Male headship also applied to the church, where "some governing and teaching roles are restricted to men." See "About Us," http://www.cbmw.org/ (accessed May 26, 2012).

The group's first act was to issue the Danvers Statement (on the CBMW website and at http://www.swbts.edu/index.cfm?pageid=1727), which argued that God created Adam to exercise headship in marriage and that "distinctions in masculine and feminine roles are ordained by God is part of the created order, and should find an echo in every human heart." For an insider's account of the formation of the CBMW, see Wayne Grudem, "Personal Reflections on the History of CBMW and the State of the Gender Debate," *Journal for Biblical Manhood and Womanhood* 14, no. 1 (2009): 12–17. Looking back on the twelve years following the Danvers Statement, Grudem notes that the CBMW had defended it in "hundreds of articles, books, and internet publications," and served as a "key player in stopping what was in 1985 a flood of evangelical feminism sweeping through the evangelical world almost completely unchallenged."

Recent studies, such as R. Marie Griffith's influential *God's Daughters: Evangelical Women and the Power of Submission* (Berkeley: University of California Press, 1997), have demonstrated that many evangelical marriages practice "mutual submission" between husband and wife. This is not the case in the evangelicals highlighted here. They argue that Ephesians 5 designates the unique authority of husbands in marriage and conclude that the notion of mutual submission in marriage is "a myth without foundation in Scripture at all." See Wayne Grudem, "The Myth of Mutual Submission," *Journal for Biblical Manhood and Womanhood*," 1, no. 4 (1996), http://www.cbmw.org/Journal/Vol-1-No-4/The-Myth-of-Mutual-Submission. More flamboyantly, David and Tim Bayly made the case for patriarchal authority and "father-rule" in a blog post titled "Mutual Submission Is Rebellion. . . ." See BaylyBlog, September 18, 2006, http://baylyblog.com/blog/2006/09/mutual-submission-rebellion#.T8JHHMXpykc (accessed May 24, 2012).

    Events at the Southern Baptist Convention in the 1980s and 1990s evidenced the battle between those two views of authority and submission. In 1984 the convention passed a resolution opposing the ordination of women because the Apostle Paul "excludes women from pastoral leadership to preserve the submission God requires because man was first in creation and the woman was first in the Edenic fall." In 1998 delegates at the convention's annual meeting defeated a proposal by moderate egalitarians calling for mutual submission in marriage and adopted a statement insisting that a wife was bound to submit to her husband and serve him as his God-given helper. See Kvam, Schearing, and Ziegler, *Eve and Adam*, 373, and Margaret Bendroth, "Last Gasp Patriarchy: Women and Men in Conservative American Protestantism," *The Muslim World* 91 (2001): 45–54. Anthony Jordan, the author of the statement, told *The News Hour with Jim Lehrer* that it was not intended as a "put down" of women. "If a husband loves his wife like Christ loved the Church, then the wife has nothing to worry about," he counseled. "Love, Honor, and Obey?" *News Hour with Jim Lehrer Transcript*, June 10, 1998, http://www.pbs.org/news hour/bb/religion/jan-june98/baptist_6-10.html (accessed May 21, 2012).

10   Bob Lepine, "The Husband Is Prophet, Priest, and King," in *Building Strong Families*, ed. Dennis Rainey, Kindle ed. (Wheaton, Ill.: Crossway Books, 2002), locations 1232–61, 1589. Lepine and Rainey are cohosts of the nationally syndicated *FamilyLife Today*. Life at the Lepine home must be exciting. He writes of taking every opportunity to proclaim the truth of God to his wife. On late-night drives, he tells of quizzing her, "What is the Latin phrase that means 'at once sinful and justified'?" If she claims she's too tired to play, he doesn't take no for an answer. Lepine also writes mission statements for his wife and maps out five-year plans for their marriage. To model a warrior spirit for his three sons, he chases down thieves in his truck. See locations 1224, 1276–85, 1594, 1635. For an excellent critique of Lepine, see Cheryl Schatz, "The Husband Is King over the Wife," Women in Ministry, January 22, 2008, http://strivetoenter.com/wim/2008/01/22/the-husband-as-king-over-the-wife/ (accessed May 5, 2012).

11   John Piper, "'The Frank and Manly Mr. Ryle'—The Value of a Masculine Ministry," January 31, 2012, http://www.desiringgod.org/resource-library/conference-messages/the -frank-and-manly-mr-ryle-the-value-of-a-masculine-ministry (accessed May 14, 2012). Piper gave this tribute to nineteenth-century pastor John Charles Ryle and masculine ministry at the Desiring God 2012 Conference for Pastors (theme: God, Manhood and Ministry: Building Men for the Body of Christ). The address is reprinted in the *Journal for Biblical Manhood and Womanhood* 17, no. 1 (2012): 10–22.

12   Elizabeth Esther, "On So-Called 'Biblical Womanhood,'" November 9, 2010, http://www.elizabethesther.com/2010/11/on-so-called-biblical-womanhood.html (accessed May 5, 2012).

13   For more on the on the use of Genesis 1–3 to legitimate the subordination of women to men as well as institution of southern slavery, see Kvam, Schearing, and Ziegler, *Eve and Adam*, 309–15, 323–39.

Chapter 1

1 Joshua Harris, *Boy Meets Girl: Say Hello to Courtship* (Sisters, Ore.: Multnomah, 2000), 45. Harris describes God as "the author of romance" on this page. *Boy Meets Girl* is a follow-up to Harris' *I Kissed Dating Goodbye: A New Attitude toward Romance and Relationships* (Sisters, Ore.: Multnomah, 1997).

2 Tim and Beverly LaHaye, *The Act of Marriage: The Beauty of Sexual Love*, rev. ed. (Grand Rapids: Zondervan, 1998) and Ed and Gaye Wheat, *Intended for Pleasure: Sex Technique and Sex Fulfillment in Christian Marriage* (Old Tappan, N.J.: Fleming H. Revell, 1977).

3 LaHaye and LaHaye, *Act of Marriage*, 32.

4 LaHaye and LaHaye, *Act of Marriage*, 32.

5 LaHaye and LaHaye, *Act of Marriage*, 28.

6 LaHaye and LaHaye, *Act of Marriage*, 24–25.

7 LaHaye and LaHaye, *Act of Marriage*, 27, 31.

8 Popular as courtship is among evangelical Christians, there are conservative groups that argue that courtship resembles dating too closely. These Christians advocate "biblical betrothal," in which a man and woman become irrevocably engaged before becoming romantically involved. Because betrothal involves an unbreakable covenant to marry—unlike courtship or dating—its proponents argue that betrothal safeguards the tender and breakable hearts of those who practice it. Many books and websites promote Christian betrothal. For readers who are interested in pursuing this movement, good places to start include a bibliography at http://polynate.net/books/courtship/bibliography.html, pro-courtship essays at http://boldchristianliving.com/articles/youthful-romance/ and http://www.biblicalbetrothal.com/, and two articles from the popular press: Laurie Goodstein, "New Christian Take on the Old Dating Ritual," *New York Times*, September 9, 2001, and Jillian Melchior, "They Plight Their Troth—and Mean It," *Wall Street Journal*, April 11, 2008.

9 Elisabeth Elliot, *Through Gates of Splendor* (Wheaton, Ill.: Living Books, 1981), originally published by Harper & Row in 1957, and now available in a number of editions, including a comic book version edited by Al Hartley (Old Tappan, N.J.: Spire Christian Comics, 1974).

10 Harris, *I Kissed Dating Goodbye*, 12.

11 Elisabeth Elliot, *Passion and Purity: Learning to Bring Your Love Life Under Christ's Control* (Old Tappan, N.J.: Fleming H. Revell, 1984), 11.

12 Elliot, *Passion and* Purity, 179.

13 Elisabeth Elliot, *Let Me Be a Woman: Notes to My Daughter on the Meaning of Womanhood* (Wheaton, Ill.: Tyndale House, 1976), ix.

14 Elliot, *Let Me Be a Woman*, 134, 50, 112. This argument from anatomy echoes a similar text in *Passion and Purity* (109), where Elliot notes, "Males, as the physical design alone would show, are made to be initiators. Females are made to be receptors, responders."

15 Elliot, *Passion and Purity*, 29.

16 Elliot, *Passion and Purity*, 175.

17 Elliot, *Let Me Be a Woman*, 97.

18 Elliot, *Let Me Be a Woman*, 136.

19 Elliot, *Let Me Be a Woman*, 118–19.

20 Elliot, *Let Me Be a Woman*, 44.

21 Elliot, *Passion and Purity*, 84–90.

22 Elliot, *Passion and Purity*, 109–10.

23 Elliot, *Passion and Purity*, 97; *Let Me Be a Woman*, 16.

24 Harris, *I Kissed Dating Goodbye*, 97.

25 Harris, *Boy Meets Girl*, 117. Harris claims on p. 119 that there are a few areas in which women can take charge. "Encouraging men to lead and to initiate doesn't mean that girls never start a conversation or have ideas for activities," he explains. "My coworker Dawn and her three roommates make a practice of inviting a group of guys over for dinner every two weeks."

26 Harris, *Boy Meets Girl*, 110–11.

27 Harris, *Boy Meets Girl*, 151.

28 Harris, *Boy Meets Girl*, 145.

29 Harris, *Boy Meets Girl*, 165–66. Emphasis in original.

30 Harris, *Boy Meets Girl*, 145.

31 Harris, *Boy Meets Girl*, 12.

32 Harris, *Boy Meets Girl*, 218.

33 Harris, *Boy Meets Girl*, 220.

34 Joshua Harris, *Not Even a Hint: Guarding Your Heart Against Lust* (Sisters, Ore.: Multnomah, 2003), 86. Harris warns here that temptation is gender specific: "Men are tempted by the *pleasure* lust offers, while women are tempted by the *power* lust promises."

35 Harris, *Not Even a Hint*, 66–67, 76, 86, 91.

36 Harris, *Not Even a Hint*, 91–92, 137–38, 149.

37 Harris' website is http://www.joshharris.com/; the Ludys' is http://www.ellerslie.com/Eric_and_Leslie_Ludy.html.

38 It would not be surprising if Harris concludes in the future that men and women should not sit together (or perhaps not even in sight of one another) during worship.

39 Peggy Orenstein, *Cinderella Ate My Daughter: Dispatches from the Front Lines of the New Girly-Girl Culture* (New York: HarperCollins, 2011), 34–35, 23.

40 Orenstein, *Cinderella Ate My Daughter*, 23–25. Emphasis in original.

41 Sheila Walsh, *God's Little Princess Devotional Bible* (Nashville, Tenn.: Thomas Nelson, 1999). Her companion boys' Bible is *God's Mighty Warrior Devotional Bible* (Nashville, Tenn.: Thomas Nelson, 2007).

42 PINC is an acronym for "Purity & Identity in Christ" (http://www.pincministries.com). See http://www.pincministries.com/video.php for an appropriately pink video introduction to the site (accessed August 11, 2011). On the PINC website (www.pincministries.com), there are articles on "healthy holiday tips," "how to PINC your church," etc.

43 http://www.reviveourhearts.com/aboutus/nancy.php (accessed August 11, 2011).

44 "The True Woman Manifesto," http://www.truewoman.com/?id=980 (accessed June 7, 2012).

45 http://www.pureinheartconference.com/about/ (accessed August 11, 2011).

46 http://www.pureinheartconference.com/faq/ (accessed August 11, 2011).

47 http://www.pureinheartconference.com/video/ (accessed August 11, 2011).

48 Jennie Bishop and Susan Henson, *Life Lessons from the Princess and the Kiss: Planting Seeds of Purity in Young Hearts* (Niles, Mich.: Revive Our Hearts, 2004). The girls' series was so successful that it spawned a series for boys in 2004 called *The Squire and the Scroll*.

49 Bishop and Henson, *Life Lessons from the Princess and the Kiss*, 52–57.

50 Bishop and Henson, *Life Lessons from the Princess and the Kiss*, 32–33, 36.

51 http://uniquelyfashionedforhisglory.blogspot.com/p/committed-to-being-christs-valentine.html (accessed August 11, 2011).

52 http://www.facebook.com/pages/Christian-PrinceSS-TM/157409616070 (accessed August 11, 2011).

53 Sarah Mally, *Before You Meet Prince Charming: A Guide to Radiant Purity* (Cedar Rapids, Iowa: Tomorrow's Forefathers, 2009), 228–30.

54 Pam Farrel and Doreen Hanna, *Raising a Modern-Day Princess: Inspiring Purpose, Value, and Strength in Your Daughter*, A Focus on the Family Book (Carol Stream, Ill.: Tyndale House, 2009), back cover, 2. The book was conceived as a companion to Robert Lewis' *Raising a Modern-Day Knight*, A Focus on the Family Book, rev. ed. (Carol Stream, Ill.: Tyndale House, 2007), aimed at boys.

55 Farrel and Hanna, *Raising a Modern-Day Princess*, 89–90, 226.

56 Farrel and Hanna, *Raising a Modern-Day Princess*, 108.

57 Farrel and Hanna, *Raising a Modern-Day Princess*, 90.

58 Danna Gresh, *8 Great Dates for Moms & Daughters: How to Talk True Beauty, Cool Fashion, and . . . Modesty!* (Eugene, Ore.: Harvest House, 2010), back cover. The front cover has the following endorsement from James Dobson: "I wish Secret Keeper Girl had been available when our daughter was moving through her tweens. She and her mother would have loved sharing these 'great dates' together." In the acknowledgments, Gresh also thanks Dobson for recommending *8 Great Dates* in his book *Bringing Up Girls* (Carol Stream, Ill.: Tyndale House, 2010).

   Hair care is something of an obsession with Gresh—she devotes an entire page to it later in the book, including detailed instructions on how much shampoo to use, how to massage it into the scalp, how to rinse effectively, and when to brush.

59 Gresh, *8 Great Dates*, 98–99.

60 Gresh, *8 Great Dates*, 35, 47, 50–51.

61 Gresh, *8 Great Dates*, 29, 81, 142. Gresh explains how her daughter Lexi respects Jesus with her take on the punk rock look. "She never compromises on keeping the look full of life. She pairs black jeans with a black-and-white striped T-shirt, then add a splash of real-life color to it with a hot-pink scarf."

62 "Because we cherish our daughters as regal princesses," Purely Woman School of Grace, http://generationsoflight.myicontrol.com/html/theschoolofgrace.html (accessed July 6, 2012).

63 "About the Event," Vision Forum, http://www.visionforumministries.org/events/fdr/008/ (accessed June 7, 2012).

64 See the Vision Forum home page at http://www.visionforum.com/ (accessed June 6, 2012).

65 The premise that Christian parents should abjure birth control and have as many children as God gives them is known in evangelical Protestantism as the Quiverfull Movement. See Rick and Jan Hess, *A Full Quiver: Family Planning and the Lordship of Christ* (Nashville, Tenn.: Wolgemuth & Hyatt, 1989) for a classic statement of the position. For a critique—including materials on Vision Forum and the stay-at-home daughter movement—see Kathryn Joyce, *Quiverfull: Inside the Christian Patriarchy Movement* (Boston: Beacon, 2009). Kate Dixon's article "Multiply and Conquer: How to Have 17 Children and Still Believe in Jesus," from *Bitch: Feminist Response to Popular Culture* 37 (2007) is available at http://bitchmagazine.org/article/multiply-and-conquer (accessed June 7, 2012). For an example of a family practicing Quiverfull principles, see the Duggars at their family website, http://duggarfamily.com/ (accessed June 7, 2012), and at The Learning Channel, http://tlc.howstuffworks.com/tv/19-kids-and-counting (accessed June 7, 2012).

   Quivering Daughters is a website that seeks to address the consequences faced by daughters raised in families that practice biblical patriarchy, as does another site called No Longer Quivering. See http://www.quiveringdaughters.com/ (accessed June 7, 2012) and http://nolongerquivering.com/ (accessed June 7, 2012). Cheryl Lindsey Seelhoff, who left the movement after a spectacularly contentious brouhaha, tells some of her story in "Confronting the Religious Right," *Off Our Backs* 36, no. 3 (2006): 18–25. For more of Seelhoff's work, see Women's Space, http://womensspace.wordpress.com/some-articles-and-books-about-me-or-relevant-to-my-life-and-history/ (accessed June 7, 2012).

66   "The Tenets of Biblical Patriarchy," http://www.visionforumministries.org/home/about/biblical_patriarchy.aspx. Vision Forum offers innumerable products related to biblical patriarchy. An indication of its dedication to this theme is that the "Patriarchy Made Simple" set has fifteen compact discs. Readers can browse the Vision Forum catalog at http://www.visionforum.com/browse/productlist/?cid=625 (accessed June 7, 2012). An anonymous contributor to the Wartburg Watch has satirized Vision Forum culture and products in a piece called "Life in Vision Forum Land." The inhabitants of Vision Forum Land exist in "a place called Perfect" in which men run the show while women and children exist at the margins ("men vote for the household. And women do not vote at all"), young girls dream of ideal relationships ("pretty girls marry Vision Forum interns. And the not-so pretty ones stay home with Mother and Father"), and family life is seen as a means to a very specific end ("having a baby is referred to as Militant Fecundity. And you name your child Modeste Perseverance Truth"). See "Doug Phillips—Home-schooling Guru and QF Proponent," http://thewartburgwatch.com/2009/07/21/doug-phillips-homeschooling-guru-and-qf-proponent/ (accessed August 9, 2011). For a cri-tique of Vision Forum by a former adherent, see "The Search for the Perfect Church," Jen's Gems, December 10, 2006, http://jensgems.wordpress.com/2006/12/10/the-search-for-the-perfect-church/ (accessed August 9, 2011).

67   Geoffrey Botkin, *Training Dominion-Oriented Daughters*, DVD (San Antonio, Tex.: Vision Forum Ministries, 2008). Botkin goes on at length to explain the domestic sciences involved in a tea party: "[T]he tablecloth, you look at that, it represents advanced . . . tex-tile and sewing arts. Civilizations need that—textile, textile arts. The china represents advanced artistry in porcelain and specialization in honorable utensils. It also repre-sents we're living in a time of peace: our dishes are not being broken up by the advancing hordes. The food—advanced chemistry and creativity in nutrition and culinary delights as well as animal husbandry. Flowers represent plant husbandry and gardening. The flow-ers that will be on our table today—they're healthy, they're not all eaten up by bugs and diseases. Girls, if we can plant flowers and care for them, that means we can plant other things for Dominion."

68   Emily Rose of Indiana, "The 2010 Vision Forum Father Daughter Retreat," simply vintage-girl, http://www.simplyvintagegirl.com/blog/index.php/2010/04/05/the-2010-vision-forum-father-daughter-retreat/ (accessed June 7, 2012).

69   "2010 Father and Daughter Retreat," Vision Forum Ministries, http://www.visionforumministries.org/events/fdr/gallery/181/ (accessed June 7, 2012).

70   "The Father & Daughter Retreat," Vision Forum Ministries, http://www.visionforumministries.org/events/fdr/ (accessed June 7, 2012), offers pictures of fathers and daugh-ters bonding at the retreats.

71   See Anna Sofia and Elizabeth Botkin, *So Much More: The Remarkable Influence of Vision-ary Daughters on the Kingdom of God* (San Antonio, Tex.: Vision Forum, 2005). See also the website Overcoming Botkin Syndrome at http://botkinsyndrome.blogspot.com/ (accessed June 7, 2012). The site defines Botkin Syndrome as the "dysfunctional dynamics and long-term effects of the teachings of the Botkin Sisters and Vision Forum (Covert/emotional incest, non-sexual but gender related incest intermingled with the . . . teachings of patriarchy/patriocentricity)." Other Internet resources critical of the Botkins and biblical patriarchy include Gina McGalliard's "House Proud: The Troubling Rise of Stay-At-Home Daughters," *Bitch Magazine*, http://bitchmagazine.org/article/

house-proud (accessed June 7, 2012); and a site called Free Jinger Quiver Full of Snark (http://freejinger.org/viewforum.php?f=8). Original discussions are at "Candid Reality Shows," Television without Pity, http://forums.televisionwithoutpity.com/index .php?showtopic=3120234 (accessed June 7, 2012); current ones can be found at "Quiver Full of Snark," "Quiver Full of Chatter," "Quiver Full of Worldly Distractions," http:// freejinger.org/index.php (accessed August 9, 2011); and the numerous articles at Wartburg Watch, http://thewartburgwatch.com/?s=Botkin (accessed August 9, 2011).

Critics often express a horrid fascination with the Botkin sisters, uncertain whether their enthusiasm about subordinating themselves to men is genuine or an example of Stockholm syndrome. Geoffrey Botkin suggests that the problem is not with his daughters, but with their detractors, whom he describes as either so "intimidated or impressed by what they see that it's as though my daughters are on the offensive and all they're doing is standing there like ladies and responding in a Godly Christ-honoring way. And literally it is completely intimidating to the wicked." See his *Training Dominion-Oriented Daughters* DVD.

72 Anna Sofia and Elizabeth Botkin, *The Return of the Daughters*, DVD (Centerville, Tenn.: Western Conservatory of the Arts and Sciences, 2007); Anna Sofia and Elizabeth Botkin, *What Is Biblical Femininity? Cultivating Sturdy Virtue in Today's Daughters*, DVD (San Antonio, Tex.: Vision Forum Ministries, 2008).

73 Anna Sofia and Elizabeth Botkin, "Authoritative Parents, Adult Daughters, and Power Struggles," Visionary Daughters, May 14, 2007, http://visionarydaughters .com/2007/05/authoritative-parents-adult-daughters-and-power-struggles (accessed August 9, 2011), and *What Is Biblical Femininity?*

74 Botkin and Botkin, "Authoritative Parents, Adult Daughters."

75 Botkin and Botkin, *So Much More*, 35, 40.

76 Quoted in Anna Sofia and Elizabeth Botkin, "The Baucham Family," in *Return of the Daughters*. Jasmine Baucham has written a book about being a stay-at-home daughter titled *Joyfully at Home: A Book for Young Ladies on Vision and Hope* (San Antonio, Tex.: Vision Forum, 2010). By 2012 she was working with a publisher on a possible two-book contract, about to finish an online BA, and considering a master's degree in humanities, philosophy, or American literature as well as helping to care for her five siblings aged five and younger. See All She Has to Say, http://allshehastosay.blogspot.com/search?updated -min=2012-01-01T00:00:00-06:00&updated-max=2013-01-01T00:00:00-06:00 &max-results=6 (accessed June 7, 2012). See August 1, 2010, http://allshehastosay .blogspot.com/ and July 27, 2010, http://allshehastosay.blogspot.com/2011/06/on -schooling.html#more (accessed August 9, 2011).

77 Douglas W. Phillips, *Sleeping Beauty and the Five Questions: A Parable about the Hearts of Fathers and Daughters*, CD audio book (San Antonio, Tex.: Vision Forum, 2004).

78 Phillips, *Sleeping Beauty and the Five Questions*.

79 Botkin and Botkin, *So Much More*, 328.

80 Botkin and Botkin, *What Is Biblical Femininity?*

81 Douglas Phillips, "Never Been Kissed: A Home-School Love Story," Vision Forum, June 9, 2001, http://www.visionforum.com/news/newsletters/newsletter.aspx?id=07-19-01 (no longer active).

82 Geoffrey Botkin, "What Is Biblical Femininity? More Than Tea and Tassels," in *What Is Biblical Femininity?* In a similar passage, Doug Phillips describes the Christian family as a vibrant vehicle of cultural transformation and contends that the war confronting the present generation of American Christians is the battle for the family (*Sleeping Beauty and the Five Questions*).

83   Anna Sofia Botkin, in *What Is Biblical Femininity?*

84   Phillips, *Sleeping Beauty and the Five Questions.*

85   Botkin, "What Is Biblical Femininity?"

86   Elizabeth Botkin, in *What Is Biblical Femininity?*

87   Elizabeth Botkin, in *Return of the Daughters.*

88   Elizabeth Botkin, *What Is Biblical Femininity?*

89   "Who Is Eric Ludy?," http://www.ericludy.com/Home.html (accessed August 5, 2011).

90   Eric and Leslie Ludy, *Wrestling Prayer: A Passionate Communion with God* (Eugene, Ore.: Harvest House, 2009), 5–6.

91   Eric Ludy, *The Bravehearted Gospel: The Truth Is Worth Fighting For* (Eugene, Ore.: Harvest House, 2007), 19–20. In an interview with Israel Wayne (April 19, 2011), Eric described bravehearted Christianity as "martyr-ready" and "the stuff of Jesus Christ [that] . . . should be drilled into the bedrock of every believing soul." He urged women of faith to be completed by the "strength, boldness, courage, and fortitude of Christ," calling them to live the gospel with "epic grandeur." Israel Wayne, "The Bravehearted Gospel—Interview w/Eric Ludy," Christian Worldview, http://www.christianworldview.net/2011/the-bravehearted-gospel-interview-w-eric-ludy/ (accessed August 5, 2011).

92   Eric and Leslie Ludy, *When God Writes Your Love Story* (Sisters, Ore.: Multnomah, 1999), 141.

93   Leslie Ludy, *Authentic Beauty: The Shaping of a Set-Apart Young Woman* (Sisters, Ore.: Multnomah, 2003), 56.

94   Leslie Ludy, *Authentic Beauty*, 36–37. The desire for a prince is essentially countercultural, she claims. Unfortunately, most men are sexual predators, not princes; secular science reduces romance and sexuality to biological urges; and women learn to look out for themselves, not to yield in trust to their knight in shining armor. In short, "we live in a world that seeks to destroy all that is princesslike and feminine within us" (37).

95   Leslie Ludy, *Authentic Beauty*, 56–59, 106–7, 189. Emphasis in original.

96   Leslie Ludy, *Authentic Beauty*, 169.

97   Eric Ludy, "The Making of Warriors," in Leslie Ludy, *Authentic Beauty*, http://www.scribd.com/doc/94031463/Authentic-Beauty-The-Shaping-of-a-Set-Apart-Young-Woman (accessed June 7, 2012); Eric Ludy, *God's Gift to Women: Discovering the Lost Greatness of Masculinity* (Sisters, Ore.: Multnomah, 2003), 56–59, 62, 123, 213.

98   Eric Ludy, *God's Gift to Women*, 187, 253. Emphasis in original.

99   Eric and Leslie Ludy, *The First 90 Days of Marriage: Building the Foundation of a Lifetime* (Nashville, Tenn.: Thomas Nelson, 2006), 98–99.

100   Ludy and Ludy, *First 90 Days of Marriage*, 113, 95–96.

101   Ludy and Ludy, *First 90 Days of Marriage*, 99–100. Emphasis in original.

102   Ludy and Ludy, *First 90 Days of Marriage*, 100.

103   Leslie Ludy, *Authentic Beauty*, 233–34. In *When God Writes Your Love Story*, Eric's chapter, "The Art of Faithfulness," is similarly confident, describing fidelity as a "skill to learn long before the wedding vows" (113). Harris admiringly describes the Ludys' marriage as highly physical (suggesting that they cannot keep their hands off one another) and is impressed that before their marriage they were able to refrain from physical contact without undue struggle. Harris, *I Kissed Dating Goodbye*, 56.

104   Leslie Ludy, *Authentic Beauty*, 123. At times, that means cutting back on their Christian ministry. As Leslie notes, "In modern Christian ministry, Eric and I have discovered that it is all too easy to become so preoccupied with pointing others to Jesus Christ that we can easily forget to point *ourselves* to Him on a daily basis. . . . We put restrictions on how many speaking engagements we would accept each year. We did not hold ministry-related

meetings on weekends or during evenings. We set aside uninterrupted time every morning of the week for prayer, Bible study, and personal spiritual growth. We set aside time during the week for focusing on each other" (151).

105 Eric Ludy, "The Making of Poets," http://www.scribd.com/doc/94031463/Authentic -Beauty-The-Shaping-of-a-Set-Apart-Young-Woman (accessed June 7, 2012). The most he will concede here is that relational intimacy will lead to "increased sexual passion."

Chapter 2

1 Harris, *Boy Meets Girl*, 43.

2 Adam Meet Eve, for example, states, "Attention Christian website owners, and webmasters: earn more money—help single Christians. Increase your site revenue when you host a banner or text links on your website. For each single Christian you send to our website who joins as a paying member you earn 40% of the total subscription fees + 40% for all renewal fees!" See http://www.adammeeteve.com/pages/link2us.html (accessed June 7, 2012).

3 See Adam Meet Eve, http://www.adammeeteve.com/pages/home.html (accessed June 7, 2012).

4 For a full list of Spark Networks holdings, see http://www.spark.net/sites.htm (accessed February 17, 2012).

5 Mary Madden and Amanda Lenhart, *Online Dating* (Washington, D.C.: Pew Internet & American Life Project, 2006), available in full online at http://www.pewinternet.org/ Reports/2006/Online-Dating/01-Summary-of-Findings.aspx (accessed June 7, 2012).

6 Soul Mate for Christians, targeting African Americans, http://www.soulmateforchris tians.com/index.php (accessed January 21, 2012); Adam and Eve Singles, http://adam andevesingles.com; Christian Soulmate, http://www.christiansoulmate.com; Christian Soulmates, http://christiansoulmates.com; Adam Meet Eve, http://www.adammeeteve .com/pages/home.html; ChristianityOasisSoulMateSearchers,http://www.christianity oasis.com/SoulMateSearchers.

7 This text is also referenced by Jesus in Matthew 19:4-6.

8 Mature Singles Only, http://www.maturesinglesonly.com; Mature Professional Singles, http://www.matureprofessionalsingles.org; Senior People Meet, http://lps.senior peoplemeet.com; Top 10 Best Dating Sites, http://www.top10bestdatingsites.com; Double Your Dating, http://www.doubleyourdating.com; Catch Him & Keep Him, http:// www.catchhimandkeephim.com; Catholic Mingle, http://www.catholicmingle.com.

9 Christian Soulmates, http://christiansoulmates.com/aboutus.aspx (accessed January 21, 2012).

10 Christian Soulmates, http://www.christiansoulmates.com/Index.aspx?noaccess=yes (accessed January 21, 2012). Another page specifies that members must be at least eighteen years old, so the reference to "girls" as well as women is presumably inadvertent. See http://www.christiansoulmates.com/Welcome.aspx (accessed January 30, 2012).

11 Christian Soulmates, http://www.christiansoulmates.com/MySearchAdmin.aspx (accessed January 21, 2012).

12 Adam Meet Eve, http://www.adammeeteve.com/pages/home.html (accessed January 21, 2012). The home page notes that while Christians should not feel compelled to marry—the site concedes that Jesus did not—for those in whom "God has planted . . . the desire for a mate there is nothing 'wrong' with seeking a Godly Christian mate."

13 Adam Meet Eve, http://www.adammeeteve.com/pages/bornagain.html (accessed November 13, 2011).

14 Adam Meet Eve, http://www.adammeeteve.com/#christian-dating-sites-reviews (accessed November 13, 2011).

15   Adam Meet Eve, http://www.adammeeteve.com/pages/spotlight.html (accessed January 21, 2012).

16   Rose Sweet, *Dear God, Send Me a Soul Mate* (Chattanooga, Tenn.: AMG, 2002).

17   Adam Meet Eve, http://www.adammeeteve.com/pages/statement.html (accessed January 21, 2012).

18   Adam Meet Eve, http://www.adammeeteve.com/pages/bornagain.html (accessed January 21, 2012).

19   Joining Adam Meet Eve entails joining ChristianCafe, which charges $47.97 for a three-month membership. See ChristianCafe, http://www.christiancafe.com/membership/index.jsp? (accessed January 21, 2012).

20   Adam Meet Eve, http://www.adammeeteve.com/pages/tell2.html (accessed January 21, 2012).

21   Christian Dating Watchdog (whose masthead reads "Keeping 'Christian' in Christian Dating") reports that Neil Clark Warren, eHarmony's founder, now declines appearances on Dobson's radio show and that Warren bought back the rights to the three books he authored that Focus on the Family published, including *Finding the Love of Your Life* and *Learning to Live with the Love of Your Life*. Watchdog has withdrawn its support for eHarmony, calling Warren a humanist and criticizing eHarmony because it "does not reject on the basis of religion." Watchdog also objects to Warren's willingness to help other sites match gays and lesbians and notes, disapprovingly, that Warren told NPR's Terri Gross that he was not concerned that eHarmony members were likely to have premarital sex. See http://www.christiandatingwatchdog.com/eharmony.html (accessed January 21, 2012).

22   See "eHarmony Sued for Exclusion of Homosexuals," n.d., Date Hookup, http://www.datehookup.com/content-eharmony-sued-for-exclusion-of-homosexuals.htm;   Beth DeFalco, "eHarmony Agrees to Provide Same-Sex Matches," MSNBC, November 20, 2008, http://www.msnbc.msn.com/id/27821393/ns/technology_and_science-tech_and_gadgets/t/eharmony-agrees-provide-same-sex-matches/#.T8E90MXpykc; Elizabeth Holmes, "EHarmony's Same-Sex Dating Site Launches," *Wall Street Journal*, March 31, 2009, http://blogs.wsj.com/digits/2009/03/31/eharmonys-same-sex-dating-site-launches/ (all accessed May 26, 2012).

23   As Nick Paumgarten put it in "Looking for Someone: Sex, Love, and Loneliness on the Internet" (*The New Yorker*, July 4, 2011), "The clean-shaven gentleman on the couch, with the excellent posture, the pastel golf shirt, and that strangely chaste yet fiery look in his eye? That would be eHarmony. EHarmony is the squarest of the [online dating] sites, but one most overtly geared toward finding your spouse." http://www.newyorker.com/reporting/2011/07/04/110704fa_fact_paumgarten (accessed August 1, 2012).

24   "Meet the Man behind eHarmony," eHarmony, http://www.eharmony.com/ (accessed January 21, 2012). The site claims that "millions of people of all ages, ethnicities, and religious backgrounds have used eHarmony's patented Compatibility Matching System™ to find the love of their lives." Since 2006, eHarmony has been operating a "marriage wellness" program as well as its dating service. See "Company Overview," http://www.eharmony.com/servlet/about/eharmony (accessed January 21, 2012).

25   Even in a Christian thread, the participants are likely to answer a question like "What exactly does a Christian guy want?" with a cheeky reply like this from Mystikchik: "What christian [*sic*] guys want is a servile chick who will shut up in church and at home, someone who will submit to the headship of some guy simply because both the man and their god have penises." See http://advice.eharmony.com/?page=view_thread&TID=10232 (accessed January 30, 2012). Or in answer to the question "Is There One Perfect Person for

Me?" a member may announce, "i believe that we live many lifetimes in order to grow and learn the necessary lessons needed for spiritual enlightenment. This means that we must also spend many lifetimes with each other. so i believe that a soul mate is someone you are already familiar with although you may not realize or know why you are drawn to them." See Yeeshababy, http://advice.eharmony.com/?page=view_thread&TID=743&start=1 (accessed January 30, 2012).

26 At eHarmony, see "Ask a Dating Expert," http://advice.eharmony.com/boards/dating -advice/ask-dating-expert/; "Dating Advice Boards," http://advice.eharmony.com/ boards/; and "Groups," http://advice.eharmony.com/boards/off-topic/groups/ and http://advice.eharmony.com/boards/on-topic/groups/ (all accessed January 21, 2012).

27 Google search, https://www.google.com/search?hl=en&q=Find+your+soulmate&oq= Find+your+soulmate&aq=f&aqi=g6g-s1g3&aql=&gs_sm=e&gs_upl=185225l18653 6l0l1871002l2l0l0l0l0l191l28411.1l2l0, and https://www.google.com/search?q=find +your+soulmate (accessed February 3, 2012).

28 "My Matches," eHarmony, http://www.eharmony.com/singles/servlet/welcome?cmd =welcome (accessed April 18, 2008), and http://www.eharmony.com/singles/servlet/ about/difference (accessed April 23, 2008).

29 "Meet Christian Singles on eHarmony," http://www.eharmony.com/christian-dating (accessed February 3, 2012).

30 Neil Clark Warren with Ken Abraham, *Falling in Love for All the Right Reasons: How to Find Your Soul Mate* (New York: Center Street, 2005), xiv.

31 Warren and Abraham, *Falling in Love for All the Right Reasons*, 236, 30.

32 Neil Clark Warren, "Is There One Perfect Person for Me?," eHarmony, http://advice .eharmony.com/dating/important-questions/is-there-one-perfect-person-for-me (accessed February 3, 2012).

33 "Why eHarmony?," eHarmony, http://www.eharmony.com/singles/servlet/about/ difference (accessed April 23, 2008).

34 "Focus on the Family: Single Ministry Discussion," ChristianCafe, http://www.christian cafe.com/blog/253/focus-on-the-family (accessed February 17, 2012).

35 More precisely, Moorcroft defines ChristianCafe's niche as "primarily born-again/evan-gelical/fundamentalist/non-denominational/Biblical Christian/Conservative Prot-estants." See David Evans, "ChristianCafe.com and Single Christian Network Merge," Online Dating Insider, May 29, 2009, http://onlinedatingpost.com/archives/2009/05/ christiancafecom-and-single-christian-network-merge/ (accessed January 10, 2012).

36 "Surf and Ye Shall Find: Christian Dating on the Internet," Canadian Christianity, http:// canadianchristianity.com/bc/bccn/0907/04surf.html (accessed February 15, 2012).

37 Krystyna Slivinski, "Catering to Christian Daters," University of Western Ontario News, March 27, 2008, http://communications.uwo.ca/com/alumni_gazette/alumni_stories/ catering_to_christian_daters_20080327441902/ (accessed December 19, 2011).

38 "Contacting Members," http://www.christiancafe.com/membership/index.jsp? (accessed February 17, 2012).

39 David Evans, "How to Run a Successful Online Dating Site," Online Dating Insider, June 19, 2009, http://onlinedatingpost.com/archives/2009/06/how-to-run-a-successful -online-dating-site/ (accessed January 10, 2012).

40 "How to Write an Appealing Dating Profile," ChristianCafe, http://www.christiancafe .com/members/help/howto_write_better_profile.jsp? (accessed November 16, 2011). Moorcroft offers virtually identical advice at the "How to Write an Appealing Dat-ing Profile," JewishCafe, http://www.jewishcafe.com/members/help/howto-write _better_profile.jsp? (accessed February 18, 2012).

41 ChristianCafe discussion threads on these topics include "Soul Mate," http://www

.christiancafe.com/members/forums/thread.jsp?id=874&category=23; "Do You Believe in Soulmates?" http://www.christiancafe.com/members/forums/thread.jsp?id=6476&category=41; "*Soul Mate* Versus Kindred Spirit," http://www.christiancafe.com/members/forums/thread.jsp?id=4581&category=41; "Finding the One," http://www.christiancafe.com/members/forums/thread.jsp?id=2845&category=24; "How Do You Know That He Is 'the One'?" http://www.christiancafe.com/members/forums/thread.jsp?id=4515&category=41; "Should the Man Make the First Move?" http://www.christiancafe.com/members/forums/thread.jsp?id=2268&category=23; "Women Taking the Lead," http://www.christiancafe.com/members/forums/thread.jsp?id=6932&category=41; "Emailing Guys," http://www.christiancafe.com/members/forums/thread.jsp?id=5042&category=23; "How to Let a Guy Lead," http://www.christiancafe.com/members/forums/thread.jsp?id=2353&category=23 (all accessed February 19, 2012).

42   Apkerr536, "What's the Point," ChristianCafe, September 17, 2011, http://www.christiancafe.com/members/forums/thread.jsp?id=5305&category=28 (accessed February 19, 2012).

43   The 139 posts in this thread titled "Feminism? Or a Biblical woman?" at ChristianCafe began on March 7, 2011, at http://www.christiancafe.com/members/forums/thread.jsp?id=641&category=24 (accessed December 19, 2011) and run for fourteen pages. All quotations from ChristianCafe members in this section come from this thread.

44   Sam Moorcroft and Lisa Anderson, host of *The Boundless Show*, "Focus on the Family: Singles Ministry Discussion," Christian Blog, December 1, 2010, http://www.christiancafe.com/blog/253/focus-on-the-family (accessed February 14, 2012).

45   Lisa Anderson, in "Focus on the Family: Singles Ministry Discussion." Anderson quotes Carolyn McCulley, "Men trust God by risking, whereas women trust God by waiting."

46   For insiders in the online dating world, the announcement did not come out of the blue. Sam Moorcroft had a long association with Focus on the Family. Boundless had interviewed him; he had interviewed Boundless writers for his own blog; he had written articles for Boundless; and Boundless had run a number of articles on ChristianCafe, including an October first-person narrative about joining ChristianCafe and writing a dating profile. David Evans in Online Dating Insider opined that ChristianCafe could not "get much closer to your optimum customer" than Boundless and congratulated Moorcroft on the "partnership win." David Evans, "ChristianCafe.com's Future Is Boundless," Online Dating Insider, November 7, 2011, http://onlinedatingpost.com/archives/2011/11/christian-cafe-coms-future-is-boundless/ (accessed December 19, 2011).

47   Boundless did not close its own online dating service or merge Marry Well with ChristianCafe.

48   After acquiring Single Christian Network in 2009, Moorcroft announced, "We look forward to working with other direct competitors in the near future, as things consolidate even more. If you are one of those, we'd love to talk!" Evans, "How to Run a Successful Online Dating Site.".

49   Focus on the Family claims to reach 238 million people in over 130 countries. See "Boundless.org Joins Forces with Online Dating Service ChristianCafe.com," Focus on the Family, November 7, 2011, http://www.focusonthefamily.com/about_us/news_room/news-releases/20111107-boundless-focus-on-the-familys-outreach-to-single-adults-joins-forces-with-christian-cafe.aspx (accessed February 21, 2012).

50   Fred, "Dating 101—Dating Advice from a Christian Perspective," ChristianCafe, November 11, 2011, http://www.christiancafe.com/members/blog/index.jsp? (accessed February 21, 2012).

51   Bestcompanion621 kicked off the conversation by condemning Focus on the Family's "political posturing" and "simplistic understandings." He warned, "ChristianCafe should not assume that we are all of one conservative stripe that thinks FOTF are a great bunch. I do not." Tmar229 dubbed the partnership "a terrible idea" and suggested that Christian-Cafe was only concerned about "how they can put more money in their pockets." All the posts cited here are from a ChristianCafe thread titled "Focus on the Family Alliance," begun on November 14, 2011, http://www.christiancafe.com/members/forums/thread .jsp?id=6543&category=30 (accessed February 21, 2012).

52   Albert Mohler, "Reflecting on 'The Mystery of Marriage,'" Boundless, March 19, 2010, http://www.boundless.org/2005/articles/a0001244.cfm (accessed January 10, 2012). All citations from this article are from this site.

53   Albert Mohler, "About," http://www.albertmohler.com/about/ (accessed May 26, 2012).

54   Alex and Brett Harris, "Addicted to Adultescence," Boundless Webzine, February 16, 2006 , http://www.boundless.org/2005/articles/a0001217.cfm (accessed February 24, 2012). The Harrises were eighteen when this article was published.

55   Psalm67 commenting on Motte Brown, "Did Tebow 'Kiss Dating Goodbye'?" The Lodge, January 18, 2012, http://lodge.marrywell.org/2012/01/tebow-kiss-dating-goodbye/ (accessed February 21, 2012).

56   Drew Dyck, "Pursue Her," Boundless Webzine, May 16, 2008, http://www.boundless .org/2005/articles/a0001750.cfm (accessed May 26, 2012).

57   Michael Lawrence, "Real Men Risk Rejection," Boundless Webzine, February 8, 2007, http://www.boundless.org/2005/articles/a0001443.cfm (accessed February 28, 2010).

58   Scott Stanley, "Myths about Soul Mates," Boundless Webzine, June 4, 2009, http://www .boundless.org/2005/articles/a0001123.cfm (accessed November 16, 2011).

59   Gary Thomas, "Soul Mates or Sole Mates?," Boundless Webzine, October 13, 2005, http://www.boundless.org/2005/articles/a0001156.cfm (accessed November 16, 2011).

60   Scott Croft, "Biblical Dating: Navigating the Early Stages of a Relationship," Bound-less Webzine, May 31, 2007, http://www.boundless.org/2005/articles/a0001512.cfm (accessed November 11, 2011).

61   Scott Croft, "Brother, You're Like a Six," Boundless Webzine, October 19, 2009, reis-sued June 1, 2012, http://www.boundless.org/2005/articles/a0001371.cfm (accessed December 2, 2011). Emphasis in original.

62   Gary Thomas, "Mary Sooner Rather Than Later," Boundless Webzine, March 15, 2009, http://www.boundless.org/2005/articles/a0001992.cfm (accessed February 24, 2012).

63   Thomas, "Soul Mates or Sole Mates?"

64   Croft, "Biblical Dating."

65   Suzanne Hadley Gosselin, "Trusting God with Relationships, Part 2," Boundless Web-zine, February 12, 2010, http://www.boundless.org/2005/articles/a0002235.cfm (accessed February 20, 2012). Hadley Gosselin was very much with the program in this article, contending that "God worked in spectacular and specific ways" to bring her and her husband together.

66   Candice Watters, quoted in Beth Brown, "Seizing Opportunities, Part 1," The Lodge, November 18, 2011, http://lodge.marrywell.org/2011/11/seizing-opportunities-part-1/ (accessed November 28, 2011). Watters confided elsewhere that she "almost didn't like it" the first time her future husband kissed her, but that over time she came to find him attractive—though ultimately what she most valued about her marriage was the com-panionship. See Candice Watters, "Not Attracted to Him," Boundless Webzine, May 10, 2010, http://www.boundless.org/2005/answers/a0002285.cfm (accessed November 29, 2011). In an interview with the Christian Broadcasting Network, Watters advised that,

to avoid unrealistic expectations, the best attitude to take into marriage was as follows: "'I have found the best possible mate that I can find given where I live, who I know and what I bring to the relationship.'" Given all this, no one will accuse Watters of excessive romanticism. Jennifer E. Jones, "Praying Boldly for a Husband," Christian Broadcasting Network, n.d., http://www.cbn.com/family/datingsingles/jej_candicewatters0108.aspx (accessed May 26, 2012).

67   Michael Lawrence, "I'm Just Not Attracted to Her, Part 2," Boundless Webzine, May 13, 2011, http://www.boundless.org/2005/articles/a0001528.cfm (accessed November 28, 2011).

68   Croft, "Brother, You're Like a Six." Emphasis in original.

69   A Girl's Guide to Marrying Well (Focus on the Family, 2009), 56–57, http://publ.com/BookData/QTCzP0p/seo/toc.html (accessed June 8, 2012).

70   Candice Gage, "You Never Marry the Right Person," The Lodge, January 16, 2012, http://lodge.marrywell.org/2012/01/marry-person/ (accessed February 25, 2012). Gage was quoting from Timothy and Kathy Keller's book, The Meaning of Marriage (New York: Dutton, 2011).

71   Gary Thomas, "Marry Sooner Rather Than Later," Boundless Webzine, March 13, 2009, http://www.boundless.org/2005/articles/a0001992.cfm (accessed February 24, 2012).

72   Camerin Courtney, "Is Singleness a Sin?" Christianity Today International, November 24, 2009, online at Crosswalk, http://www.crosswalk.com/11621125/ (accessed January 3, 2012); Gina R. Dalfonzo, "God Loves a Good Romance," Christianity Today, October 12, 2010, http://www.christianitytoday.com/ct/2010/octoberweb-only/51-21.0.html (accessed January 3, 2012).

73   Gina R. Dalfonzo, "The Good Christian Girl: A Fable," Christianity Today, July 9, 2010, http://www.christianitytoday.com/ct/2010/julyweb-only/59-11.0.html (accessed January 3, 2012).

74   "Marry Well 'Guy Drive,'" The Lodge, January 29, 2010, http://lodge.marrywell.org/2010/01/marry-well-guy-drive/ (accessed December 27, 2011).

75   USALady63, November 18, 2011, and JJD78, November 10, 2011, "Share Your Online Dating Experience," The Lodge, http://lodge.marrywell.org/2011/11/share-online-dating-experience/ (accessed November 20, 2011).

76   Motte Brown, "Marry Well Isn't for Everyone, But . . . ," The Lodge, January 21, 2011, and 1ForHistory comment, January 22, 2011, http://lodge.marrywell.org/2011/01/marry/ (accessed December 21, 2011).

77   Marry Well frequently reiterated that its "emphasis on men taking leadership in the relationship" made it distinctive in the world of online dating. See "Connecting," Marry Well, n.d., http://marrywell.org/connect/connect.php (accessed November 28, 2011).

78   Steve Watters, "Soul Mate Standard Leaving Many Americans Unmarried," The Lodge, December 7, 2010, http://lodge.marrywell.org/2010/12/soul-mate-standard-leaving-many-middle-americans-unmarried/ (accessed December 21, 2011).

79   David Murrow, "Where Have the Men Gone?" Boundless Webzine, January 25, 2012, http://www.boundless.org/2005/articles/a0002510.cfm (accessed February 21, 2012). Murrow argued that the single men remaining in the church were testosterone-challenged losers who were either Bible geeks, musical, asexual, predators, or social misfits.

80   Steve Watters, "Christian Boy Meets Christian Girl," The Lodge, May 25, 2011, http://lodge.marrywell.org/2011/05/christian-boy-meets-christian-girl/ (accessed December 21, 2011); and Susan Olasky, "Christian Boy Meets Christian Girl," World, June 4, 2011, http://www.worldmag.com/articles/18064 (accessed February 26, 2012).

81   Comment by Ehaven, May 28, 2011, on Watters, "Christian Boy Meets Christian Girl."

82   Comment by elena, May 27, 2011, on Watters, "Christian Boy Meets Christian Girl."

83   Comment by MissLea, March 7, 2011, on Motte Brown, "Soul Mate Babe," The Lodge, March 4, 2011, http://lodge.marrywell.org/2011/03/soul-mate-babe/ (accessed December 21, 2011).

84   Lydiann at Watters, "Christian Boy Meets Christian Girl."

85   MissLea at Motte Brown, "Ask Marry Well: Is It Okay for Women to Initiate?" The Lodge, January 24, 2011, http://lodge.marrywell.org/2011/01/marry-well-women-initiate/ (accessed December 21, 2011).

86   "Ask Marry Well: How Does a Woman 'Make Herself Known'?," The Lodge, March 24, 2010, http://lodge.marrywell.org/2010/03/ask-marry-well-how-does-a-woman-make -herself-known/ (accessed February 26, 2012).

87   Brown, "Ask Marry Well: Is It Okay for Women to Initiate?"

88   Candice Watters, "Pulling a Ruth, Part 2," Boundless Webzine, August 7, 2003, http:// www.boundless.org/2005/articles/a0001856.cfm (accessed February 26, 2012).

89   Candice Watters, "Ruth Revisited," Boundless Webzine, September 21, 2006, http:// www.boundless.org/2005/articles/a0001352.cfm (accessed February 26, 2012). In an unrelated work, Jackie Kendall also advises unmarried Christian women to avoid the bozos and find themselves a Boaz. See *A Man Worth Waiting For: How to Avoid a Bozo* (Nashville, Tenn.: FaithWords, 2008).

90   Candice Watters, *Get Married: What Women Can Do to Help It Happen* (Chicago: Moody, 2008). Watters was also enthusiastic about Debbie Maken's *Getting Serious about Getting Married: Rethinking the Gift of Singleness* (Wheaton, Ill.: Crossway Books, 2006). See Watters' "Getting to Marriage: What You Can Do," Boundless Webzine, April 20, 2006, http://www.boundless.org/2005/articles/a0001254.cfm (accessed June 8, 2012). Another Boundless author, A. J. Kiesling, wrote *Where Have All the Good Men Gone? Why So Many Christian Women Are Remaining Single* (Eugene, Ore.: Harvest House, 2008).

91   "Who We Are," Marry Well, http://marrywell.org/connect/about_us.php (accessed May 26, 2012).

92   Dennis Rainey, "Thinking Biblically about Marriage," *FamilyLife Today*, December 6, 2010, http://www.oneplace.com/ministries/familylife-today/listen/thinking -biblically-about-marriage-148975.html (accessed May 26, 2012).

Chapter 3

1   *Colbert Report*, "Yahweh or No Way: Online Christian Dating and Seven Days of Sex," January 17, 2012, http://www.colbertnation.com/the-colbert-report-videos/406123/ january-17-2012/yahweh-or-no-way---online-christian-dating---seven-days-of-sex. Colbert first reported on Young's sexperiment in January, 2009. Online at http://www .colbertnation.com/the-colbert-report-videos/216624/january-26-2009/ed-young (accessed March 23, 2012).

2   Ed and Lisa Young, *Sexperiment: 7 Days to Lasting Intimacy with Your Spouse* (New York: Faith Words, 2012).

3   Matthew Lee Anderson, "The Trouble with Ed Young's Rooftop Sexperiment," *Christianity Today*, January 12, 2012, http://www.christianitytoday.com/ct/2012/january web-only/ed-young-sexperiment.html (accessed March 14, 2012).

4   See the *New York Times*, http://www.nytimes.com/best-sellers-books/2012-01-22/ hardcover-advice/list.html (accessed March 23, 2012).

5   Mark and Grace Driscoll, *Real Marriage: The Truth about Sex, Friendship, & Life Together*, Kindle ed. (Nashville, Tenn.: Thomas Nelson, 2012), locations 1871, 2542.

6   Driscoll and Driscoll, *Real Marriage*, locations 3616, 3684–4157.

7   There are exceptions, naturally. Numerous online evangelical groups offer advice and sex

toys for married Christian couples interested in spicing up their love life. Christian Love Toys offers free Bibles to customers purchasing oils, lubes, vibrators, and penis pumps. See http://www.christianlovetoys.com/pages/Resources.html (accessed March 14, 2012). Intimacy of Eden (http://www.intimacyofeden.com) offers similar products, and sites like The Marriage Bed and Adam's Rib: A Wife's Biblical Perspective provide articles and advice columns. Christian Nymphos, dedicated to teaching "every women to walk in sexual freedom with their husbands," has a section of the website dedicated to anal sex and anal play. Christian Nymphos also lists Focus on the Family as a resource. See http://christiannymphos.org; http://christiannymphos.org/category/anal-sex/; and http://christiannymphos.org/resources (accessed March 14, 2012).

8   David Sessions, "Mark Driscoll's Sex Manual 'Real Marriage' Scandalizes Evangelicals," *The Daily Beast*, http://www.thedailybeast.com/articles/2012/01/13/mark-driscoll-s -sex-manual-real-marriage-scandalizes-evangelicals.html (accessed March 14, 2012).

9   David Vanderveen, quoted in Churchmouse Campanologist, "Mark Driscoll's Real Marriage—Where's the Sanctity?" http://churchmousec.wordpress.com/tag/health/ (accessed March 9, 2012).

10   A number of evangelicals have argued that Christian domestic discipline is a distortion of the God-ordained submission required of Christian wives. See, e.g., Paul and Lori, "Domestic Discipline at Odds With the Word of God," January 1, 2006, http://site .themarriagebed.com/domestic-discipline. Conversely, in *Woman Submit! Christians and Domestic Violence* (Auburndale, Fla.: One Way Cafe Press, 2007), Jocelyn Andersen contends on pp. 60–61 that the gender hierarchy laid out in Genesis 3:16 ("your desire shall be for your husband, and he shall rule over you") is descriptive of the sinful desire for male supremacy resulting from the fall. "Because of this," she maintains, "there are men who feel they have a mandate from God to reign supreme within their homes and some will take that mandate to an abusive, dangerous—even deadly—extreme. Instead of detaching herself from these disrespectful attitudes and maltreatment; instead of a result that love of loss and desire for her abusive husband on the woman's part, the natural female response often seems to be an even more intense desire for her husband's love, affection, and acceptance. . . . I have chosen to call this perfectly normal, predictable, and prophesied response . . . the *Eve* Syndrome." Another useful source is Kathryn Joyce, "Biblical Battered Wife Syndrome: Christian Women and Domestic Violence," *Religion Dispatches*, January 22, 2009, http://www.religiondispatches.org/archive/1007/some _pastors_believe_abuse_is_biblical_grounds_for_divorce/ (accessed March 9, 2012).

11   Leah Kelley, "Other—Family & Relationships," *Yahoo! Answers*, July 22, 2006, http://answers.yahoo.com/question/index;_ylt=AvTfs2xZbYH7ljW6VJZr7QQjzKIX; _ylv=3?qid=20060722174903AAAbWPA (accessed March 23, 2012). Kelley's name appears to be a pseudonym.

12   Kelley explained at the Yahoo Christian Domestic Discipline group (hereinafter the Yahoo group), "It's obvious I find spanking sexy in theory (just look at my fiction and you'll be able to see that)." "Are the Benefits Worth the Risk?" October 3, 2006, http://dir.groups.yahoo.com/group/christiandomesticdiscipline/message/25211 (accessed March 6, 2012).

13   Leah Kelley, *Christian Domestic Discipline Bible Study for Wives* (n.p.: Christian Domestic Discipline, 2006), 46.

14   The Yahoo group was http://dir.groups.yahoo.com/group/christiandomesticdiscipline/. This group was founded on March 26, 2003. As of August 14, 2012, it claimed 3,824 members and had published 88,157 messages. Other Yahoo groups active as Kelley gained notoriety included Catholic Mentoring/Loving Discipline; Couples Christian Domestic

Discipline; Traditional Marriage (http://groups.yahoo.com); CDD Personals; Christian DD Moms; and Christian Singles Domestic Discipline (http://groups.yahoo.com/group/ChristnSinglesDomDis/). A website comparable to Leah Kelley's was Christian Domestic Discipline at http://www.christiandd.com/. Non-Christian sites frequently consulted by CDD groups included Taken in Hand (http://www.takeninhand.com/) and "Mr. Lovingdd's" Loving Domestic Discipline (http://lovingdd.blogspot.com/). Other sources of frequent referrals were romantic spanking fiction sites such as Lulu .com and Bethany's Woodshed (http://www.herwoodshed.com/).

15   Leah Kelley, "Making the Switch," Christian Domestic Discipline, hereinafter Kelley CDD, http://www.christiandomesticdiscipline.com (accessed July 17, 2008, but no longer active); Kelley, *Christian Domestic Discipline Bible Study for Wives*, 38; "Newsletter," April 2007 and November 13, 2008 (accessed May 21, 2009 but no longer active). Kelley claimed that there was so much traffic at her site that she had to ask her sister Kaliee for assistance in running it. She also commented that her husband loved to touch her when she was wearing a baby doll dress and that she had been forced to sew her own because those available in stores were too short given her "no-panty policy." Even then, she said, she was behind posting pictures of the new longer dresses because she "modeled my newest pink one for my husband and . . . well . . . let's just say it will have to be freshened up before I can take pictures of it now." Kelley CDD, http://web.archive.org/web/20070602013403/http://christiandomesticdiscipline.com/ (accessed May 21, 2009).

16   Web Direct, "H[a]ve You Ever Heard of Leah Kelley?" http://www.wdirect.com/hve-ever-heard-leah-kelley-cWEtMjAwODA0MjIxNTU2NDNBQTFFFS2xz.html (accessed May 6, 2012).

17   Anne Johnson, "The Gods Are Bored: In Nausea We Trust," May 14, 2007, http://godsrbored.blogspot.com/2007/05/in-nausea-we-trust.html (accessed May 21, 2009).

18   Gen. J. C. Christian, "She's No Pervert," Jesus' General, May 12, 2007, http://patriotboy.blogspot.com/2007/05/shes-no-pervert.html (accessed March 31, 2012).

19   Recursion, "Loving Wife Spanking in a Christian Marriage," Democratic Underground, June 2, 2007, http://www.democraticunderground.com/discuss/duboard.php?az=show_mesg&forum=105&topic_id=6571414&mesg_id=6571467 (accessed April 1, 2012).

20   Greta Christina, "Christian Spanking Porn," Greta Christina's Blog, September 2, 2007, http://freethoughtblogs.com/greta/2007/09/02/christian-spank/ (accessed May 6, 2012), originally published at Blowfish Blog.

21   Mathman, The Wolf Web, August 2, 2007, http://thewolfweb.com/message_topic.aspx?topic=486641 (accessed April 14, 2012).

22   For an interesting discussion of BDSM, Ephesians 5, and egalitarian versus complementarian understandings of marriage by blogger Hugo Schwyzer of Pasadena City College, see his " 'Domestic Democracy,' Ephesians 5:21, and BDSM in the Christian Marriage," October, 10, 2003, http://www.hugoschwyzer.net/2007/10/03/domestic-democracy-ephesians-521-and-bdsm-in-the-christian-marriage/ (accessed May 28, 2012).

23   Jules Markham, *Domestic Discipline* (Toronto: Adlibbed, 2007), 3–12, 111–35. In the only scholarly article we were able to find on Christian domestic discipline, R. Clair Snyder-Hall points to the difficulties involved in reconciling feminism and CDD. Practitioners typically denigrate feminism, and feminists are hard put to condone the sexism and violence inherent in CDD. Yet there are women who freely choose CDD, and a basic goal of feminism is to empower women to make their own choices. See R. Clair Snyder-Hall, "The Ideology of Wifely Submission: A Challenge for Feminism?," *Politics & Gender* 4, no. 4 (2008): 563–86.

In an article in *Bitch* titled "Slap Happy" (39 (2008): 63–68), Jessica Wakeman examines the paradoxical situation created when feminists ask their male partners to enter into a domestic discipline arrangement with them. For couples who have difficulty settling disputes, she reports, domestic discipline can function as a kind of relationship therapy. She postulates that domestic discipline may provide women a kind of absolution.

The relationship between feminism and domestic discipline is debated outside of academia as well. In a 2007 discussion thread titled "Ok Which One of You Guys Wrote This . . ." at spankingclassics.com, members expressed a variety of opinions about the relationship of feminism and domestic discipline. Since feminism "was all about choice," a member named Penny argued, women were free to choose domestic discipline. Victory replied, "I'm saying that IMO there are some lifestyles, including the male HOH DD model, that contradict feminism."

Pagan commented, "The old status quo told us that women belonged in the home. The new status quo says were not supposed to want that. Just who gets to define 'full human being'?" Lunacyn opined that "people who need women to fit into their idea of what a feminist should or should not be are the ones impeding the women's movement." Lambasting women for choosing to be spanked, she continued, was "no different then [*sic*] when we were told that we couldn't work, wear pants, play sports, etc. etc. The fight was (and still is) so that women could choose what they want for themselves. What they choose is irrelevant." And Copine answered, "[M]y practically useless degree in Women's Studies seems to be urging me to type . . . there is no such thing as Feminism. There are, however, feminisms. . . . What I perceive in this thread is a disagreement between those who both started and stopped listening to a version of feminism that was popularized in the 70's (and was quickly oversimplified by some of the movement as well as those who wish to put an end to it)." See Spanking Classics thread, http://www.spankingclassics .com/discus/messages/109/97620.html?1181016445 (accessed May 13, 2012).

Spanking Classics is a rich site. It lists over eight thousand members and provides free spanking fiction, role-playing opportunities, autobiographical accounts of spankings, spanking discussions, a storyboard, a poetry board, and essays and articles on spanking. It is run by Bethany Burke and her partner Jim, who also operate Bethany's Woodshed (http://www.herwoodshed.com/home.html), which describes itself as the web's original and largest spanking fiction store.

24 In the scholarly world, spanking typically is classified as a form of sadomasochism (SM). While "sadomasochism has received limited attention from researchers," scientific studies have shown that, in consensual SM encounters that go well, both the dominant and the submissive partner exhibit decreases in salivary cortisol—a hormone associated with stress—and increases in relationship closeness. This finding suggests that engaging in SM activities can produce increased intimacy between partners, as practitioners of BDSM, DD, and CDD maintain. See Brad J. Sagarin, Bert Cutler, Nadine Cutler, Kimberly A. Lawler-Sagarin, and Leslie Matuszewich, "Hormonal Changes and Couple Bonding in Consensual Sadomasochistic Activity," *Archives of Sexual Behavior* 38 (2009): 186–87, 192, 196–98.

25 Markham, *Domestic Discipline*, 51–53, 12.

26 As scholar William Simon observes, "Erotic cultures, like certain kinds of religious cultures, specialize in transforming the real or nearly real into the possibility of the hyperreal. . . . Like religious cultures, erotic cultures struggle to routinize the exceptional and, like religious cultures, they succeed more often than we realize." Simon suggests that SM "directly touches and sometimes embarrassingly illuminates the degree to which hierarchy, with the immediate application of power and control, permeates virtually

all aspects of social life. . . ." Sexual SM, he says, "can become an occasion for a visceral confirmation of a *version* of self that is not obtainable in other configurations of the self." *Postmodern Sexualities*, Kindle ed. (New York: Taylor & Francis, 2004), locations 3661, 3203–57. Emphasis in original.

Scholars Trevor Butt and Jeff Hearn strike a similar note on the way spanking reveals larger realities. "Corporal punishment," they say, "may be located as part of several, perhaps many, other broader discourses, and so be given meanings *as something else*." See "The Sexualization of Corporal Punishment: The Construction of Sexual Meaning," *Sexualities* 1, no. 2 (1998): 223. Emphasis in original. Sociologist Rebecca F. Plante provides an illuminating discussion of ways in which people who practice adult sexual spanking legitimate an activity that the majority culture regards as deviant. "To address these stigmatizing interests," she says, "individuals must develop coping strategies and design culturally and subculturally meaningful 'sexual stories.'" One way to render the sexual self, Plante argues, is "to construct a story describing its attributes, tracing its history, and locating it within the nexus of cultural sexual scripting." This, we are arguing, is precisely what the theology of biblical manhood and womanhood does. See Rebecca F. Plante, "Sexual Spanking, the Self, and the Construction of Deviance," *Journal of Homosexuality*, 50, nos. 2–3 (2006): 65–66.

27 Kelley, "Silicone Spatulas Are Evil!!!," Kelley CDD, October 30, 2006, http://web .archive.org/web/20070427100123/http://blog.christiandomesticdiscipline.com/ (accessed April 24, 2012).

28 Kelley, "Making the Switch"; Kelley, *Christian Domestic Discipline Bible Study for Wives*, 38; Kelley, CDD Newsletter, April 2007 and November 13, 2008.

29 Kelley, Kelley CDD, http://forums.about.com/n/pfx/forum.aspx?tsn=1&nav=message s&webtag=ab-usliberals&tid=14926 (accessed April 1, 2012). Exchanges such as these exacted a toll on Kelley. Her insistence on defending herself at the Women's Studies division of Yahoo Answers—when she ran out of nice things to say, she just quoted Scripture—resulted in being expelled from Yahoo. That meant scrambling to find a new server for her website. Kelley said that she was also threatened with having her children removed from her custody because of her advocacy of CDD. Kelley has left her website for others to run for several years. In 2011 she opened a new site called traditionalchristianmarriage. com. That site is no longer operative. Kelley announced her return to the Yahoo group in December 2011. See Kelley, "New Member Introduction," December 11, 2012, http:// groups.yahoo.com/group/christiandomesticdiscipline/message/78216 (accessed April 21, 2012). She also joined the Yahoo Biblical Christian Domestic Discipline group in 2010. See Kelley, "Introduction," in December 2010, http://groups.yahoo.com/group/Biblical ChristianDomesticDiscipline/message/180 (accessed April 20, 2012).

Kelley then dropped out of sight until May 2012, when she announced to the Yahoo group that her husband had left her in 2010 and that she was now divorced and living in a different state. Kelley expressed embarrassment over the divorce but also looked forward to getting back to writing about CDD. She disclosed that she was engaged to a "goodhearted, tough-as-nails redneck that wears his dominance like a second skin" she met through an online dating service. So far she had failed to work up the nerve to tell him about CDD, though she knew he believed in belt spankings, and that scared her. Naturally one of the male members of the Yahoo group immediately admonished her: "I strongly suggest you reveal your writtings [*sic*] to him and be clear that you believe in Biblical submission. . . . You then need to accept his decision on how he will hold you accountable, your job is to [be] obedient to his leadership however he chooses to lead you." "Hello Old Friends!" thread, May 3, 2012, http://dir.groups.yahoo.com/group/christiandomestic

discipline/messages/88301?threaded=1&m=e&var=1&tidx=1 (accessed May 7, 2012). Kelley has begun a new blog at Leah Kelley, http://leah-kelley.blogspot.com/.

30 Meloff, comment on "Church Discipline: Open Discussion on Domestic Discipline and Patriarchy," Church Discipline, January 16, 2008, http://church-discipline.blogspot. com/2008/01/open-discussion-on-domestic.html (accessed May 6, 2012).

31 Brent Riggs, "A Reader Asks: My Husband Has Been Reading a Lot of Christian 'Domestic Discipline' Where the Husband Has the Duty . . . ," On Having Serious Faith, August 26, 2009, http://www.seriousfaith.com/2009/08/a-reader-asks-my-husband-has-been -reading-a-lot-of-christian-domestic-discipline-where-the-husband-has-the-duty/ (accessed March 9, 2012).

32 Greta Christina, comment on Christina, "Christian Spanking Porn."

33 Mary, comment on "Bible Thumpers against Domestic Discipline," Punishment Book, June 4, 2007, http://www.punishmentbook.org/2005/05/bible_thumpers_.html (accessed April 3, 2009).

34 Leah Kelley, Christian Domestic Discipline 101 (n.p.: Christian Domestic Discipline, 2007), 8.

35 Kelley, Christian Domestic Discipline Bible Study for Wives, 40. See also Leah Kelley's Amazon Blog, "Answering About.com: Love a Correction or Domestic Violence (Part 2)," http://www.amazon.com/Christian-Domestic-Discipline-Spanking-Collection/ dp/1430309199/ref=sr_1_1?ie=UTF8&s=books&qid=1239983065&sr=1-1.

36 Kelley, Christian Domestic Discipline Bible Study for Wives, 6, 10, 12; "Trouble in Paradise," Kelley CDD (accessed May 27, 2009, but no longer active).

37 Kelley, Christian Domestic Discipline Bible Study for Wives, 14–16.

38 Leah Kelley, Consensual Christian Domestic Discipline (n.p.: Christian Domestic Discipline, 2007), 14–23. Emphasis in original.

39 Christian Domestic Discipline FAQs, Kelley CDD, http://www.christiandomestic discipline.com/cddfaqs.html (accessed June 5, 2012).

40 Kelley, Christian Domestic Discipline 101, 21–23, 54. That spanking regimen may seem complicated, but it is a simplification of the system advocated by an author known only as Mr. Lovingdd. Between the exhaustive descriptions of spanking techniques at his website (http://lovingdd.blogspot.com/) and in his books, Mr. Lovingdd set the field's descriptive standard. His first book on loving discipline delineated at least eleven types of spanking: introductory (or practice), maintenance, punishment, disobedience, preemptive, unjust, just because (or submission), multiple, casual, play, and transformational (or avoid at all costs). He identified over twenty possible spanking positions and considered a wide range of spanking implements as well. CDD websites in the mid- and late 2000s typically advised readers to consult the Mr. Lovingdd's website. Kelley posted links to Mr. Lovingdd (see http://www.christiandomesticdiscipline.com/links.html) at her site, and the Yahoo group continues to do so (http://groups.yahoo.com/group/christian domesticdiscipline/links, accessed April 23, 2012), even though the Loving Domestic Discipline site is currently inactive. Kelley's site ran articles by Sir Don, who either was Mr. Lovingdd or was plagiarizing him. Compare, for example, Sir Don's article on maintenance discipline at Kelley CDD, http://www.christiandomesticdiscipline.com/ maintenancediscipline.html (accessed April 23, 2012) with p. 55 of the chapter on maintenance discipline in Mr. Lovingdd's LDD, 7th ed. (n.p., 2007).

Sir Don offered these immortal words on the importance of spanking slowly: "When you cook a steak, and use high heat to sear the top, and then try to eat it you will find the steak cold and unsatisfying, just like a woman might feel after a very brief but hard spanking, yes she cried but only out of pain and learned only pain from the spanking. But slowly warming her bottom up, you will be able to spank her longer. The painful and longer spanking will allow her to submit to her HOH better, by humbling her." See "Warm Up Is Very Important," Kelley CDD, http://web.archive.org/web/20080124153234/http://blog.christiandomesticdiscipline.com/2007/04/14/warm-up-is-very-important .aspx (accessed May 21, 2009).

Only one significant CDD site raised questions about Mr. Lovingdd's material: Christian Domestic Discipline, http://www.christiandd.com/. This site, run by women, included a link to Loving Domestic Discipline until two of the moderators read Mr. Lovingdd's second book, *Advanced Loving Discipline*. There the author explored disciplinary techniques designed to humiliate women, such as toilet discipline, in which the HOH urinated in his woman's mouth. The moderators concluded—and we concur, having reached this opinion separately—that the LDD literature was an elaborate sham that Mr. Lovingdd concocted out of his imagination (or plagiarized from others). See http://www.christiandd.com/bookreviews/mrlovingdd/mrlovingddbyannie.html (accessed April 23, 2012). The Christiandd site, which provided links to CDD fiction unavailable at Kelley's site, remains online but no longer appears to be active.

41   Kelley, *Christian Domestic Discipline 101*, 37–45. As she notes with regard to punishment spankings on p. 37, "The husband should be prepared to give his wife a spanking that hurts. Otherwise, he is wasting his time. He needs to be prepared to ignore her pleas and give her an appropriate spanking if he wants the CDD relationship to be effective."

42   Kelley, Kelley CDD, "Suggestions for Introducing Christian Domestic Discipline to Your Husband," http://www.christiandomesticdiscipline.com/introducingtospouse.html (accessed May 21, 2009).

43   Kelley CDD, "Christian Domestic Discipline FAQs," http://www.christiandomestic discipline.com/cddfaqs.html (accessed June 5, 2012); Kelley, *Christian Domestic Discipline 101*, 59.

44   K, "In This Moment, I Am His," Kelley CDD, http://www.christiandomesticdiscipline .com/inthismoment.html (accessed June 5, 2012).

45   Kelley, *Christian Domestic Discipline 101*, 52, 59.

46   Leah Kelley, *Dream in Black and White* (n.p., TCM, 2006).

47   Leah Kelley, *Captive Dreams* (n.p., TCM, 2006).

48   These descriptions appeared in Kelley's CDD Spanking Romance Story section of Lulu. com on January 6, 2007. Kelley defined "moderate spanking" content as "more than 2 spankings, usually very thorough, or in shorter stories, one or two thorough spankings." Kelley claimed that none of the fiction on this list depicted severe spankings, which she described as "not for the faint of heart." The moderate spankings in these titles include belt whippings applied to the front and back of the thighs, a razor strop spanking imposed upon a wife whose hands were tied, anal rape, and the repeated use of an elephant-hide whip. See Lulu.com, http://www.lulu.com/shop/leah-kelley/spanking-romance-stories -punished-wives/paperback/product-6455776.html (accessed March 6, 2012).

49   See "Re: Are the Benefits Worth the Risk?" http://dir.groups.yahoo.com/group/christiandomesticdiscipline/message/25211 (accessed March 6, 2012), and "Re: Wanting a Punishment Spanking?" April 17, 2007, http://dir.groups.yahoo.com/group/christiandomesticdiscipline/message/33043?threaded=1&l=1 (accessed March 7, 2012). It was fine with Kelley if other women were attracted to milquetoast Prince Charmings, but she liked bad boys. See "Traditional Christian Marriage Advice for Husbands," Traditional Christian Marriage, 2010, http://www.traditionalchristianmarriage .com/christiandomesticdiscipline* (accessed August 19, 2011). It is not possible to provide the entire URL address as the domain name has lapsed and the Way Back Machine can no longer retrieve this file.

In a 2010 blog entry, she waxed poetic about the Showtime series *Weeds*. Her adult children had watched several seasons of *Weeds*, but Kelley ignored it until a drug cartel owner named Esteban appeared. Esteban was not hesitant to throw Nancy, his marijuana-dealing significant other, over his knee for a brisk spanking. That was all Kelley needed to become hooked. "Many of you will find this is inappropriate," she observed, "but I can't help it. I love that show." Kelley conceded that Esteban was not the most wholesome character: "Yes, yes . . . I know he was a drug lord and an all-around bad guy." Yet he knew how to dominate a woman, and that's what excited Kelley. "He was an alpha male that *spanked*. Sigh. . . . Now do you understand why that was my favorite show?" "I Miss Esteban!," Traditional Christian Marriage, December 8, 2010, http://blog .traditionalchristianmarriage.com/2010/12/08/i-miss-esteban* (accessed December 8, 2010, no longer active).

50 Leah Kelley, "The Love of the Father," in *Christian Domestic Discipline Spanking Romance Love Novella Series* (n.p.: Christian Domestic Discipline Fiction, 2006), 18.

51 The prissy feminist, for example, now appears in a new light: "The skirt swirled around her slender ankles as she walked. He'd never seen her in such a feminine ensemble, and he was in awe. Her face bore only a hint of makeup, but she looked even more beautiful in her natural state, and her hair was styled with a *ribbon* around her head, no less. She bore little resemblance to the feminist he knew." See Kelley, "Love of the Father," 28. Emphasis in original.

52 Leah Kelley, "The Love of the Husband," in *Christian Domestic Discipline Spanking Romance Love Novella Series*, 58–59.

53 For example, see this text from "Love of the Father," 118: "Her husband continued to whip her until her screams died out and all she could do was sob and beg while her legs moved slowly up and down in a bicycling motion. She'd never been in such pain, and she'd never regretted anything more in her life than lying to her husband." A similar passage is found in *Bridling the Tongue* (Christian Domestic Discipline, 2007), 19, in which a wife endures harsh discipline from her husband: "It was the worse whipping he'd ever given her. . . . Gradually her heart softened and she accepted how very wrong she'd been to speak such harsh words against another, no matter what the girl had done. With the realization came surrender, and she sobbed into her pillow, no longer fighting the horrible pain of the belt." And from "The Check," *Christian Domestic Discipline Spanking Romance Short Story Collection* (n.p., Christian Domestic Discipline Fiction, 2006), 118: "She sobbed into her pillow, the pain unspeakable, yet Clay continued to whip her without mercy until she was so spent she could do no more than cry quietly."

54 Leah Kelley, "The Women's Rebellion," in *Christian Domestic Discipline Spanking Romance Short Story Collection*, 8–11.

55 Leah Kelley, "To Train Up a Wife," in *Christian Domestic Discipline Spanking Romance Short Story Collection*, 112: "By the time he entered the bedroom, Lizzie lay stiffly on her side of the bed. . . . Sometimes he was rough with their lovemaking after a light spanking, but tonight had been rather severe. He pulled her into his arms and kissed her gently."

56 "Love of the Husband," 176: "Shoshana looked up at him, her expression so earnest he couldn't resist a kiss to her reddened lips. . . . He knew his wife looked at a spanking as real punishment rather than a game and he preferred it that way, but it took quite a bit of coaxing on his part to get her to respond to his lovemaking." In a story called "The Love of the Father," 118–19, it is not clear if the wife is more than an onlooker during sex: "She watched him through wide eyes while he moved into position and clung to him while he made love to her with exquisite care. When he finished she sighed and curled against his body where she fell sound asleep only moments later."

57   In *Christian Domestic Discipline Bible Study for Wives*, 46, Kelley advises, "never, never, *never* turn him down when he wants sex. Your body belongs to him. He should know he's always welcome there." She also urges wives to experiment. "Does your husband like pirates? Be the sexiest wench he's ever laid eyes on. Does he like to spank your bottom? Put on some drop-seat pantaloons and lay out the paddle.... Whatever works for the two of you behind closed doors is fine with God." (Emphasis in original.)

58   Kelley, "Re: Wanting a Punishment Spanking?," April 17, 2007, http://groups.yahoo.com/group/christiandomesticdiscipline/message/33043?threaded=1&l=1 (accessed March 7, 2012). Kelley explained that she dreaded spankings and found them humiliating. In deference to her feelings, Kelley's husband had quit giving her maintenance spankings, and even during punishment spankings he was careful not to spank too hard because they both knew, as Kelley put it, that "I'm a weinie [*sic*]." December 2 and 7, 2007, Kelley CDD, http://web.archive.org/web/20070623034022/http://leahslife.christiandomesticdiscipline.com/ (accessed May 21, 2009).

59   Kelley gave her husband credit for understanding that a "Christian wife is an intelligent being" who should have "little need for her husband's correction." See "Role of Play in a CDD Marriage," April 19, 2007, Kelley CDD Blog, http://web.archive.org/web/20080325075321/http://blog.christiandomesticdiscipline.com/2007/04/19/role-of-play-in-a-cdd-marriage.aspx#Comment (accessed April 12, 2012).

60   She denounced enemas and anal plugs, for example, when the Yahoo group did not.

61   See the article on "Silent Spanking," http://groups.yahoo.com/group/christiandomesticdiscipline/files/ (accessed April 19, 2012). The group "neither endorses nor condemns" disciplinary enemas. See http://groups.yahoo.com/group/christiandomesticdiscipline/message/45210 (accessed April 19, 2012). For a thread on figging, see http://groups.yahoo.com/group/christiandomesticdiscipline/message/52619 (accessed April 19, 2012). For a thread on anal plugs, expand the messages at http://groups.yahoo.com/group/christiandomesticdiscipline/messages/50179?threaded=1 (accessed April 19, 2012).

62   Yahoo group, http://dir.groups.yahoo.com/group/christiandomesticdiscipline/ (accessed April 8, 2012).

63   The forum at Kelley's website supported considerable traffic from 2005 through 2010, when the forum moved to a Yuku site (http://cddforum.yuku.com), which is now closed. For archived posts from 2005–2010 and 2011, see Christian Domestic Discipline Forum, http://wayback.archive.org/web/query?q=type%3Aurlquery+requestexactscheme%3Ayes+url%3Ahttp%3A%2F%2Fwww.christiandomesticdiscipline.com%3A80%2F&count=40000&start_page=1 (accessed April 8, 2012). The forum is currently online at its original site: http://christiandomesticdiscipline.com (accessed April 12, 2012).

64   On April 24, 2012, for example, Bulldog's *Order of Marriage and Christian Domestic Discipline* was available free of charge at the Yahoo group (http://groups.yahoo.com/group/christiandomesticdiscipline/files/), the Biblical Christian Domestic Discipline group (http://groups.yahoo.com/group/BiblicalChristianDomesticDiscipline/files/Bulldog%27s%20Articles), the CDD_HOH Husbands group (http://groups.yahoo.com/group/CDD_HOH_Husbands/files/), and the CDDHOH Couples group (http://groups.yahoo.com/group/CDDHOH/files). It can also be purchased in the Amazon Kindle store and at Lulu.com.

65   The only practitioner of CDD we discovered making this argument was Suzanne, who observed that the Hebrew word used for "helper" or "helpmeet" was also used to describe Yahweh's relationship to Israel. "If God is a 'helper' to us," Suzanne argued, "we cannot imply that somehow he is in any way 'following the lead' of the one He is helping.

Similarly, Eve being a helpmate from creation also wouldn't imply that. . . . Perhaps these verses are simply pointing out the way it will be once we are in heaven, back in 'Eden' . . . no male or female roles or hierarchy, just perfect harmony with God alone as the 'head.' In the meantime, I agree that it feels good right to finally be submitting to my husband." engineersuzy, "Re: Gender Equality," April 23, 2007, http://dir.groups.yahoo. com/group/christiandomesticdiscipline/message/33415 (accessed March 7, 2012).

66　Messianic Rabbi, "Care to Share?," Christian Domestic Discipline Forum, June 3, 2009 (accessed December 4, 2009, but no longer active).

67　William, "Welcome Jessica and Sigurd," November 30, 2009, http://groups.yahoo.com/ group/BiblicalChristianDomesticDiscipline/message/39 (accessed March 9, 2012).

68　Bulldog, "Easy Going Men," location 1215; Mrs. Bulldog, "My Beloved's Reasoning Concerning CDD," location 2000–2008, in Bulldog, *Order of Marriage and Christian Domestic Discipline*, vol. 2, Kindle ed. (n.p., n.d.).

69　Heather, "What Is It," November 4, 2009, http://dir.groups.yahoo.com/group/christian domesticdiscipline/message/67598 (accessed November 9, 2009). Heather marveled at the intimacy CDD had brought to her marriage, and she clearly used Genesis 1–3 to explain it. Before CDD, she said, she often resented her husband for not leading her. After CDD, she understood that if her husband was not leading her it was because she had usurped his place. She could confess her sin to him, and he would punish her. "I do this because I respect him," she asserted. "I WANT him to be the man in this relationship. I want to be what I was created to be." (Emphasis in original).

70　Nikita14576, "Re: What It Is," November 7, 2009, http://dir.groups.yahoo.com/group/ christiandomesticdiscipline/message/67623 (accessed April 9, 2012).

71　Belinda, apostledbm, and Lilibeth, "Why I Want CDD," Kelley CDD Blog, June 4, 2007, December 13, 2007, and January 15, 2008, http://web.archive.org/ web/20080213064624/http://blog.christiandomesticdiscipline.com/2007/05/22/ why-i-want-cdd.aspx (accessed April 11, 2012).

72　In one of the more surreal clips on YouTube, viewers can observe Bulldog and his wife instruct a thoroughly irreverent Australian couple about Christian domestic discipline and teach the man how to spank. http://www.youtube.com/watch?v=H_6jUjQAnrc (accessed April 24, 2012).

73　London Tanners is a popular supplier for the Yahoo CDD group members and offers a "complete domestic discipline series" that includes a loopy johnny as well as a domestic discipline paddle, strap, grandma slipper paddle, boudoir paddle, French martinet, and free carrying case for £340, or about $550. See https://www.thelondontanners .com/?p=152 (accessed April 12, 2012). The Yahoo group moderators also recommend the loopy johnny at Adam and Gillian's Sensual Whips and Toys (http://www.aswgt .com/loopy.html). For more of the moderators' recommendations, see http://dir.groups .yahoo.com/group/christiandomesticdiscipline/links/Implements_001145921488/ (accessed April 12, 2012).

74　See http://f1.grp.yahoofs.com/v1/YFCHT97a4VY4ZL338a62QQbzG5Lvo0-mhsp PuEl2LDNsIctrXI6cpfUeSTgNqjGtgGz-CyVgmOIxgZIsjuc3gJEiGICGKhCLlSU- tUQ/Silent%20Spanking%20-%20Capzasin%20Cream (accessed April 12, 2012). Talon warned men to be sure they wore gloves when applying capsaicin and urged them to realize just how painful it was. The result, he said, "is often a crying woman bare bottomed on the bed waiting for the flames of Hades to leave her poor bottom!" See "Re: Capsaicin," October 15, 2011, http://groups.yahoo.com/group/christiandomesticdisci- pline/message/86266 (accessed April 25, 2012). Some men use capsaicin during or after spankings to intensify them. AJ38320 described the effect as "absolute H*LL" see "Re:

Capsaicin," October 15, 2011, http://groups.yahoo.com/group/christiandomesticdiscipline/message/86266 (accessed April 25, 2012). Nancy argued that applying capsaicin after a spanking would produce intolerable pain and was, in her opinion, abusive. See "Re: What's Christian about CDD," January 27, 2006, http://groups.yahoo.com/group/christiandomesticdiscipline/message/1984427 (accessed April 25, 2012).

75 Deanna, "I Think He Was To[o] Severe," June 18, 2008, http://dir.groups.yahoo.com/group/christiandomesticdiscipline/message/48844 (accessed April 15, 2009).

76 Deanna, "I Think He Was To[o] Severe—Tonite Too!!!," June 19, 2008, http://dir.groups.yahoo.com/group/christiandomesticdiscipline/message/48936 and http://dir.groups.yahoo.com/group/christiandomesticdiscipline/message/48974 (accessed April 15, 2009).

77 Deanna, "I Think He Was To[o] Severe—Hoping for Replies before 8:00 If Possible," June 20, 2008, http://dir.groups.yahoo.com/group/christiandomesticdiscipline/message/49016, and June 21, 2008, http://dir.groups.yahoo.com/group/christiandomesticdiscipline/message/49030 (accessed April 15, 2009).

78 Corinne Taylor, "I Think He Was To[o] Severe—Tonite Too!!!," June 20, 2008, http://dir.groups.yahoo.com/group/christiandomesticdiscipline/message/48988 (accessed April 15, 2009).

79 Paul, "I Think He Was To[o] Severe," June 19, 2008, http://dir.groups.yahoo.com/group/christiandomesticdiscipline/message/48954 (accessed April 15, 2009).

80 Monica, "I Think He Was To[o] Severe—Hoping for Replies before 8:00 If Possible," June 22, 2008, http://dir.groups.yahoo.com/group/christiandomesticdiscipline/message/49064 (accessed April 15, 2009).

81 Two members sided with Deanna. Tina (who appears to have joined the group to offer critiques of CDD) responded to Deanna's question if anyone else besides her thought her HOH was being too severe with this answer: "God and the authorities." "I Think He Was To[o] Severe," June 19, 2008, http://dir.groups.yahoo.com/group/christiandomesticdiscipline/message/48894 (accessed April 15, 2009). Ros argued that relationships involve two people, not one, and that both Deanna and her HOH needed to believe in physical discipline for it to work. See "I think he was to[o] severe tonight too!!!" June 21, 2008, http://dir.groups.yahoo.com/group/christiandomesticdiscipline/message/49024?threaded=1&l=1 (accessed April 15, 2009).

82 aj38320, "Retraining Complete . . . or . . . Just Beginning," November 19, 2009, http://dir.groups.yahoo.com/group/christiandomesticdiscipline/message/67799 (accessed December 4, 2009).

83 EmmyGV, cddforum Message Board, Christian Domestic Discipline Forum, November 6, 2009, http://cddforum.yuku.com/topic/1189 (accessed December 9, 2009).

84 Samuel and Tonna, "Refocusing Versus Maintenance Spankings," Christian Domestic Discipline, February 11, 2012, http://christiandomesticdiscipline.wordpress.com/2012/02/11/refocusing-versus-maintenance-spankings/ (accessed March 25, 2012).

85 In response to a member who posted an "Am I Being Abused?" questionnaire at the website, moderators at the Yahoo CDD group announced in 2009 that they would no longer post discussions about domestic abuse. Too many people, they said, were joining the group simply to accuse "all those that practice CDD of being in an abusive relationship. There are numerous groups to support the advocacy or interests of those people," the moderators concluded, "and it is the intent of the owners and moderators of this forum to protect the members hear from those types of attacks. . . . [W]e do not believe that this forum in any way condones or encourages women to stay in an abusive relationship. Recent suggestions that it does are in error and we wish to take this opportunity

to express that those views are not acceptable." See Moderators, "~Abuse~Message to Forum," June 5, 2009, http://dir.groups.yahoo.com/group/christiandomesticdiscipline/messages/62680 (accessed March 20, 2012). On July 24, 2008, members received a moderator reminder that "while some may disagree with what the husband decides for his own home and his wife, we do NOT allow husband bashing on this group. Nor will we allow anyone to say a husband is being abusive if he decides on something that you don't agree with." See http://dir.groups.yahoo.com/group/christiandomesticdiscipline/message/50060 (accessed March 20, 2012).

86   Kai, "Reminder [*sic*] Spankings or Maintanance [*sic*]," July 25, 2008, http://dir.groups .yahoo.com/group/christiandomesticdiscipline/message/50097 (accessed April 13, 2012).

87   Teri Sexton, "Bruising & Doctor's Appt.," March 23, 2007, http://groups.yahoo.com/group/christiandomesticdiscipline/message/31049?threaded=1&l=1 (accessed March 24, 2012).

88   Jim, "I'm Not the Ogre Teri Makes Me Appear!," March 6, 2007, http://groups.yahoo .com/group/christiandomesticdiscipline/message/29562 (accessed March 24, 2012).

89   Sarah Dinah, "Re: I Am Not Sure I Belong Here," April 22, 2007, http://groups.yahoo .com/group/christiandomesticdiscipline/message/33363?threaded=1&l=1 (accessed March 7, 2012).

90   Joanne Graves, "Re: I'm Not Sure If I Belong Here," April 19, 2007, http://groups.yahoo. com/group/christiandomesticdiscipline/message/33202?threaded=1&l=1 (accessed March 7, 2012).

91   Mr. John Havelin, "Re: Jim Says I Need to Confess and Ask for Forgiveness," February 16, 2007, http://groups.yahoo.com/group/christiandomesticdiscipline/message/28924 (accessed March 7, 2012.)

92   Moderators, "Re: I Am Not Sure I Belong Here," April 20, 2007, http://groups.yahoo .com/group/christiandomesticdiscipline/message/33273 (accessed March 7, 2012); Kelley, "Re: I Am Not Sure I Belong Here," http://groups.yahoo.com/group/christiando-mesticdiscipline/message/33250 (accessed March 7, 2012).

93   Teri Sexton, "Re: I Am Not Sure If I Belong Here," April 20, 2007, http://groups.yahoo .com/group/christiandomesticdiscipline/message/33273?threaded=1&l=1 (accessed March 7, 2012).

94   Joinedbygod9, "Ready to Give Up," November 5, 2009, http://groups.yahoo.com/group/christiandomesticdiscipline/message/67605 (accessed April 14, 2012). Thirty-four posts and six weeks later, members were still unable to solve joinedbygod9's problem, and the women respondents were particularly doubtful of success. They agreed that men did not respond well to criticism, so joinedbygod9 would be wise not to confront her husband with his failures. And there was no point in joinedbygod9 telling her husband to man up and spank her, because men hated it when women bossed them around. Engineer Suzie suggested the situation was hopeless, just "as when it comes to sex." A woman can ask a man to pleasure her, she observed, but "if it's not something that interests him, it just doesn't happen." Kai concurred. You can encourage some men till the cows come home, she said, and they still "will never change or step up to the plate. In the end they are who they are and nothing short of God will ever change that." See "Ready to give up" thread, messages 67657 and 68162, November 5–December 19, 2009, http://dir.groups.yahoo .com/group/christiandomesticdiscipline/msearch?ST=%22ready+to+give+up%22&SM=contains&pos=30&cnt=10 (accessed April 14, 2012).

95   Bethany Burke and Jim, "From Bethany's Advice Column," Spanking Classics, January 28, 2003, http://www.spankingclassics.com/discus/messages/435/437.html?1043980462 (accessed May 12, 2012).

96 As Snyder-Hall observes, "The ideology of wifely submission requires the husband to pay a lot of attention to his wife, which makes a woman feel valued and loved. . . . CDD requires that a husband monitor his wife's behavior, as she needs to constantly feel his authority." Snyder-Hall, "Ideology of Wifely Submission," 573–74.

Wakeman notes of women in domestic discipline relationships: "The crux of domestic discipline is that women's behavior is inherently rife with transgressions, and the discipline provided by their intimate partner will be a leveling force. . . . Their fallibility frustrates and overwhelms them. They want someone to be profoundly disappointed in them when they are disappointing; being spanked is comforting because it shows that someone cares enough to punish them." See "Slap Happy," 65–66.

97 This paragraph is indebted to the work of Brame, Brame, and Jacobs. They compare the "joy, completion, or relaxation" that a submissive person feels following a spanking to "postcoital feelings." They also argue that spankees "enjoy the feeling that an authoritarian figure has assumed total control." And they describe the "happy ending" of a spanking: "The person spanked feels that he or she has been taught a valuable lesson and somehow improved. The authority feels satisfied at having corrected the submissive behavior and by the sheer physical control of a willing partner. Couples often complete the scenario with cuddles and kisses." See William Brame, Gloria Brame, and Jon Jacobs, *Different Loving: The World of Sexual Dominance and Submission*, Kindle ed. (New York: Villard Books, 1993), locations 5118–5228.

It is Wakeman who postulates that domestic discipline may provide women a kind of absolution. "Many American women strongly feel the drive to be perfect: to be educated, to be a breadwinner, to be a good mother, to be a good wife, and to be beautiful, to boot," she observes. "Is it possible some women—whether kinkily inclined, formerly abused, neither, or both—turn to domestic discipline the same way others find solace in punishing behaviors like eating disorders, cutting, or obsessively working out?" See "Slap Happy," 65–68.

98 Boss, "How to Make Her Remember," April 11, 2012, http://groups.yahoo.com/group/christiandomesticdiscipline/message/88052?threaded=1&l=1 (accessed April 15, 2012); and "Re: Need Some Advice," July 27, 2011, http://groups.yahoo.com/group/christiandomesticdiscipline/message/85000 (accessed April 15, 2012).

99 Deanna, "Re: Need Advice," March 16, 2012, message 87842, and March 22, 2012, message 87897, in thread http://dir.groups.yahoo.com/group/christiandomesticdiscipline/msearch?date=any&DM=------------&DD=----&DY=----&DM2=------------&DD2=----&DY2=----&AM=contains&AT=&SM=contains&ST=%22Need+advice%22&MM=contains&MT=&charset=UTF-8; and "Re: Maintenance Man!," April 9, 2012, http://groups.yahoo.com/group/christiandomesticdiscipline/message/88031?threaded=1&l=1 (accessed April 15, 2012).

100 Deanna, April 23, 2012, message 88168, and other respondents in the Yahoo group thread,http://dir.groups.yahoo.com/group/christiandomesticdiscipline/msearch?date=any&DM=------------&DD=----&DY=----&DM2=------------&DD2=----&DY2=----&AM=contains&AT=&SM=contains&ST=%22Belt+to+my+hands%22&MM=contains&MT=&charset=UTF-8 (accessed April 25, 2012).

101 The most obvious example is the 1987 Danvers Statement issued by the Council on Biblical Manhood and Womanhood: "Distinctions in masculine and feminine roles are ordained by God as part of the created order, and should find an echo in every human heart. . . . Both Old and New Testaments also affirm the principle of male headship in the family." See http://www.cbmw.org/core-beliefs/ (accessed June 6, 2012).

102 Gayle, February 10, 2008, http://groups.yahoo.com/group/christiandomestic discipline/message/45616?threaded=1&l=1 (accessed June 6, 2012).

103 Disco Stu, "Re: Opinions?" May 18, 2009, http://groups.yahoo.com/group/christian domesticdiscipline/message/61778; and "Training Wheels Off. Shining Like Gold," October 7, 2009, http://dir.groups.yahoo.com/group/christiandomesticdiscipline/ message/66602 (accessed May 4, 2012).

104 Disco Stu, "What Happened Sunday Morning. Teaching the Cleaning Lady, RE: Welcome Home," Alpha Males and Their Submissive Women (hereinafter AMATSW), February 21, 2010, http://groups.yahoo.com/group/AMATSW/message/406 (accessed December 17, 2010); and Mark, message 224, December 6, 2009, and messages 225, 245, 246, 247 at http://groups.yahoo.com/group/AMATSW/messages/64?threaded=1&m =e&var=1&tidx=1 (accessed April 16, 2012). Disco Stu's additional messages are numbered 225, 243, 255, 258, 259.

105 Angel, "I Am an AMAZON WOMAN!" June 18, 2010, http://dir.groups.yahoo.com/ group/christiandomesticdiscipline/message/73985?threaded=1&l=1 (accessed March 19, 2012).

106 Angel, "Care to Share?" Christian Domestic Discipline Forum, June 2, 2009 (accessed December 4, 2009, but no longer active).

107 Disco Stu, "Epilogue to a Sunday Lesson," AMATSW, March 11, 2010, and March 9, 2010, http://groups.yahoo.com/group/AMATSW/message/516 (accessed December 17, 2010). And "Re: Prayer Needed (for HOH)," December 14, 2010, http://dir.groups .yahoo.com/group/christiandomesticdiscipline/message/78322 (accessed December 17, 2010).

108 Disco Stu, "Epilogue to a Sunday Lesson," AMATSW, March 11, 2010, http://groups. yahoo.com/group/AMATSW/message/516 (accessed December 17, 2010).

109 Disco Stu, "The Power of the Voice," April 2, 2010, http://groups.yahoo.com/group/ AMATSW/message/607 (accessed November 17, 2010), and "Spiritual Leadership," March 23, 2010, http://groups.yahoo.com/group/AMATSW/message/581 (accessed November 17, 2010).

110 Angel, "I Stop Feeling Sorry for Myself," April 25, 2011, http://dir.groups.yahoo.com/ group/christiandomesticdiscipline/message/82949 (accessed June 6, 2012).

111 Angel, "Re: Do You Need to Remind Them?" March 24, 2012, http://dir.groups.yahoo .com/group/christiandomesticdiscipline/messages/87924 (accessed April 26, 2012).

112 Disco Stu, "What Maintenance Did to Me," April 7, 2010, http://dir.groups.yahoo.com/ group/christiandomesticdiscipline/message/70018?threaded=1&l=1 (accessed March 19, 2012).

113 Disco Stu, "What Maintenance Did to Me," April 7, 2010, http://dir.groups.yahoo.com/ group/christiandomesticdiscipline/message/70018?threaded=1&l=1 (accessed March 19, 2012).

114 2 Corinthians 5:17 and 1 Corinthians 15:49.

115 Disco Stu didn't use any implements to spank Angel. He relied on his hand.

Chapter 4

1 According to Eric Mazur and Kate McCarthy, popular culture stands in contrast to popular religion because it "includes a much wider range of products and practices that, while they may take on religious connotations, remain ostensibly secular sites of experience that neither the participant nor the casual observer would identify . . . as religious" (3). Eric Michael Mazur and Kate McCarthy, "Introduction," in God in the Details: American Religion in Popular Culture, 2nd ed. (New York: Routledge, 2011), 3.

2   Laura Copier, Jaap Kooijman, and Caroline Vander Stichele note that the wide range of objects that qualify as popular culture artifacts are "endless" and that this is a strength:

> The strength of popular culture is its inclusiveness and boundlessness and, perhaps most importantly, its ability to appropriate other forms of couture in a widely attractive way. Popular culture can be manipulative, turning culture into commodities that audiences are seduced into buying, yet it can also be remarkably democratic, opening up space for consumers to create meaning by making it part of their daily lives. Instead of giving a strict definition, it might be more fruitful to recognize popular culture as a broad, almost arbitrary collection of cultural objects that are intertextually linked and open to a wide range of interpretations.

     Copier, Kooijman, and Vander Stichele, "Close Encounters: The Bible as Pre-Text in Popular Culture," in *The Bible in/and Popular Culture: A Creative Encounter*, ed. Philip Culbertson and Elaine M. Wainwright, Semeia Studies 65 (Atlanta: Society of Biblical Literature, 2010), 191.

3   Mazur and McCarthy, *God in the Details*, 15–18.

4   Humor is a complex area of study. Not only is it cross-disciplinary (e.g., anthropology, sociology, psychology, biology, etc.), but there are a number of theories of its function. Some of the more prominent theories are the following: Superiority theory (laughter is a way to assert one's superiority over others); relief theory (laughter enables a person to get release from pent-up emotions, etc.); incongruity theory (laughter results when the punch line is a surprise and not what one expected).

     As one author explains,

> The superiority thinkers, as represented by Aristotle and Hobbes, suggest that humor involves lowly types, people made ridiculous or, as Hobbes put it in his classic statement, humor involves a "sudden glory arising from some sudden conception of some eminency in ourselves; by comparison with the infirmity of others, or with our own formerly." (Piddington 1963: 160) The most widely held theory of humor involves the notion of incongruity, namely that there is a difference between what we expect and what we get in jokes, cartoons, plays and other humorous works. Thus Schopenhauer suggested that we laugh at the ". . . sudden perception of the incongruity between a concept and the real objects which have been thought through it in some relation, and laughter itself is just the expression of this incongruity" (Piddington 1963: 171–72). A third theory deals with the psyche and, as explained by Freud in his book *Jokes and Their Relation to the Unconscious* (1963), involves the unconscious, masked aggression, and various intrapsychic economies that humor provides. (See Grotjahn 1966).

     Arthur Asa Berger, "What's So Funny about That?," *Society* 47, no. 1 (2010): 6.

5   Charles G. Kelly, in his article "Laughing In and Out of Eden: An Analysis of Adam and Eve Jokes," remarks,

> Since Eve is the "mother of all races" and Adam is the "father of us all," by association we are automatically connected with their plight. Consequently, Adam and Eve become prime subjects and targets of numerous sexual, religious, political and racial jokes that touch a universal thread in all of us and appeal to a wide range of joke tellers—and listeners.

     Kelly, "Laughing In and Out of Eden: An Analysis of Adam and Eve Jokes," *Midwestern Folklore* 14, no. 2 (1988): 91.

6   Michelle L. Bemiller and Rachel Zimmer Schneider, "It's Not Just a Joke," *Sociological Spectrum* 30 (2010): 459–79.

7   Arthur Asa Berger, *Manufacturing Desire: Media, Popular Culture, and Everyday Life* (Edison, N.J.: Transaction, 2008), 80.

8   Bemiller and Schneider, "It's Not Just a Joke," 464, report that sexist humor is not "just a joke" and suggest, "Correlations have also been found between sexist humor, sexual harassment, and sexual discrimination (Ford 2000; Frazier et al. 1995; La France and Woodzicka 1998; Pryor 1995). Pryor (1995) asserts that sexist jokes are the most common form of sexual harassment in the workplace."

9   According to humor theorists Limor Shifman and Dafna Lemish, "[F]eminist humour differs from 'female humour': whereas the latter refers to any kind of humour generated by women, 'feminist humour' is ground in criticism of the patriarchal structure of society and aspires to reform it (Franzini 1996)." Shifman and Lemish, "Between Feminism and Fun(ny)mism: Analyzing Gender in Popular Internet Culture," *Information, Communication & Society* 13, no. 6 (2010): 873.

10 Shifman and Lemish warn, "The still somewhat ambiguous concept of post-feminism has evoked heated debate and divergent evaluations in the research literature (Lotz 2001). According to Gill (2007), 'postfeminism' can be used to describe a certain sensibility or 'gist' prevalent in contemporary media. One of the main attributes of this 'gist' is the intertwining of feminist and anti-feminist ideas." Shifman and Lemish, "Between Feminism and Fun(ny)mism," 874.

11 In their analysis of gender in popular Internet humor, Shifman and Lemish argue, "In a relatively short period of time that it has existed, the Internet has become a major player in the production and distribution of humour, in general, and humour about gender, in particular (Shifman 2007). Since comedic texts draw on prevalent ideologies, stereotypes, and cultural codes, analyses of humour offers a unique perspective for understanding contemporary perceptions and stereotypes of highly charge issues such as gender and sexuality (Billig 2005; Boskin 1997)." Shifman and Lemish, "Between Feminism and Fun(ny)mism," 870.

12 Shifman and Lemish, "Between Feminism and Fun(ny)mism," 870.

13 Julie A. Woodzicka and Thomas Ford draw attention to this fact, especially as it pertains to sexist jokes: "Access to the internet has increased the ease with which sexist jokes can be located and distributed. For example, type the words 'sexist jokes' into any web browser and a library of female denigration immediately appears." Woodzicka and Ford, "A Framework for Thinking about the (not-so-funny) Effects of Sexist Humor," *Europe's Journal of Psychology* 3 (2010): 175.

14 Limor Shifman, "Humor in the Age of Digital Reproduction: Continuity and Change in Internet-Based Comic Texts," *International Journal of Communication* 1 (2007): 190–91.

15 Limor Shifman and Dafna Lemish, "'Mars and Venus' in Virtual Space: Post-feminist Humor and the Internet," *Critical Studies in Media Communication* 28, no. 3 (2011): 254.

16 That is not to say, however, that the term *post-feminist* is easily understood. Theorists vary greatly concerning its definition and characteristics: "On the positive side, it is understood to be a new form of feminism updated to late twentieth-to early twenty-first century modes of living that incorporate achievements of previous waves of the feminist movements. . . . On the negative side, post-feminism has been understood to be a form of backlash (Faludi, 1992) that undermines the achievements of 'second wave feminism.' Wheleman (2000) applied this view in writing about 'retro-sexism,' where old sexist ideas are wrapped in new nostalgic packages." Shifman and Lemish, "'Mars and Venus,'" 255.

17 Shifman and Lemish, "'Mars and Venus,'" 255.

18 Shifman and Lemish, "'Mars and Venus,'" 257.

19 Warren St. John, "Seriously, the Joke Is Dead," *New York Times*, May 22, 2005, http://www.nytimes.com/2005/05/22/fashion/sundaystyles/22joke.html?pagewanted=all (accessed May 1, 2012).

20 Shifman, "Humor in the Age of Digital Reproduction," 195.

21 Indeed, Mary Douglas notes that a "joke cannot be perceived unless it corresponds to the form of the social experience." Mary Douglas, "Jokes," in *Rethinking Popular Culture: Contemporary Perspectives in Cultural Studies,* ed. Chandra Mukerji and Michael Schudson (1975; repr., Berkeley: University of California Press, 1991), 299.

22 As Charles Case and Cameron Lippard observe, "Humor gives individuals a greater license to express dangerous, irreverent, or even mean-spirited sentiments that would be considered inappropriate or forbidden in most 'serious' forms of discourse." Charles E. Case and Cameron D. Lippard, "Humorous Assaults on Patriarchal Ideology," *Sociological Inquiry* 79, no. 2 (2009): 241.

23 Mary Crawford, "Gender and Humor in Social Context," *Journal of Pragmatics* 35 (2003): 1420.

24 Sigmund Freud identifies the "hostile" joke as a joke type in which aggressiveness is one of its key characteristics: "[T]endentious jokes are . . . highly suitable for attack of the great, the dignified and the mighty who are protected by external circumstances from direct disparagement." Freud, *Jokes and Their Relation to the Unconscious* (New York: Norton, 1960), 105.

25 Lisa Friedland and James Allan, "Joke Retrieval: Recognizing the Same Joke Told Differently," http://maroo.cs.umass.edu/pub/web/getpdf.php?id=835 (accessed June 1, 2012).

26 Shifman and Lemish, "Between Feminism and Fun(ny)mism," 872.

27 According to Shifman and Lemish, Internet jokes about gender/sex can be divided into three categories: sexist, feminist, and post-feminist. Jokes that targeted Eve/Woman tended to utilize some of the same elements that are found in their description of "sexist" jokes: "First, such humor tends to target and ridicule women, emphasizing their inferiority in comparison to men. Second, the targeting of women can be direct and explicit, but in many cases is implicit (i.e. uses stereotypical feminine prototypes such as 'blonde' or 'wife' without signifying explicitly that the joke deals with gender). Third, sexist humor employs traditional stereotypes in which women are portrayed as stupid, dependent, illogical, and nagging sexual objects. Finally, sexist humor not only emphasizes that men and women have different features, in doing so it indicates that there is a clear hierarchy positioning women as inferior to men." Shifman and Lemish, "Between Feminism and Fun(ny)mism," 873.

28 As Janet Bing notes, not only do jokes depend on these common stereotypes, but "most stereotypes about women are negative in the fictional world of jokes." Janet Bing, "Liberated Jokes: Sexual Humor in All-Female Groups," *Humor* 20, no. 4 (2007): 340.

29 When discussing the strategy of "role reversal" (women substituting men as targets in previously sexist jokes), Bing also notes the problem presented by stereotypes of women: "Feminist have often used role reversal to create humor, but such reversals can be difficult because most stereotypes of women are predominately negative, as discussed in *Bitches, Bimbos and Ballbreakers: The Guerrilla Girls' Illustrated Guide to Female Stereotypes* (Guerrilla Girls 2003)." Janet Bing, "Liberated Jokes," 353.

30 Shifman and Lemish, "Between Feminism and Fun(ny)mism," 872–73.

31 One should note that this type of joke involves a power dynamic. As Case and Lippard observe, "[F]or the powerful, humor provides the means to ridicule and abuse subordinate groups and to justify greater privileges, statuses, and rewards for themselves (e.g. racist, sexist, and ethnic humor)." Case and Lippard, "Humorous Assaults on Patriarchal Ideology," 243.

32 "In the beginning, God created earth and rested. Then God created man and rested. Then God created woman. Since then, neither God nor man has rested. AMEN." "Adam and Eve

Jokes," http://www.yuksrus.com/religion_adam_and_eve.html (accessed October 12, 2011).

33 Kelly, "Laughing In and Out of Eden," 94.

34 "It's in the Garden of Eden and Eve is feeling a bit of relationship angst about her marriage with Adam. She asks Adam 'Do you love me?' Adam replies, 'Of course dear' and then mutters to himself, 'Do I have a choice?'" "Do You Love Me Joke," Family Friends Jokes: Jokes about Family and Friends, http://www.familyfriendjokes.com/joke/do-you-love -me-joke (accessed February 5, 2012).

35 Shifman and Lemish, "Between Feminism and Fun(ny)mism," 885.

36 Bemiller and Schneider, "It's Not Just a Joke," 471.

37 A book published in 2004 capitalized on this in its title: *Adam vs. Eve: Jokes from the Front-line in the Battle of the Sexes.* Paul Rogan and Justin Rosenholtz, *Adam vs. Eve: Jokes from the Frontline in the Battle of the Sexes* (New York: Carlton Books, 2004).

38 Shifman and Lemish, "'Mars and Venus,'" 260.

39 "Eve: Adam, Do You Love Me? – Adam: Do I Have a Choice?," D3Motivation, www .demotivation.us/eve-adam-do-you-love-me-1252596.html (accessed October 11, 2011).

40 "Adam and Eve," TFS: The Forum Site, http://www.theforumsite.com/forum/topic/ Adam-and-Eve/323232 (accessed August 15, 2011).

41 "Adam and Eve Jokes."

42 In his work on Adam and Eve jokes, Kelly likens this type of portrayal to jokes about "naïve newlyweds" who are "willing but ignorant participants." Kelly, "Laughing In and Out of Eden," 92.

43 Ironically, there is actually research on headaches and sex. See Margaret J. Redelman, "What If the 'Sexual Headache' Is Not a Joke?" *British Journal of Medical Practitioners* 4, no. 1 (2010): 40–44.

44 Shifman and Lemish, "Between Feminism and Fun(ny)mism," 873; see also Case and Lippard, "Humorous Assaults on Patriarchal Ideology," 243–45.

45 Shifman and Lemish, "Between Feminism and Fun(ny)mism," 871.

46 Case and Lippard, "Humorous Assaults on Patriarchal Ideology," 244.

47 Janet Bing, "Is Feminist Humor an Oxymoron?," *Women and Language* 27, no. 1 (2004): 24.

48 Shifman and Lemish identifies such jokes as "feminist humor" and argue that the Internet is a prime "stage" for such humor. Shifman and Lemish, "Between Feminism and Fun(ny)mism," 873.

49 "Adam and Eve Jokes."

50 "Gender Role Humor," Java Casa: Music and Media, http://javacasa.com/humor/ genderroles.htm (accessed October 5, 2011).

51 "Adam and Eve Jokes."

52 This third joke actually collects the punch lines of some of the other two-liners while adding a few different reasons. But the second reason given in this joke ("Give us someone to bitch at immediately") actually reinforces the stereotype of woman the nagging bitch and runs counter to the notion of her superiority found in the other reasons. "101 of the Best MEN Jokes," Funnygurl.com, http://www.funnigurl.com/jokes/101men.html (accessed January 10, 2012). One additional version utilizes an automobile metaphor: "God created Adam first. His first model. Then God created Eve second . . . a later model and definitely looks better and lasts longer." "Gender Role Humor," Java Casa.

53 Case and Lippard, "Humorous Assaults on Patriarchal Ideology," 248–49.

54 "Adam and Eve's Choice."

55 "Adam and Eve Jokes."

56   "Adam and Eve Jokes."

57   "Adam and Eve Jokes."

58   Shifman and Lemish label their third type of gender joke as "post-feminist" and iden-
       tify three elements of Internet jokes that they found in this category: "First, postfeminist
       humor . . . focuses on gender differences. . . . Second, focusing on difference means that
       both men and women are targeted in comedic texts, rather than either men or women. . . .
       Third, the context of postfeminist humor is the world of leisure and consumption
       rather than politics or work." Of these elements, the first two are the most helpful in
       understanding the jokes that target both Adam and Eve. Shifman and Lemish, "Between
       Feminism and Fun(ny)mism," 874–75.

59   Shifman and Lemish, "'Mars and Venus,'" 255–56.

60   Shifman and Lemish, "'Mars and Venus,'" 261–65.

61   "Gender Role Humor," Java Casa.

62   Shifman and Lemish note that "women are treated as sexual objects in the comic texts in
       significantly more ways that are men." Shifman and Lemish, "'Mars and Venus,'" 259.

63   "Adam and Eve Jokes."

64   "Adam and Eve Jokes."

65   "The Christian Thread," SmallWorlds Forum, http://www.smallworlds.com/small-
       worlds/forum/showthread.php?t=364386&page=45 (accessed October 1, 2011).

66   As an interesting side note, Kelly, in his analysis of Adam and Eve jokes, makes the follow-
       ing remarks:
       "Adam had the great privilege of naming all the animals. As the parade of beasts
       ended, though, he realized that there was not found a helper suitable for him" (Gene-
       sis 2:20). God then created Eve as Adam's partner to provide the kind of companion-
       ship he could not find among the beasts. The following joke, however, offers another
       possibility: "Why did God create woman? Because sheep can't cook" (Knott 1982:
       84). Reinforcing already existing stereotypes that women are only housewives and
       sex partners, the joke suggests that the only difference between women and sheep is
       the women's ability to cook, that men could just as easily satisfy themselves sexually
       with sheep. ("Laughing In and Out of Eden," 94–95)

67   One last version of this joke type expands on the description and function of woman, who
       must be gained by Adam giving up his left leg and arm. While this joke is similar in form
       to the previous two, it contains a somewhat different description of the woman. She is not
       only a satisfying sex object ("She will be great fun in bed"), but also a great companion
       ("Eve will be someone you can speak to about the deepest things in your heart and she
       will always understand."). While women's beauty is extolled prior to this in the opening
       lines, apparently men are to be loved for their "spiritual qualities" alone. The image of
       woman that emerges is of one who will never challenge man's decisions and always be
       supportive. Moreover, although she is smart, she will never reveal just how smart she is
       and thus allow man to live with the illusion that he is the one in charge. Of course, since
       this woman is not the one given to the man (because he was not willing to pay the price),
       the result is an explanation of why men and women do not get along as "smoothly" as
       the divine intent this joke describes. "Garden of Eden Jokes," Joke Library, http://www
       .jokelibrary.net/religion/eden.html (accessed September 15, 2011).

68   "And God Made Man: Men vs. Women Jokes," Croc Jokes.com, http://crocjokes.com/dirty
       jokes.php?ID=1370&o=23&R=80&S=RANK&cat=mvsw (accessed October 7, 2011).

69   Gender Role Humor," Java Casa.

70   "Adam and Eve," aznlover, http://www.aznlover.com/community/archive/index.php/
       t-2284.htm (accessed September 15, 2011).

71 Shifman and Lemish argue that in post-feminist humor, men are sometimes portrayed as with an "uncultured primitiveness." By this they mean that men are imaged as "simple, underdeveloped, vulgar, 'beast-like,' uncultured, childish, unrestrained, and dirty." Shifman and Lemish, "'Mars and Venus,'" 263.

72 Bing, "Is Feminist Humor an Oxymoron?" 30.

73 Case and Lippard, "Humorous Assaults on Patriarchal Ideology," 242.

Chapter 5

1 Sal Randazzo, in his book *Mythmaking on Madison Avenue* suggests that "myths are more than entertaining little stories about gods, goddesses, and heroic characters. The universality of myths, the fact that the same myths recur across time and many cultures, suggests that they originate somewhere inside of us. . . . Advertisers sell products by mythologizing them, by wrapping them in our dreams and fantasies . . . advertising is not simply in the business of 'selling soap' . . . advertising turns products into brands by mythologizing them—by humanizing them and giving them distant identities, personalities, and sensibilities that reflect our own." Randazzo, *Mythmaking on Madison Avenue: How Advertisers Apply the Power of Myth & Symbolism to Create Leadership Brands* (Chicago: Probus, 1993), ix, xii, 1.

2 As Peter Daly notes, "In contemporary advertising the text identifies Paradise, the meaning of which is secularized and hedonized. Adam and Eve inhabit a Garden of Advertising, where Eden is used to push the pleasure principle or awaken the acquisitive instincts of consumers" (84). Daly, "Adam and Eve in the Garden of Advertising," in *European Iconography: Selected Papers of the Szeged International Conference, June 9–12, 1993*, ed. György E. Szőnyi (New York: Brill, 1996).

3 As John Harms and Douglas Kellner suggest,

> [T]he "marketplace" should be seen as a "cultural system" (1986, p. 263ff.) and not just as a mechanism for moving commodities and money. Furthermore, it is cultural symbolism and images that provide crucial insights into the nature and functions of advertising. The authors' analysis of the "persuasive" form of modern advertising indicates how cultural forms of social communication create meanings through non-discursive visual imagery which come to shape consciousness and behavior subtly by sanctioning some forms of thought and behavior while delegitimating others.

John Harms and Douglas Kellner, "Toward a Critical Theory of Advertising," Illuminations: The Critical Theory Project, http://gseis.ucla.edu/faculty/kellner/Illumina%20 Folder/kell6.htm (accessed June 7, 2012).

4 As Jean Kilbourne argues, "Advertising is an over 100 billion dollar a year industry and affects all of us throughout our lives. We are each exposed to over 2000 ads a day, constituting perhaps the most powerful educational force in society. The average American will spend one and one-half years of his or her life watching television commercials. The ads sell a great deal more than products. The sell values, images, and concepts of success and worth, love and sexuality, popularity and normalcy. They tell us who we are and who we should be. Sometimes they sell addictions." Kilbourne, "Beauty . . . and the Beast of Advertising," Center for Media Literacy, http://www.medialit.org/reading-room/ beautyand-beast-advertising (accessed August 13, 2012).

5 This is especially important since, as Sut Jhally argues,

> While every culture has to work to define for its members what gender relationships should be, no other culture in history, I believe, has been this obsessed with explicit portrayals of gender relations. Gender and sex have never been as important as they

are in our culture . . . through advertising, in our cultural discourse, questions of sex and gender have been elevated to a privileged position.

This may also offer an answer as to where the power of advertising derives from. The representations of advertising are part of the context within which we define or understand gender. Advertising draws us into *our* reality.

Jhally, *The Codes of Advertising: Fetishism and the Political Economy of Meaning in the Consumer Society* (New York: St. Martin's, 1987), 136. Emphasis in original.

6   John Harms and Douglas Kellner lament in their article "Toward a Critical Theory of Advertising" that more work needs to be done on "the socio-economic functions of advertising and the ways that ads actually shape and influence perception and behavior which reproduce the existing social systems." The same need exists concerning how advertising uses biblical materials to strengthen traditional interpretations and to challenge them.

7   Ancient writers suggested a host of plausible ways that Eve could have "persuaded" Adam to eat the forbidden fruit. As John A. Phillips observes,

The stark biblical verse, "She also gave some to her husband, and he ate," leaves everything to the imagination, and 20 centuries of male rationalizing have indeed imagined just about everything to account for what must have transpired between Adam and his wife, and Adam and his own conscience. As perfectly strong as Adam is, he cannot withstand the onslaught of the now superhuman Eve. She makes use of her feminine powers and weaknesses alike to press her evil design: She lies, appeals to his marital faith, impugns his courage, whines, scolds, . . . And, of course she is seductive.

Phillips, *Eve: The History of an Idea* (San Francisco: Harper & Row, 1984), 74.

8   "Adam & Eve," Baldwinstone Agency, http://www.baldwinsone.com/AgencyProfile. html (accessed November 11, 1998; no longer active).

9   Richard Lacayo argues that "no matter what everyone else may think, we say the world's oldest profession is marketing. How else can you describe a pursuit that makes an appearance in the Book of Genesis? What we mean here is the part in which the serpent sells Eve on that apple. Even granting that she was an early example of insufficient sales resistance, that was a masterpiece of promotion." Lacayo, "Marketing: Search for a Perfect Pitch," *Time*, July 23, 2001, http://www.time.com/time/magazine/article/0,9171,1000378,00 .html (accessed May 28, 2011, no longer active).

David Bullard, an online writer for Ad Focus (an IT services company), agrees: "You probably won't like it, but I reckon the first advertising executive was the serpent in the Garden of Eden. Not only does he get Eve to eat forbidden fruit by telling her that it will make her as good as a god (typical industry hype) but he also fires the starting pistol for the whole advertising industry of the future." Bullard, "Section 4: Odd Kind of Therapy," Ad Focus, May 23, 2003, http://www.adfocus.co.za/adfocus2003/d10.htm (accessed March 3, 2006; no longer active).

10 In his book *Value-Added Selling*, Tom Reilly defends "persuasion" from its detractors by arguing that in Eve we have the first salesperson: "Persuasion often takes a bad rap. People hear the word and think it means manipulation and mind control. Here's a reality check: persuasion has existed from the time that Eve persuaded Adam to take a bite from the Apple." Reilly, *Value-Added Selling: How to Sell More Profitably, Confidently, and Professionally by Competing on Value, Not Price*, 2nd ed. (New York: McGraw-Hill, 2002), 89.

11 In his article "What Makes People Buy?" Tom Kuegler implies that Eve originally had help from the snake in her marketing research:

When TV was introduced, did it totally change the core of what marketing does? NO. You still had to put forth a compelling message, entice someone to act, and then help shorten the sales cycle. That's marketing. It hasn't changed at all since Eve marketed to Adam to eat the forbidden fruit. If it happened today, Eve would still have to do her research (probably without the help of a snake), create a message targeted to her audience, refine the message, and then help close the deal. Kuegler, "What Makes People Buy?" ClickZ: Marketing News & Expert Advice, May 5, 2000, http://www.clickz.com/clickz/column/1694804/what-makes-people-buy (accessed June 7, 2011).

12 Richard C. Christian, for example, discusses sales meetings in the *Journal of Marketing* and begins by saying: "SALES MEETINGS—big ones, little ones, short ones, long ones, dull ones, stimulating ones, regional ones, national ones—have been a going thing since shortly after Adam, Eve, and the apple got together." Christian, "Industrial Marketing: Are You Conducting Sales Meetings . . . or Marketing Meetings?" *Journal of Marketing* 25.1 (1960): 72.

13 Evan Sohn, "Lessons from the First Salesman—The Serpent," Biznik, April 8, 2008, http://biznik.com/articles/lessons-from-the-first-salesman-the-serpent (accessed June 9, 2011).

14 Sohn, "Lessons."

15 Noel Bussey, "Adam & Eve Opens Its Doors for Business," Brand Republic, January 17, 2008, http://www.brandrepublic.com/news/777310/ (accessed June 9, 2011).

16 Gemma Charles, "Adam & Eve Leads 2010 Agency Winners," *Marketing*, December 2010, http://www.marketingmagazine.co.uk/news/1045296/Adam---Eve-leads-2010-agency-winners/ (accessed January 7, 2012).

17 Joe Fernandez, "Phones4u appoints Eden to £10m media account," *MarketingWeek*, 2010, http://www.marketingweek.co.uk/phones4u-appoints-eden-to-%C2%A310m-media-account/3008977.article (accessed January 8, 2012).

18 "Adam & Eve," IPA: Promoting the Value of Agencies, http://www.ipa.co.uk/Agencies/Adam-Eve (accessed January 3, 2012).

19 John O'Shaughnessy and Nicholas J. O'Shaughnessy, *Persuasion in Advertising* (New York: Routledge, 2003).

20 "Original Sin," *SPC. Soap, Perfumery, and Cosmetics* 69 (1996): 8.

21 "All about Eve Cali Rand 1997," http://universparfum.netai.net/joop/viewer.swf (accessed October, 31, 2012).

22 "All About Eve by Joop Fragrances," ParfumesRaffy.com, http://www.parfumsraffy.com/women/all-about-eve-perfume-for-women-by-joop-fragrances.html (accessed January 8, 2012).

23 "All About Eve Perfume—by Joop Perfumes," Gift Scents, http://www.gift-scents.com/detail.php?id=2270&pid=12876 (accessed April 11, 2003; no longer active).

24 In the 1990s, Joop launched its "What about Adam?" cologne. Amazon.com describes its fragrance as being a combination of "citrus, spice, woods and lavender" and recommends its use in "daytime." Unlike its "co-product" All About Eve, there is no seduction implied in its packaging (other than its phallic shape?) or marketing copy. "What about Adam," Amazon, http://www.amazon.com/Joop-Set-edt-Ounces-Deodorant-Aftershave/dp/B000C1VYFM/ref=sr_1_1?ie=UTF8&qid=1325454285&sr=8-1 (accessed January 1, 2012).

25 "Monica Bellucci, Dior's Hypnotic Poison," stylefrizz, http://stylefrizz.com/200811/monica-bellucci-diors-hypnotic-poison/ (accessed January 7, 2012).

26 "Monica Bellucci, Dior's Hypnotic Poison."

27 As one perfume reviewer noted, it is
> [a]n advertising that plays to the stereotype or archetype of Eve. The bottle of Hypnotic Poison becomes or rather suggests the (red) apple Eve bit into as she was seduced into it by the serpent in the garden of Eden.

After Eve/Monica Bellucci gets expulsed from Eden she takes on the attributes of the snake in order, in her turn, to ssssseduce unwitting men.
Marie-Helene Wagner, "Monica Bellucci Plays Daughter of Eve for Dior Hypnotic Poison Ad," The Scent Salamander, November 11, 2008, http://www.mimifroufrou.com/scented salamander/2008/11/monica_bellucci_plays_daughter.html (accessed January 1, 2012).

28 "Desperate Housewives Forbidden Fruit Coty for Women," Fragrantica.com., http://www.fragrantica.com/perfume/Coty/Desperate-Housewives-Forbidden-Fruit-2970.html (accessed January 1, 2012).

29 TV Addict, "Check out Mary Louise Parker Nude," theTVaddict.com, July 24, 2007, http://www.thetvaddict.com/2007/07/24/check-out-mary-louise-parker/ (accessed September, 9, 2007).

30 "Weeds Downloads: Monday Nights Are Tempting," Showtime, http://www.sho.comweeds/downloads.do (accessed October 17, 2007; no longer active).

31 "Desperate Housewives," ABC Medianet, http://abcmedianet.com/showpage/show-page.aspx?program_id=001653&type=lead (accessed June 14, 2011; no longer active).

32 Tim Nudd, "'Housewives' Gets Biblical on Us," Adweek, September 9, 2005, http://www.adweek.com/adfreak/housewives-gets-biblical-us-20254 (accessed September 14, 2007).

33 "yU + co Opens ABCs Desperate Housewives: Title Sequence Looks at Women Scorned through the Ages," Broadcast Newsroom, November 12, 2004, http://facilities.broad-castnewsroom.com/articles/viewarticle.jsp?id=29118 (accessed May 14, 2012).

34 "Desperate Housewives," yU + co, http://www.yuco.com/projects/desperate-house wives (accessed May 14, 2012).

35 "Desperate Housewives," ABC, http://abc.go.com/shows/desperate-housewives/about-the-show (accessed May 17, 2012).

36 Senthil Ganesan, "Case Study: Benetton Group: Unconventional Advertising," Global CEO (November 2002): 55.

37 Maxey Hackworth, "United Campaign of Benetton," Cavalier Daily, http://www.cavalierdaily.com/CVArticle.asp?ID=14004&pid=931 (accessed April 9, 2006; no longer active).

38 Ganesan, "Case Study," 53.

39 Eric J. Lyman, "The True Colors of Oliviero Toscani," adageglobal, http://www.ericjlyman.com/adageglobal.html (accessed May 17, 2012).

40 Ganesan, "Case Study," 53.

41 Ganesan, "Case Study," 54–55.

42 Christopher Turner, "Benetton's Most Controversial Advertising Campaigns: 5. Black Woman Breastfeeding White Baby (July 1989)," Fashionist, July 28, 2010, http://www.fashionist.ca/2010/07/benettons-most-controversial-advertising-campaigns.html (accessed January 1, 2012).

43 Ganesan, "Case Study," 56.

44 Christopher Turner, "Benetton's Most Controversial Advertising Campaigns: 2. Aids—David Kirby (February 1992)," Fashionist, July 28, 2010, http://www.fashionist.ca/2010/07/benettons-most-controversial-advertising-campaigns.html (accessed January 1, 2012; no longer active).

45 "The Red Ribbon of AIDS Prevention—1997," http://www.regimbald.ca/Benetton/html/1997.html (accessed April 9, 2006; no longer active).

46 "Bird." http://www.regimbald.ca/Benetton/html/1992.html (accessed April 9, 2006; no longer active).

47 "Looking at Death in the Face: In the Year 2000, Benetton Is Launching Its Worldwide

Communication Campaign about Capital Punishment," United Colors of Benetton, January 7, 2000, http://www.benettongroup.com/node/469 (accessed May 17, 2012).

48 "About Benetton—Our Campaigns," United Colors of Benetton, http://press.benetton group.com/ben_en/about/campaigns/history/?t=print (accessed June 14, 2011; no longer active).

49 "About Benetton—Our Campaigns."

50 "United Superstars of Benetton," http://www.regimbald.ca/Benetton/html/1988.html (accessed April 9, 2006; no longer active).

51 Ken McGorry, "History Repeats Itself at Kirshenbaum Bond: Randy Cohen Helps Skewer Ancient Lore for Liberty Mutual," *Post*, April 1, 2005, http://www.highbeam .com/doc/1G1-132230571.html (accessed May 14, 2012).

52 Amy Corr, "Out to Launch," MediaPost, April 13, 2005, http://www.mediapost.com/ publications/article/29196/out-to-launch.html (accessed September 6, 2007; no longer active).

53 Beck Finley, "Liberty Mutual 'Adam & Eve,'" DigitalContentProducer.com, July 1, 2005, http://digitalcontentproducer.com/mil/clips/video_hot_spots_88/ (accessed September 12, 2007).

54 As Peter Daly explains, "A case in point is Jesuit emblem book *Typus Mund* (1697). . . . This engraving simplifies the [Garden] scene and focuses on Eve and the serpent. Here the picture of the snake has a telling new detail: the snake has the head of a woman. If the source of evil is the snake, and the snake is equated with woman, then the entry of evil into the human world is caused by woman." Daly, "Adam and Eve in the Garden of Advertising," 77.

55 Corr, "Out to Launch."

56 McGorry, "History Repeats Itself."

57 "Eve Shared That Apple and Look What Happened. Don't You Make the same mistake. Twix: Two for Me, None for You," Legacy Tobacco Documents Library #2069546430, University of California, San Francisco, http://legacy.library.ucsf.edu/tid/rnx32d00 (accessed May 10, 2012). For a scanned picture of the ad in color, go to http://bytesmedi arecaps.blogspot.com/ (accessed May 10, 2012).

58 Daniel Chandler, "Impulse: Chance Encounter (1998)," Media Semiotics, http://www .aber.ac.uk/media/Modules/MC30820/impulse.html (accessed April 17, 2003).

59 Chandler, "Impulse."

60 Chandler, "Impulse."

61 Ian Furgusson, "British TV ad uses gay theme," CNN World News, May 19, 1998, http:// edition.cnn.com/WORLD/europe/9805/19/gay.ad/ (accessed April 1, 2006).

62 "TV & Radio Blog: Where have all the gay men gone in TV ads?" *Guardian*, http://www .guardian.co.uk/culture/tvandradioblog/2008/may/22/whereareallthegaymenint (accessed January 1, 2012).

63 Rabbinical commentators understood the fruit as either figs (*Genesis Rabbah* 15:7) or grapes (*Genesis Rabbah* 19:5).

64 Alex Santoso, "The Evolution of Tech Companies' Logos," Neatorama, February 7, 2008, http://www.neatorama.com/2008/02/07/the-evolution-of-tech-companies-logos/ (accessed January 9, 2012).

65 Santoso, "Evolution of Tech Companies' Logos."

66 Steven Weyhrich, "The Apple I," Apple II History, http://apple2history.org/history/ ah02/ (accessed April 24, 2003).

67 "The Apple Logo," TAM: The Apple Museum, http://www.theapplemuseum.com/indec. php?od=44 (accessed September 6, 2007; no longer active).

68 "Apple Logo."

69   "1979 Apple II 'Adam Ad;' Gallery One: 1976–1979," Apple Advertising and Brochure Gallery, http://www.macmothership.com/gallery/MiscAds/AdamAd.JPG (accessed January 7, 2012).

70   "Coleco Adam Computer," http://oldcomputers.net/adam.html (accessed November 7, 2007).

71   "Logical Challenges Coleco's 'Adam,'" *New York Times*, June 17, 1983, http://www.nytimes.com/1983/06/17/business/logical-challenges-coleco-s-adam.html (accessed September 11, 2011).

72   "Logical Products—The Adam Computer," Logical, http://www.logicalbusiness.com/p_adam.htm (accessed September 11, 2007).

73   Paul Atkinson, "The Origin of PCs: Perspectives on the History of the Office Computer," http://www.dancingmind.co.uk/cuba%202000/Ponencias/P%20Paul%20Atkinson.htm (accessed September 18, 2007; no longer active).

74   "Logical Products."

75   "What Do the Scriptures Say?" http://www.scripturessay.com/article.php?cat&id=667 (accessed May 10, 2012; no longer active).

76   As one writer explains,

> The relationship of gambling and religion goes back to the dawn of human time. Was the snake tempting Adam and Eve with a gamble when he suggested that they disobey God and go ahead and eat of the fruit of the tree of knowledge? Could they have known where that quest of knowledge would lead them? Could they have contemplated the nature of life had they not searched for something different?

William Norman Thompson, "Religion and Gambling," in *Gambling in America: An Encyclopedia of History, Issues, and Society* (Santa Barbara, Calif.: ABC-CLIO, 2001), 318.

77   "Winning over Gambling Addiction," The Bridge of Overcomers Outreach, http://overcomersoutreach.org/blog/winning-over-gambling-addiction/ (accessed March 12, 2012).

78   "Garden of Eden Slots—Game Review," Online Casino Directory, http://online.worldcasinodirectory.com/playtech/garden-of-eden (accessed January 9, 2012).

79   "Garden of Eden Slot Machine," Slots, http://www.slots-gambling.com/slots/review-pt-garden-of-eden.html (accessed January 9, 2012).

80   "Forbidden Fruit Slot," 24hSlots.com, http://24hslots.com/guide/forbidden-fruit-slot (accessed January 9, 2012).

81   "Adameve: The Genesis of Poker," Adameve.com, http://www.adamevepoker.com/main/index.php (accessed January 9, 2012).

82   "Adameve Casino Review," grem.net, http://www.grem.net/casino-reviews/adameve-casino-review (accessed January 9, 2012).

83   "Richard A. Canfield: America's First Casino King," Poker Player, May 21, 2006, http://www.pokerplayernewspaper.com/node/5212 (accessed May 2, 2012).

84   "Richard Albert Canfield," in *The Columbia Encyclopedia*, 6th ed., 2008, Encyclopedia.com, http://www.encyclopedia.com/doc/1E1-CanfieldR.html (accessed January 10, 2012).

85   "Some Cool Gambling Quotes," 4onlinegambling.com, http://www.4online-gambling.com/gamblingquotes.htm (accessed January 10, 2012).

86   *Genesis Rabbah* 19:5.

87   *Sanhedrin* 70a; *Genesis Rabbah* 19:5.

88   "Absolut Merlet," Absolutad.com, http://www.absolutad.com/absolut_lists/ads/pictures/?id=1271&_s=ads (accessed January 10, 2012).

89   "Smirnoff Green Apple Twist: Adam & Eve," Ads of the World, 2006, http://adsoftheworld.com/media/print/smirnoff_green_apple_twist_adam_eve (accessed November 7, 2011).

90 Forbidden Fruit Winery, http://www.forbiddenfruitwines.com/ (accessed April 20, 2012).

91 "Cathedral Square Forbidden Fruit Apple Ale," The Beer Taster, 2011, http://beer-taster
.com/beer-reviews/beer-taster/cathedral-square-forbidden-fruit-apple-ale/ (accessed
May 10, 2012).

92 "Forbidden Fruit Liqueur" has been discontinued but was used as an ingredient in the
"Adam and Eve" cocktail listed on the Good Cocktails.com website (http://www.good
cocktails.com/recipes/ingredient.php?ing=151).

93 "Hoegaarden: Labels, Coasters, and Other Media for Hoegaarden," Brewpalace, http://
www.brewpalace.com/CompanyDetails.asp?DrillValue=Hoegaarden&CompanyTab=
Media (accessed January 1, 2012).

94 Lucy Sanders, "Food and Beer at the Esplanade Bier Markt, Toronto," Beercook.com,
http://www.beercook.com/articles/biermarkt.htm (accessed September 11, 2007).

95 Michael Jackson, "Europe's Stylish Summer Whites," The Beerhunter, 1997, http://www
.beerhunter.com/documents/19133-000113.html (accessed October 29, 2007).

96 As Davidson notes, "Advertising for alcoholic beverages is full of sexual messages, the
most common being that drinking the product will help bring on some exciting sexual
encounter." D. Kirk Davidson, Selling Sin: The Marketing of Socially Unacceptable Products
(Westport, Conn.: Praeger, 1996), 157.

97 "Marketing & Product Management: From Eden to New York," ScanFlux, http://www
.scanflux.com/en/products/originalsin/about.php (accessed September 5, 2007; no longer active).

98 "Eve Poster," http://origsin.com/v4/shop/eve-poster/ (accessed January 1, 2012).

99 "Marketing & Product Management."

100 St. Augustine, "On Marriage and Concupiscence," book 1, ch. 27.

101 "Original Sin," Ben E. Keith, Co., http://www.benekeith.com/beverage/brands/329
(accessed January 2, 2012).

102 "Shop: Posters," Original Sin, http://origsin.com/v4/shop/ (accessed May 27, 2012).

103 "Shop: Tee-shirts," Original Sin, http://origsin.com/v4/shop/original-sin-pinup-t-shirt
-womens/ (accessed May 27, 2012; no longer active).

104 "Labels and Posters," Great Sex Brewing Co., http://www.greatsexbrewing.com/labels
-posters.htm (accessed January 2, 2012).

105 "The Gemütliche Brother's Fable," Great Sex Brewing Co., http://www.greatsexbrewing
.com/fable.htm (accessed September 6, 2007).

106 "Great Merchandise from Great Sex Brewing," Great Sex Brewing Co., http://www
.greatsexbrewing.com/merchandise.htm (accessed January 2, 2012).

107 In his book Selling Sin: The Marketing of Socially Unacceptable Products, D. Kirk Davidson notes that producers of such products face challenges not faced by other products.
While marketing usually takes place in a positive/neutral environment, for example, the
marketers of products such as alcohol, tobacco, and "adult" products face hostility, not
from the consumers but from "some portion of our society, large enough in numbers or in
importance to make their views significant, considers these products to be unacceptable."
Davidson, Selling Sin, 1.

108 "Tobacco Advertising Themes: Eve," Stanford School of Medicine, http://tobacco.stan-
ford.edu/tobacco_main/images.php?token2=fm_st037.php&token1=fm_img0978
.php&theme_file=fm_mt013.php&theme_name=Women's%20Cigarettes&subtheme
_name=Eve (accessed May 20, 2012).

109 "Pollay Advertisements: You've Come a Long Way Baby," Tobacco Documents Online,
http://tobaccodocuments.org/pollay_ads/Virg03.07.html?ocr_position=hide_ocr
(accessed January 1, 2012).

110 "A Stacked Deck (1985)," http://www.jimsburntofferings.com/adsvsjokers.html
(accessed April 6, 2006).

111 This is carefully documented in Allan M. Brandt's book, *The Cigarette Century: The Rise, Fall, and Deadly Persistence of the Product That Defined America* (New York: Basic Books, 2007).

112 Andrew Lindstrom, "40 Gorgeous Vintage Tobacco Advertisements," Well-medicated, http://wellmedicated.com/lists/40-gorgeous-vintage-tobacco-advertisements/ (accessed January 2, 2012).

113 Tertullian, *On the Apparel of Women* 1.2, http://www.drury.edu/ess/values/tertulian.html (accessed August 8, 2012).

114 "There's a Little Eve in Every Woman," Tobacco Documents Online, http://tobaccodocuments.org/pollay_ads/Eve_01.15.html?ocr_position=hide_ocr (accessed January 2, 2012).

115 "There's a Little Eve in Every Woman."

116 Rob H. Kamery, Sarah T. Pitts, and Cayce R. Lawrence, "Ethical and Socially Responsible Advertising: Can It Be Achieved?" *Academy of Marketing Studies Journal* 6.2, January-July, 2002, http://www.alliedacademies.org/publications/papers/amsj%20vol%206%20no%201%20and%20no%202%202002%20p%20103-117.pdf (accessed October 31, 2012).

117 "Pollay Advertisements: Farewell to the Ugly Cigarette. Smoke Pretty. Eve," Tobacco Documents Online, http://tobaccodocuments.org/pollay_ads/Eve_02.12b.html (accessed January 2, 2012).

118 "Tobacco Advertising Themes: Eve."

119 Jane Brody, "Study Ties Women's Brands to Smoking Increase for Girls," *New York Times*, 1994, http://www.nytimes.com/1994/02/23/us/study-ties-women-s-brands-to-smoking-increase-for-girls.html?pagewanted=all&src=pm (accessed May 10, 2012).

Chapter 6

1 Gary Anderson, "Celibacy or Consummation in the Garden? Reflections on Early Jewish and Christian Interpretations of the Garden of Eden," *Harvard Theological Review* 82, no. 2 (1989): 124–48.

2 "R. Johanan b. Hanina said: "The day consisted of twelve hours. In the first hour, his [Adam's] dust was gathered; in the second, it was kneaded into a shapeless mass; in the third, his limbs were shaped; in the fourth, a soul was infused into him; in the fifth, he arose and stood on his feet; in the sixth, he gave [the animals] their names; in the seventh, Eve became his mate; in the eighth, they ascended to bed as two and descended as four; in the ninth, he was commanded not to eat of the tree; in the tenth, he sinned; in the eleventh, he was tried; and in the twelfth he was expelled [from Eden] and departed, for it is written, *Man abideth not in honour.*" Sanhedrin 38b. Another tradition preserved in *Genesis Rabbah* 22:2 states that two (Adam and Eve) went to bed and seven (Adam, Eve, Cain + his twin sister and Abel + twin sisters) got up.

3 AND 'THE MAN KNEW, etc.' R. Huna and R. Jacob in R. Abba's name said: "No creature ever copulated before Adam: it is not written, man knew, but 'and the man knew' intimates that he made known sexual functions to all." *Genesis Rabbah* 22.2.

4 "R Eleazar said: Any man who has no wife is no proper man; for it is said, *Male and female created he them and called their name Adam.* . . . R Eleazar further stated: What is meant by the Scriptural text, *This is now bone of my bones, and flesh of my flesh?* This teaches that Adam had intercourse with every beast and animal but found no satisfaction until he cohabited with Eve." *Yebamoth* 63a. Emphasis in original.

5 "For R. Johanan stated: When the serpent copulated with Eve, he infused her with lust. The lust of the Israelites who stood at Mount Sinai, came to an end, the lust of the idolaters who did not stand at Mount Sinai did not come to an end." *Yebamoth* 103b. See also *Shabbat* 145b–146a and *Abodah Zarah* 22b.

6   *Targum Pseudo-Jonathan* 4:1-2, 5:1-3. See also the *Pirke de Rabbi Eliezer* 11–12. They interpreted Cain's hostility toward Abel as sibling rivalry in history's first blended family.

7   "R. Simon said: "THE MOTHER OF ALL LIVING means, the mother of all life." For R. Simon said: "Throughout the entire one hundred and thirty years during which Adam held aloof from Eve the male demons were made ardent by her and she bore, while the female demons were inflamed by Adam and they bore." *Genesis Rabbah* 20:11.

8   "Know and understand that, when Adam was separated for 130 years from Eve, he slept alone, and the first Eve—that is Lilith—found him, and being charmed with his beauty, went and lay by his side, and there were begotten from her demons, spirits, and imps in thousands and myriads, and whomever they lighted upon they injured and killed outright, until Methushelah appeared and besought the mercy of God." *Chronicles of Jerahmeel* 23.

9   As one commentator explains,

> According to Hebrew legend, the first woman God created as a companion for the first man Adam was a strong-willed lady named Lilith. . . . As both had been created from dust, Lilith considered herself equal to Adam. (They differed anatomically, of course, with the Bible referring to a male as one who "pisseth against the wall" [1 Sam 25:34; 1 Kgs 14:10, 21:21].) Lilith objected to having to lie beneath Adam during sexual intercourse, but Adam would have it no other way. Lilith up and left him, winding up in rabbinic tradition as a baby-killing demoness who seduces sleeping men. . . .
>
> With Lilith departed, Adam was back where he started, being without a fit helper. According to a Hebrew tradition . . . God let Adam watch while he put a second woman together. The process of anatomical assemblage was so disgusting that Adam found the woman repulsive even though she was beautiful when finished. God sent this first Eve away and tried again: while Adam slept, Yahweh created the Eve found in Genesis 2 from Adam's rib. God presented her to Adam, who said happily, "This is now bone of my bones, and flesh of my flesh: she shall be called Woman, because she was taken out of Man" (Gen 2:23).

Ronald L. Decker, "Gender: 'Male and Female Created He Them,'" in *And Adam Knew Eve: A Dictionary of Sex in the Bible*, http://www.ronaldecker.com/andg.htm (accessed February 1, 2012).

10 According to Elaine Pagels, "Tatian blamed Adam for inventing marriage, believing that for this sin God expelled Adam and his partner in crime from Paradise." Pagels, *Adam, Eve, and the Serpent* (New York: Random House, 1988), 27.

11 Jerome, *Letter to Eustochium*, XXII.19.2–3, in *The Letters of St. Jerome*, Ancient Christian Writers 33, trans. Charles Christopher Mierow (New York: Newman, 1963), 150–51.

12 Decker, "Adam and Eve," in *And Adam Knew Eve: A Dictionary of Sex in the Bible*, http://www.ronaldecker.com/anda.htm#ADAM (accessed February 1, 2012).

13 "Sex in the '80's: The Revolution Is Over," *Time*, April 9, 1984, A Date in Time: Vintage Magazines and Collectibles—Our Specialty, http://www.tias.com/11804/PictPage/1923090169html (accessed January 10, 2012; no longer active).

14 "POM Wonderful 'Eve' TV Commercial," http://vimeo.com/15536322 (accessed October 25, 2012).

15 Editor, "Readers Say Naked Angela Simmons PETA Ad Missed the Mark," *It's Not Enough to Dream: The Magazine*, October 13, 2011, http://itsnotenoughtodream.com/readers-say-naked-angela-simmons-peta-ad-missed-the-mark/ (accessed April 12, 2012).

16 Tressugar, "A Look at PETA's Serious Sexualized Stunts," The Good Men Project, March 16, 2012, http://goodmenproject.com/sex-relationships/a-look-at-petas-serious-sexualized-stunts/ (accessed May 30, 2012).

17 "'Adam & Eve,' Print Ad for Durex Condoms by Mccann Erickson Belgium," Coloribus: Creative Advertising Archive, http://www.coloribus.com/adsarchive/prints/durex
-condoms-adam-eve-5049105/ (accessed December 30, 2011).

18 "Adam and Eve, 1597," Peter Paul Rubens: Works Gallery, Orazio Centaro's Art Images
on the Web, http://www.ocaiw.com/galleria_maestri/image.php?id=623&catalog=pitt
&start=&lang=en&letter=&id_img=1978&name= (accessed January 25, 2012).

19 "Adam and Eve Viagra/Jardim," Advertolog: Advertising & Commercials, http://www
.advertolog.com/admirror/adam-and-eve-theme/10580255/.

20 "Adam and Eve Viagra/Jardim."

21 "Adam and Eve Viagra/Jardim."

22 "Adam and Eve Viagra/Jardim."

23 "Adam and Eve Viagra/Jardim."

24 "Adam & Eve, Outdoor Advert for Sensuelle by Sulzer Sutter," Coloribus: Creative
Advertising Archive, http://www.coloribus.com/adsarchive/outdoor/sensuelle-adam
-eve-7870105/ (accessed January 14, 2012).

25 "Adam and Eve Framed Giclee Print, Lucas Cranach the Elder," U4Posters.com, http://
www.u4posters.com/a/Adam-and-Eve-Lucas-Cranach-the-Elder.html (accessed January 14, 2012).

26 The copy at the top of the page is in German: *Für Frauen, die auch alleine Zurechtkommen.*
"Adam & Eve, Outdoor Advert."

27 Phillip Feemster, "Smirnoff Twist," http://rivetingthought.com/site_frames/smirnoff
_twist_apple.html (accessed January 10, 2012).

28 Feemster, "Smirnoff Twist."

29 "Eve's Garden History," Eve's Garden, http://evesgarden.com/eves-garden-history.html
(accessed May 30, 2012).

30 "Eve's Garden History."

31 Dell Williams, *Revolution in the Garden: Memoirs of the Gardenkeeper* (San Francisco: Silverback Books, 2005).

32 Williams, *Revolution in the Garden*, 18–19.

33 Emily Johnson, "Good Vibes: Eve's Garden Founder Appears in West Side Benefit for
Women," West Side: The Spirit, April 13, 2011, http://evesgarden.com/eves-garden-in
-the-news.html (accessed May 30, 2012).

34 Johnson, "Good Vibes."

35 Jay Cheshes, "Hard-Core Philanthropist: How Can a Vibrator in Topeka Help Halt the
Spread of AIDS in Hanoi? Just Ask Phil Harvey, Porn Magnate and Social Entrepreneur,"
MotherJones.com, November 1, 2002, http://www.motherjones.com/toc/2002/11
(accessed April 20, 2008).

36 "Phil D. Harvey," DKT International, http://www.dktinternational.org/about-dkt/
board/ (accessed May 20, 2012).

37 "Philip D. Harvey, King of Porn, Master of Charity," afrik-news.com, December 17, 2007,
http://www.afrik-news.com/article12407.html (accessed October 20, 2011).

38 Phil Harvey, *The Government vs. Erotica: The Siege of Adam & Eve* (Amherst, N.Y.: Prometheus, 2001), 41.

39 Harvey, *Government vs. Erotica*, 41–42.

40 Looking back on this action, Harvey said, "But we decided to go ahead and take our
chances." Steve Almond, "Sex Aid: Phil Harvey built a porn empire to save the Third
World," Nerve, July 17, 2002, http://www.nerve.com/dispatches/almond/sexaid
(accessed June 2, 2012).

41 Harvey, *Government vs. Erotica*, 43–44.

42   "About the Adam & Eve Catalogue," Adam & Eve, http://www.adameve.com/silos/retro/About2.html (accessed January 20, 2012).

43   "PSI at a Glance," PSI, http://www.psi.org/about-psi/psi-at-a-glance?phpMyAdmin=D673WcPmz30VmXaIcHmZXgbNRE3 (accessed January 30, 2012).

44   "Mission & Values," PSI, http://www.psi.org/about-psi/mission?phpMyAdmin=D673WcPmz30VmXaIcHmZXgbNRE3 (accessed January 30, 2012).

45   "Mission & Values."

46   "DKT is one of the largest private providers of family planning and reproductive health products and services in the developing world, serving 22 million couples in 2011." DKT International, http://www.dktinternational.org/ (accessed January 30, 2012).

47   Malcolm Potts, Bixby Professor of Family Planning and Population at the University of California, Berkeley, remarks,

>   Harvey is the guru of social marketing. . . . From selling condoms in pharmacies owned by nuns in the Philippines to the use of a defunct Land Rover as a rolling condom storehouse, this book makes its point clearly and in easy to read fashion. . . . A blueprint to confront the mounting problems facing the international community as it struggles to implement the Cairo agenda of universal access to family planning and slowing AIDS with limited resources.

>   http://dktinter.s463.sureserver.com/wp-content/uploads/2011/04/EveryChildBeWanted.pdf (accessed September 20, 2011).

48   President Jimmy Carter, http://dktinter.s463.sureserver.com/wp-content/uploads/2011/04/EveryChildBeWanted.pdf (accessed September 20, 2011).

49   Cheshes, "Hard-Core Philanthropist."

50   "Founding: Adam & Eve Fact Sheet," Adam & Eve, filecache.drivetheweb.com/mr5/186230/download/Presskit2012.pdf (accessed May 5, 2012).

51   "Well Endowed: Phil Harvey Sells Sexual Excitement to the Rich, Then Helps the Poor," Economist, October 7, 2004, http://www.economist.com/node/3262292 (accessed January 30, 2012).

52   Rushe Dominic, "Birth Control Charity Turned into Sex Giant," Sunday Times, October 2, 2002, 11.

53   Harvey, Government vs. Erotica, 45.

54   "About AdamandEve.com," Adam & Eve, http://www.adameve.com/silos/retro/About3.html (accessed January 14, 2012).

55   "A Brief Timeline of the Adult Industry," Adam & Eve, http://www.adameve.com/silos/retro/About3.html (accessed January 14, 2012).

56   "A Brief Timeline of the Adult Industry."

57   "Adam & Eve Blazes New Trail with First Adult Nationwide Commercial," PR Newswire, United Business Media, February 12, 2002, http://www.prnewswire.com/news-releases/adam--eve-blazes-new-trail-with-first-adult-nationwide-commercial-75968527.html (accessed January 12, 2012).

58   Loren Baker, "Amazon.com Gets Sex Appeal with Adam & Eve Deal," SEJ: Search Engine Journal, November 3, 2004, http://www.searchenginejournal.com/amazoncom-gets-sex-appeal-with-adam-eve-deal/1020/ (accessed January 1, 2012).

59   "Adam & Eve Productions Announces the Premiere of 'Reality-X: the Search for Adam and Eve,'" News Releases, May 2, 2005, http://mediaroom.adameve.com/index.php?s=24512&item=59835 (accessed May 21, 2012; no longer active).

60   "Twitter," Adam & Eve, http://www.adameve.com/silos/retro/About3.html (accessed January 14, 2012).

61   "Customers: Adam & Eve Fact Sheet," Adam & Eve, http://webcache.googleuser

content.com/search?q=cache:QVoGWPoVUu8J:filecache.drivetheweb.com/mr5/
186230/download/Presskit2012.pdf+Adam+and+Eve+fact+sheet&cd=2&hl=en&ct=
clnk&gl=us (accessed May 3, 2012).

62 Holman W. Jenkins Jr., "Pornography, Main Street to Wall Street," *Policy Review* 105
(February 1, 2001), http://www.hoover.org/publications/policy-review/article/7065
(accessed January 1, 2012).

63 "Customers: Adam & Eve Fact Sheet."

64 "Well Endowed."

65 Adam & Eve: Celebrating Our 40th Anniversary (1971–2011), http://www.adameve
.com/silos/retro/index.html (accessed January 14, 2012).

66 "Retail: Adam & Eve Fact Sheet," Adam & Eve, http://webcache.googleusercontent
.com/search?q=cache:QVoGWPoVUu8J:filecache.drivetheweb.com/mr5/186230/
download/Presskit2012.pdf+Adam+and+Eve+fact+sheet&cd=2&hl=en&ct=clnk&gl
=us (accessed May 3, 2012).

67 One blogger remarked, "[U]nlike any other sex-based retail stores I have encountered,
they [Adam & Eve stores] have eliminated the creepy factor from their stores. . . .
The stores are designed as large warehouse boutiques, so they are well-lit, clean stylish spaces." "Adam & Eve Stores," Sexpertesse, January 15, 2011, http://sexpertesse
.blogspot.com/2011/01/adam-eve-stores.html (accessed May 18, 2012).

68 "Why Franchise?" Adam & Eve, http://www.adamevestores.com/Fanchising/Why
-Franchise-aspx (accessed January 14, 2012).

69 "Our Sex Positive Policy: Laying Out the Details," Adam & Eve, http://www.adameve
.com/t-sex_positive.aspx (accessed January 1, 2012).

70 Harvey, *Government vs. Erotica*, 38.

71 Harvey, *Government vs. Erotica*, 47–48.

72 Phil Harvey as quoted by Michael Joseph Gross, "Good Sex," Spring 2007, http://
www.02138mag.com/magazine/article/1211.html (accessed April 20, 2008; no longer
active).

73 Harvey as quoted by Gross, "Good Sex."

74 Harvey, *Government vs. Erotica*, 193.

75 Harvey, *Government vs. Erotica*, 192.

76 Opinions vary as the specific types of harm, but they include such ideas as "(a) increased
callousness towards women; (b) trivialization of rape as a criminal offense; (c) distorted
perception about sexuality; (d) increased appetite for more deviant and bizarre types of
pornography (escalation and addiction); (e) devaluation of the importance of monogamy; (f) decreased satisfaction with partner's sexual performance, affection and physical
appearance; (g) doubts about the value of marriage; (h) decreased desire to have children; and (i) viewing non-monogamous relationships as normal and natural behavior
(Drake 1994)." Jill C. Manning, "The Impact of Internet Pornography on Marriage and
the Family: A Review of the Research," *Sexual Addiction & Compulsivity* 13 (2006): 135.

77 Mary Eberstadt and Mary Anne Layden, *The Social Costs of Pornography: A Statement of
Findings and Recommendations* (New York: Witherspoon Institute, 2010).

78 Harvey as quoted by Gross, "Good Sex."

79 Brian Alexander, "The Sex Mogul of Hillsborough, North Carolina," in *America Unzipped:
In Search of Sex and Satisfaction* (New York: Harmony Books, 2008), 42.

80 Harvey, *Government vs. Erotica*, 216.

81 Harvey, *Government vs. Erotica*, 216–23.

82 Harvey, *Government vs. Erotica*, 221.

83 Harvey, *Government vs. Erotica*, 223.

84 "Entrepreneur and Philanthropist: Phil Harvey IS the American Dream," Sex Herald.com 7, no. 1, http://www.sexherald.com/sex-industry-interviews/entrepreneur_and_philan thropist-_phil_harvey_is_the_american_dream.html (accessed January 1, 2012).

85 Vincent J. Miller, *Consuming Religion: Christian Faith and Practice in a Consumer Culture* (New York: Continuum, 2005), 29–31.

86 Miller, *Consuming Religion*, 72.

87 Miller, *Consuming Religion*, 72.

88 Miller, *Consuming Religion*, 72.

89 Miller, *Consuming Religion*, 30.

90 "The Brand: What Is the Value of a Brand?" http://www.adamevestores.com/ Franchising/The-Brand.aspx (accessed January 14, 2012).

91 "Why Franchise?"

92 Interview with a colleague.

Conclusion

1 In recognition of this fact and its importance to biblical studies, the Society of Biblical Literature convened a section on the study of the Bible and popular culture in 2005, and the first session appeared in the 2006 national program. The coauthors of this book are founding members of the section.

2 As Copier, Kooijman, and Vander Stichele note,

> [I]t would be useful to understand the bible as "pre-text" in relation to its many dif-
> ferent manifestations in popular culture. A "pre-text" in this case is what comes
> before, *but does not fully determine*, a later text. . . .
>
> . . . [T]he bible informs, yet never fully determines, the reading of popular mani-
> festations of biblical themes, figures, motifs, etc.

Copier, Kooijman, and Vander Stichele, "Close Encounters," 193–94. Emphasis in original.

3 Copier, Kooijman, and Vander Stichele, "Close Encounters," 194.

4 Philip Culbertson argues that even traditional biblical scholars can learn something from this dialogue:

> [P]opular culture not only influences biblical interpretation but also opens up new
> perspectives and challenges and confronts the conventional, stylized hermeneutical
> frameworks of the "industry" of the academic study of biblical texts. (71)

Philip Culbertson, "'Tis a Pity She's (Still) a Whore: Popular Music's Ambivalent Resistance to the Reclamation of Mary Magdalene," in Culbertson and Wainwright, *Bible in
and Popular Culture*.

SELECTED BIBLIOGRAPHY

[This bibliography references hard copy materials only. For information regarding online sources, please consult the endnotes.]

Alexander, Brian. *America Unzipped: In Search of Sex and Satisfaction*. New York: Harmony Books, 2008.

Andersen, Jocelyn. *Woman Submit! Christians and Domestic Violence*. Auburndale, Fla.: One Way Cafe Press, 2007.

Anderson, Gary. "Celibacy or Consummation in the Garden? Reflections on Early Jewish and Christian Interpretations of the Garden of Eden." *Harvard Theological Review* 82, no. 2 (1989): 124–48.

Baucham, Jasmine. *Joyfully at Home: A Book for Young Ladies on Vision and Hope*. San Antonio, Tex.: Vision Forum, 2010.

Bayly, Timothy B. "Father Hunger among a Lost Generation: The Pastor's Opportunity." In *Pastoral Leadership for Manhood and Womanhood*, edited by Wayne Grudem and Dennis Rainey, Kindle ed., 1493–1502. Wheaton, Ill.: Crossway Books, 2002.

Bemiller, Michelle L., and Rachel Zimmer Schneider. "It's Not Just a Joke." *Sociological Spectrum* 30 (2010): 459–79.

Bendroth, Margaret. "Last Gasp Patriarchy: Women and Men in Conservative American Protestantism." *The Muslim World* 91 (2001): 45–54.

Berger, Arthur Asa. *Manufacturing Desire: Media, Popular Culture, and Everyday Life*. Edison, N.J.: Transaction, 2008.

———. "What's So Funny about That?" *Society* 47, no. 1 (2010): 6–10.

Bing, Janet. "Is Feminist Humor an Oxymoron?" *Women and Language* 27, no. 1 (2004): 22–34.

———. "Liberated Jokes: Sexual Humor in All-Female Groups." *Humor* 20, no. 4 (2007): 337–66.

Bishop, Jennie, and Susan Henson. *Life Lessons from the Princess and the Kiss: Planting Seeds of Purity in Young Hearts*. Niles, Mich.: Revive Our Hearts, 2004.

Botkin, Anna Sofia, and Elizabeth Botkin. *The Return of the Daughters*. DVD. Centerville, Tenn.: Western Conservatory of the Arts and Sciences, 2007.

———. *What Is Biblical Femininity? Cultivating Sturdy Virtue in Today's Daughters*. DVD. San Antonio, Tex.: Vision Forum Ministries, 2008.

Botkin, Geoffrey. *Training Dominion-Oriented Daughters*. DVD. San Antonio, Tex.: Vision Forum Ministries, 2008.

Brame, William, Gloria Brame, and Jon Jacobs. *Different Loving: The World of Sexual Dominance and Submission*. Kindle ed. New York: Villard Books, 1993.

Brandt, Allan M. *The Cigarette Century: The Rise, Fall, and Deadly Persistence of the Product That Defined America*. New York: Basic Books, 2007.

Bulldog. *Order of Marriage and Christian Domestic Discipline*. Vol. 2. Kindle ed. N.p., n.d.

Butt, Trevor, and Jeff Hearn. "The Sexualization of Corporal Punishment: The Construction of Sexual Meaning." *Sexualities* 1, no. 2 (1998): 203–27.

Case, Charles E., and Cameron D. Lippard. "Humorous Assaults on Patriarchal Ideology." *Sociological Inquiry* 79, no. 2 (2009): 240–55.

Christian, Richard C. "Industrial Marketing: Are You Conducting Sales Meetings . . . or Marketing Meetings?" *Journal of Marketing* 25 (1960): 72–74.

Copier, Laura, Jaap Kooijman, and Caroline Vander Stichele. "Close Encounters: The Bible as Pre-Text in Popular Culture." In Culbertson and Wainwright, *Bible in/and Popular Culture*, 189–96.

Crawford, Mary. "Gender and Humor in Social Context." *Journal of Pragmatics* 35 (2003): 1413–30.

Culbertson, Philip. "'Tis a Pity She's (Still) a Whore: Popular Music's Ambivalent Resistance to the Reclamation of Mary Magdalene." In Culbertson and Wainwright, *Bible in/and Popular Culture*, 61–80.

Culbertson, Philip, and Elaine M. Wainwright, eds. *The Bible in/and Popular Culture: A Creative Encounter*. Semeia Studies 65. Atlanta: Society of Biblical Literature, 2010.

Daly, Peter. "Adam and Eve in the Garden of Advertising." In *European Iconography: Selected Papers of the Szeged International Conference, June 9–12, 1993*, edited by György E. Szőnyi, 77–85. New York: Brill, 1996.

Davidson, D. Kirk. *Selling Sin: The Marketing of Socially Unacceptable Products.* Westport, Conn.: Praeger, 1996.

DeBerg, Betty A. *Ungodly Women: Gender and the First Wave of American Fundamentalism.* Minneapolis, Minn.: Fortress, 1990.

Dixon, Kate. "Multiply and Conquer: How to Have 17 Children and Still Believe in Jesus." *Bitch: Feminist Response to Popular Culture* 37 (2007): 32–37.

Dobson, James. *Bringing Up Girls.* Carol Stream, Ill.: Tyndale House, 2010.

Douglas, Mary. "Jokes." In *Rethinking Popular Culture: Contemporary Perspectives in Cultural Studies*, edited by Chandra Mukerji and Michael Schudson, 291–310. 1975. Repr., Berkeley: University of California Press, 1991.

Driscoll, Mark, and Grace Driscoll. *Real Marriage: The Truth about Sex, Friendship, & Life Together.* Kindle ed. Nashville, Tenn.: Thomas Nelson, 2012.

Eberstadt, Mary, and Mary Anne Layden. *The Social Costs of Pornography: A Statement of Findings and Recommendations.* New York: Witherspoon Institute, 2010.

Elliot, Elisabeth. *Let Me Be a Woman: Notes to My Daughter on the Meaning of Womanhood.* Wheaton, Ill.: Tyndale House, 1976.

———. *Passion and Purity: Learning to Bring Your Love Life under Christ's Control.* Old Tappan, N.J.: Fleming H. Revell, 1984.

———. *Through Gates of Splendor.* Wheaton, Ill.: Living Books, 1981. Originally published by Harper & Row in 1957, and now available in a number of editions, including a comic book version edited by Al Hartley (Old Tappan, N.J.: Spire Christian Comics, 1974).

Farrel, Pam, and Doreen Hanna. *Raising a Modern-Day Princess: Inspiring Purpose, Value, and Strength in Your Daughter.* A Focus on the Family Book. Carol Stream, Ill.: Tyndale House, 2009.

Freud, Sigmund. *Jokes and Their Relation to the Unconscious.* New York: Norton, 1960.

Gallagher, Sally K. *Evangelical Identity and Gendered Family Life.* Kindle ed. New Brunswick, N.J.: Rutgers University Press, 2003.

Ganesan, Senthil. "Case Study: Benetton Group: Unconventional Advertising." *Global CEO* (November 2002): 54–59.

Goodstein, Laurie. "New Christian Take on the Old Dating Ritual." *New York Times*, September 9, 2001.

Gresh, Danna. *8 Great Dates for Moms & Daughters: How to Talk True Beauty, Cool Fashion, and . . . Modesty!* Eugene, Ore.: Harvest House, 2010.

Griffith, R. Marie. *God's Daughters: Evangelical Women and the Power of Submission.* Berkeley: University of California Press, 1997.

Grudem, Wayne. "The Myth of Mutual Submission." *Journal for Biblical Manhood and Womanhood* 1, no. 4 (1996): 1–4.

———. "Personal Reflections on the History of CBMW and the State of the Gender Debate." *Journal for Biblical Manhood and Womanhood* 14, no. 1 (2009): 12–17.

Harris, Joshua. *Boy Meets Girl: Say Hello to Courtship.* Sisters, Ore.: Multnomah, 2000.

———. *I Kissed Dating Goodbye: A New Attitude toward Romance and Relationships.* Sisters, Ore.: Multnomah, 1997.

———. *Not Even a Hint: Guarding Your Heart Against Lust.* Sisters, Ore.: Multnomah, 2003.

Harvey, Phil. *The Government vs. Erotica: The Siege of Adam & Eve.* Amherst, N.Y.: Prometheus, 2001.

Hess, Rick, and Jan Hess. *A Full Quiver: Family Planning and the Lordship of Christ.* Nashville, Tenn.: Wolgemuth & Hyatt, 1989.

Jakes, T. D., ed. *Holy Bible: Woman Thou Art Loosed! Edition.* Nashville, Tenn.: Thomas Nelson, 1998.

Jerome. *Letter to Eustochium,* XXII.19.2–3. In *The Letters of St. Jerome.* Ancient Christian Writers 33, translated by Charles Christopher Mierow, 150–51. New York: Newman, 1963.

Jhally, Sut. *The Codes of Advertising: Fetishism and the Political Economy of Meaning in the Consumer Society.* New York: St. Martin's, 1987.

Joyce, Kathryn. *Quiverfull: Inside the Christian Patriarchy Movement.* Boston: Beacon, 2009.

Keller, Timothy, and Kathy Keller. *The Meaning of Marriage.* New York: Dutton, 2011.

Kelley, Leah. *Bridling the Tongue.* N.p.: Christian Domestic Discipline, 2007.

———. *Captive Dreams.* N.p.: TCM, 2006.

———. *Christian Domestic Discipline Bible Study for Wives.* N.p.: Christian Domestic Discipline, 2006.

———. *Christian Domestic Discipline 101.* N.p.: Christian Domestic Discipline, 2007.

———. *Christian Domestic Discipline Spanking Romance Love Novella Series.* N.p.: Christian Domestic Discipline Fiction, 2006.

———. *Christian Domestic Discipline Spanking Romance Short Story Collection.* N.p.: Christian Domestic Discipline Fiction, 2006.

———. *Consensual Christian Domestic Discipline.* N.p.: Christian Domestic Discipline, 2007.

———. *Dream in Black and White.* N.p.: TCM, 2006.

Kelly, Charles. "Laughing In and Out of Eden: An Analysis of Adam and Eve Jokes." *Midwestern Folklore* 14, no. 2 (1988): 91–97.

Kendall, Jackie. *A Man Worth Waiting For: How to Avoid a Bozo.* Nashville, Tenn.: FaithWords, 2008.

Kiesling, A. J. *Where Have All the Good Men Gone? Why So Many Christian Women Are Remaining Single.* Eugene, Ore.: Harvest House, 2008.

Kvam, Kristen E., Linda S. Schearing, and Valarie H. Ziegler, eds. *Eve and Adam: Jewish, Christian, and Muslim Readings on Genesis and Gender.* Bloomington: Indiana University Press, 1999.

LaHaye, Tim, and Beverly LaHaye. *The Act of Marriage: The Beauty of Sexual Love.* Rev. ed. Grand Rapids: Zondervan, 1998.

Lepine, Bob. "The Husband Is Prophet, Priest, and King." In *Building Strong Families,* edited by Dennis Rainey, Kindle ed., chap. 4. Wheaton, Ill.: Crossway Books, 2002.

Lewis, Robert. *Raising a Modern-Day Knight.* A Focus on the Family Book. Rev. ed. Carol Stream, Ill.: Tyndale House, 2007.

Litfin, A. Duane. "Evangelical Feminism: Why Traditionalists Reject It." *Bibliotheca Sacra* 136 (1979): 258–71.

Lovingdd, Mr. *LDD.* 7th ed. N.p., 2007.

Ludy, Eric. *The Bravehearted Gospel: The Truth Is Worth Fighting For.* Eugene, Ore.: Harvest House, 2007.

———. *God's Gift to Women: Discovering the Lost Greatness of Masculinity.* Sisters, Ore.: Multnomah, 2003.

Ludy, Eric, and Leslie Ludy. *The First 90 Days of Marriage: Building the Foundation of a Lifetime.* Nashville, Tenn.: Thomas Nelson, 2006.

———. *When God Writes Your Love Story.* Sisters, Ore.: Multnomah, 1999.

———. *Wrestling Prayer: A Passionate Communion with God.* Eugene, Ore.: Harvest House, 2009.

Ludy, Leslie. *Authentic Beauty: The Shaping of a Set-Apart Young Woman.* Eugene, Ore.: Multnomah, 2003.

Madden, Mary, and Amanda Lenhart. *Online Dating.* Washington, D.C.: Pew Internet & American Life Project, 2006.

Maken, Debbie. *Getting Serious about Getting Married: Rethinking the Gift of Singleness*. Wheaton, Ill.: Crossway Books, 2006.

Mally, Sarah. *Before You Meet Prince Charming: A Guide to Radiant Purity*. Cedar Rapids, Iowa: Tomorrow's Forefathers, 2009.

Manning, Jill C. "The Impact of Internet Pornography on Marriage and the Family: A Review of the Research." *Sexual Addiction & Compulsivity* 13 (2006): 131–65.

Markham, Jules. *Domestic Discipline*. Toronto: Adlibbed, 2007.

Marsden, George M. *Fundamentalism and American Culture: The Shaping of Twentieth-Century Evangelicalism, 1870–1925*. New York: Oxford University Press, 1980.

Mazur, Eric Michael, and Kate McCarthy. *God in the Details: American Religion in Popular Culture*. 2nd ed. New York: Routledge, 2011.

Melchior, Jillian. "They Plight Their Troth—and Mean It." *Wall Street Journal*, April 11, 2008.

Miller, Vincent J. *Consuming Religion: Christian Faith and Practice in a Consumer Culture*. New York: Continuum, 2005.

Niebuhr, H. Richard. *Christ and Culture*. New York: Harper, 1951.

Orenstein, Peggy. *Cinderella Ate My Daughter: Dispatches from the Front Lines of the New Girly-Girl Culture*. New York: HarperCollins, 2011.

O'Shaughnessy, John, and Nicholas J. O'Shaughnessy. *Persuasion in Advertising*. New York: Routledge, 2003.

Pagels, Elaine. *Adam, Eve, and the Serpent*. New York: Random House, 1988.

Paumgarten, Nick. "Looking for Someone: Sex, Love, and Loneliness on the Internet." *The New Yorker*, July 4, 2011, 36–49.

Phillips, Douglas W. *Sleeping Beauty and the Five Questions: A Parable about the Hearts of Fathers and Daughters*. CD audio book. San Antonio, Tex.: Vision Forum, 2004.

Phillips, John A. *Eve: The History of an Idea*. San Francisco: Harper & Row, 1984.

Piper, John. " 'The Frank and Manly Mr. Ryle': The Value of a Masculine Ministry." *Journal for Biblical Manhood and Womanhood* 17, no. 1 (2012): 10–22.

Plante, Rebecca F. "Sexual Spanking, the Self, and the Construction of Deviance." *Journal of Homosexuality* 50, nos. 2–3 (2006): 59–79.

Randazzo, Sal. *Mythmaking on Madison Avenue: How Advertisers Apply the Power of Myth & Symbolism to Create Leadership Brands*. Chicago: Probus, 1993.

Redelman, Margaret J. "What If the 'Sexual Headache' Is Not a Joke?" *British Journal of Medical Practitioners* 4, no. 1 (2010): 40–44.

Reilly, Tom. *Value-Added Selling: How to Sell More Profitably, Confidently, and Professionally by Competing on Value, Not Price.* 2nd ed. New York: McGraw-Hill, 2002.

Rogan, Paul, and Justin Rosenholtz. *Adam vs. Eve: Jokes from the Frontline in the Battle of the Sexes.* New York: Carlton Books, 2004.

Sagarin, Brad J., Bert Cutler, Nadine Cutler, Kimberly A. Lawler-Sagarin, and Leslie Matuszewich, "Hormonal Changes and Couple Bonding in Consensual Sadomasochistic Activity." *Archives of Sexual Behavior* 38 (2009): 186–200.

Seelhoff, Cheryl Lindsey. "Confronting the Religious Right." *Off Our Backs* 36, no. 3 (2006): 18–25.

Shifman, Limor. "Humor in the Age of Digital Reproduction: Continuity and Change in Internet-Based Comic Texts." *International Journal of Communication* 1 (2007): 187–209.

Shifman, Limor, and Dafna Lemish. "Between Feminism and Fun(ny)mism: Analyzing Gender in Popular Internet Culture." *Information, Communication & Society* 13, no. 6 (2010): 870–91.

———. "'Mars and Venus' in Virtual Space: Post-feminist Humor and the Internet." *Critical Studies in Media Communications* 28, no. 3 (2011): 253–73.

Simon, William. *Postmodern Sexualities.* Kindle ed. New York: Taylor & Francis, 2004.

Snyder-Hall, R. Clair. "The Ideology of Wifely Submission: A Challenge for Feminism?" *Politics & Gender* 4, no. 4 (2008): 563–86.

Anna Sofia and Elizabeth Botkin. *So Much More: The Remarkable Influence of Visionary Daughters on the Kingdom of God.* San Antonio, Tex.: Vision Forum, 2005.

Steinberg, Shirley R., and Joe L. Kincheloe, eds. *Christotainment: Selling Jesus through Popular Culture.* Boulder, Colo.: Westview, 2009.

Sweet, Rose. *Dear God, Send Me a Soul Mate.* Chattanooga, Tenn.: AMG, 2002.

Thompson, William Norman. *Gambling in America: An Encyclopedia of History, Issues, and Society.* Santa Barbara, Calif.: ABC-CLIO, 2001.

Wakeman, Jessica. "Slap Happy." *Bitch* 39 (2008): 63–68.

Walsh, Sheila. *God's Little Princess Devotional Bible.* Nashville, Tenn.: Thomas Nelson, 1999.

———. *God's Mighty Warrior Devotional Bible.* Nashville, Tenn.: Thomas Nelson, 2007.

Warren, Neil Clark, and Ken Abraham. *Falling in Love for All the Right Reasons: How to Find Your Soul Mate*. New York: Center Street, 2005.

Watters, Candice. *Get Married: What Women Can Do to Help It Happen*. Chicago: Moody, 2008.

Wheat, Ed, and Gaye Wheat. *Intended for Pleasure: Sex Technique and Sex Fulfillment in Christian Marriage*. Old Tappan, N.J.: Fleming H. Revell, 1977.

Williams, Dell. *Revolution in the Garden: Memoirs of the Gardenkeeper*. San Francisco: Silverback Books, 2005.

Woodzicka, Julie A., and Thomas E. Ford. "A Framework for Thinking about the (not-so-funny) Effects of Sexist Humor." *Europe's Journal of Psychology* 3 (2010): 174–95.

Young, Ed, and Lisa Young. *Sexperiment: 7 Days to Lasting Intimacy with Your Spouse*. New York: Faith Words, 2012.

INDEX